MW00893142

From Both Sides of the River

A Family Portrait

Anne Cutter Mikkelsen

WILLOW ISLAND PRESS

It can only be the hope of those who teach, that some among the thousands who are taught will use their minds to solve the riddles that face us. ~ Leeds Darrah Cutter II

About the Author

Anne Cutter Mikkelsen lives in Bellingham, Washington, with her husband Mike, an artist who has lived with the symptoms of Parkinson's disease for almost 30 years. She has four children and ten grandchildren.

Anne is a "foodie" and advocate. She is the author of several short non-fiction stories. In 2010 she completed a memoir with recipes titled, *Take Charge of Parkinson's Disease: Dynamic Lifestyle Changes to Put YOU in the Driver's Seat,* published as a DiaMedica Guide to Optimum Wellness, DiaMedica Publishing, New York, N.Y.

The third child of eight, Anne was born in New York, and grew up in Anoka, Minnesota, beside the Mississippi River. She studied classic French cooking in Provence, at *L'Ecole de Trois Gourmandes,* with Simone (Simca) Beck, Julia Child's writing and cooking partner. Anne owned and operated two restaurants, a catering business and a B&B in Minnesota. She hosted a cooking show, *Cooking with Panache,* produced by NTV in Northfield, Minnesota.

Watch for the next book: *The 1941 Dodge Convertible.* Mike's love affair began in Connecticut 1947, when he discovered and took ownership of his dream. "She" was gone when he returned from Korea. It would be after she had spent many down-and-out years in a Montana gully before he could resurrect and restore her to the full dignity and original splendor she deserved.

From Both Sides of the River: A Family Portrait
Copyright © 2011, Anne Cutter Mikkelsen
Willow Island Press
3639 Toad Lake Road
Bellingham, Washington 98226
Website: www.annecuttermikkelsen.com

Library of Congress Cataloging-in-Publication Data pending

Mikkelsen, Anne Cutter, 1944-
From Both Sides of the River: A Family Portrait

ebook ISBN: 978-0-615-41419-5
print ISBN: 978-1456425531

Book design and typography for print and ebook by Kathleen Weisel, Bellingham, Washington. (www.weiselcreative.com)

Cover art by E.A. (Mike) Mikkelsen. If you have the right artist, you really can judge a book by its cover. Mike is a life-long artist and teacher. Nature is art and his medium depends on the tools available at the moment.

Some names have been changed to protect identity and privacy.

Contents

Acknowledgements

Not to know what has been transacted in former times is to be always a child. If no use is made of the labors of the past ages, the world must remain always in the infancy of knowledge. ~Cicero

Bringing the past and present together through the stories that affected my life has been an invigorating, satisfying experience. I appreciate the extravagance of peace and space because insight, healing and reflection come with age and the luxury of time.

To virtually tag along in the company of my parents, through their writing, has been an unparalleled honor. Because they preserved their history, I had the rare opportunity to *solve the riddles that faced me.*

My husband has read drafts of this story since 2006. His belief in the importance of the message is evident in every line he lovingly etched to create the cover art. Thank you Mike for modeling the power of perseverance.

Thank you to my sister, Eightball Sarah Doll, for her contributions—both spiritual and material.

May you always remember
We did grow up in the Taj Mahal
The trees and the islands held and instructed you
May you always
Be curious about yourself
Take pride in your triumphs
And joy in our differences
May you be exuberant with your love,
Of your life
And yourself

Susan Colleen Browne, writer, author, teacher, friend. Thank you for hours and hours of inspiration, encouragement, patience and scrupulous editing.

Kate Weisel, your expert guidance and wise counsel through the final process of editing, translating and typesetting made this an even more joyful experience. Thank you.

And, my heartfelt gratitude goes to my dear friend and writing partner, Carolyn Stinson. "It's all in the timing." You generously offered your "stickler" skills at the precise moment I needed them the most.

Permissions

An excerpt of *From Both Sides of the River* was published in October, 2008, in the University of Northern British Columbia, literary journal. www. scrollinspace.com.

Excerpts of Sandwich Extraordinare and Seeds of Nurturing (Circle of Kneading) were included in the book, *Take Charge of Parkinson's Disease: Dynamic Lifestyle Changes that Put YOU in the Driver's Seat.* Author, Anne Cutter Mikkelsen, published 2011, by Diamedica Publishing, N.Y., N.Y. www.diamedicapub.com.

Dedication

This is for my children, all teachers
Sean Connolly
Geoffrey Darrah
Andrew Kenneth
Sarah Anne Conroy

and my parents
Mary Helen White Cutter
Leeds Darrah Cutter II

Foreword

There are two ways to be fooled. One is to believe what isn't true; the other is to refuse to believe what is true. ~Soren Kierkegaard

Fact or Fiction

The cooking season of 1980 in Provence was *the* ecstatic moment of her life. After forty-two years of raising children, mostly as a widow, and suffering extraordinary grief, my mother had at last transformed herself. She had just completed another term as American assistant to the revered cooking icon, Simone Beck, at her school of French cookery in the South of France. Mother was euphoric, dreaming of many more seasons in the lavender-drenched countryside.

"The very idea," she told me, "that a Minnesota woman, a granddaughter of Irish immigrants, could ascend to the pinnacle of French cooking." Mother referred to her stroke of luck as, "a surprise package, elephant and pig." In that year, she was as deliriously happy and as content as she had been in 1940—honeymooning on the Navy Base in Coronado.

"For as many years as Simca teaches," she wrote in her reflections on Provence, "I hope she will allow me to serve as her assistant." Simca must have felt the same way, because she paid special tribute to Mother in her latest book, *New Menus From Simca's Cuisine:*

> *"... to one person in particular—generous, devoted, efficient, tireless in the testing and retesting of recipes. ... My acquaintance with this gentle-spirited and exquisite woman has been one of the most fortunate of my life."*

When my father died, Mother, formerly a devoted housewife, suddenly found herself alone raising eight children, from five to nineteen years old. In addition, she was left with two businesses and an unwieldy "gentleman's farm" to run. While she skillfully managed all of that, she longed for an achievement all her own, an undeniable passion—a new love. To her utter surprise, her new love was cooking. Mother had never, ever found cooking to be an enjoyable activity; it was a chore that had to be completed every day, three times a day, multiplied by ten or more people.

As the third child and second daughter, I easily found my place next to Mother in her kitchen and in the dining room, at home and in our separate restaurants. You really get to know a cooking partner, when there's rough-to-fine chopping and deft, light folding going on in the same small work space, when the heat and tension are high in the kitchen. In her lifetime, Mother managed to establish and nurture authentic friendships with each of her adult children. Every relationship was skillfully focused on the talents and dreams of the individual child.

After Mother died, my siblings and I discovered fragments of her story and her secrets, all kept in safe places, where they could be found and explored later—much later.

Because my mother and I shared a passion for food, everyone agreed I should have the cardboard box, filled with cooking memorabilia.

When I sat down with the box to sift through Mother's accumulation of culinary treasures, I didn't expect to find anything new or shocking. I unfolded a yellowed newspaper from the Fargo-Moorhead Sunday Forum, dated 1979. I smiled at the photograph of Mother skillfully cutting a classic *genoise* loose from the edges of a spring-form pan. In the article, titled "A Cook by 'Accident,'" the staff writer described Mother's outlook on life as, "eternally optimistic and self-deprecating."

Explaining what led to her new love—cooking, Mother told the reporter, "I consider myself accident prone. My whole life's been like that. But I don't quarrel with it. Everything's turned out pretty well."

The enormously understated first *accident* she refers to was my father's death. In her grief, Mother attempted to rebuild her life with something fresh and new of her own choosing, not superimposed by what he had left undone.

On a whim, she attended a benefit luncheon in Minneapolis featuring the local French cooking teacher, Verna Meyer. Following an introduction to Meyer, Mother began cooking classes, soon becoming Meyer's assistant. Seventeen years later, because of a series of other *accidents,* Mother was invited to serve as Simca's assistant in France. I don't believe Mother owed her success to any accidents. She was exceptionally talented, hard working and very clever.

In addition to more newspaper stories about my own restaurants and notes from cooking schools Mother and I attended together, I found several letters from Simca, each beginning with, *My very dearest Mary Helen.* In one letter Simca excitedly details plans for her next visit to Mother's home at The Last House on Park Street in Anoka.

Deeper into the box, as I sorted through random recipes from *LaVarenne,* the Paris cooking school Mother attended, I uncovered an autographed copy of *Mastering the Art of French Cooking,* co-authored by Simca and Julia Child. I read stacks of Mother's recipes from Mary Helen's Kitchen, each one carefully edited by Simca, herself. Wow! I had never heard about that.

My heart ached, as I picked up several sheets of onion skin paper, and read my own lost opportunity. Apparently Mother was writing a cookbook with me, but I was unaware of this collaboration. Was I just too busy to pay attention? How could I have ignored her skill and her generosity?

Another letter from Simca outlined the itinerary for Mother's and my last trip to her cooking school in 1980. I was deliriously lost in my Mediterranean memories—the beaches in Cannes and Mother's giddy joy, as she hosted the tour of three-star restaurants from Nice to Crissier, Switzerland. Practicing her newly learned French, while she fingered her old strand of pearls, she competently ordered *aperitifs,* silken *foie gras,* veal *mousse,* and scallops in crisp puff pastry.

Hours after I started, I was surrounded by two three-foot piles of recipes, menus and newspaper clippings. Still remembering Mother's glee and the taste of that goose liver with truffles, I spotted something else in the bottom of the cardboard box, something out of place, mysterious and instantly disturbing.

Even before removing it from the box, I began devouring the story typed on three sheets of thin blue paper. All thoughts of tender morsels and warm Mediterranean beaches suddenly vanished.

The story was written by Mother, two years before she died. The setting was Simca's garden at *Domaine de Bramafan.* Her young characters, Bridget and Peter, *were* my parents. Peter, a bookish lawyer and World War II Navy pilot, and Bridget, the writer of radio soap operas and daughter of a pacifist school teacher, all sounded familiar. I couldn't put the papers down.

It was her character's shortcomings I did not recognize. Maybe I didn't really know my parents after all. Peter could not have been my father, controlling and, as Bridget claimed, "...capable of reducing her to compliance."

When I became an adult, Mother confided in me. She told stories on herself, in that self-deprecating way the reporter noticed. On the airplane going to The Great Chefs of France cooking school in California, Mother told me how she imagined the future unfolding for each of her children. She was prophetic. Why then would she not have shared the doubts she had about my father?

Bridget's charges were simply not true. What in my parents' lives would have fueled such accusations? For 22 years his children believed he was dead. But, Bridget saw him in that garden in France, and what's more, "… she was ready for him." Or was that the scene Mother wanted to believe? More jarring than anything else, her main character "understood what had, in his mind, justified his leaving and she knew just how he had managed it."

The story ended dramatically and inconclusively in mid-sentence, leaving me with questions about the reality of my childhood memories: fact or fiction.

Feeling like an accomplice, I gripped the blue papers firmly in my lap. Curiously, they were attached to a French menu and more painstaking recipes, typical of Mother's later years. The recipes were also typed, but on business-like stationery imprinted in the upper left-hand corner with a sepia photo of our childhood home beside the Mississippi River at The Last House on Park Street, Anoka, Minnesota. *Ahhh,* I thought, *there really are no accidents.*

Of course Mother knew I would receive her recipes and everything else in that box. She knew I would explore and analyze even the most innocent inferences. How, *had he managed it?* Maybe she needed to create a soap opera villain so she could feel fortunate he was gone. Was she rewriting history, rewiring her brain, convincing herself that she could survive quite well without him?

Finally, I decided Mother's account on blue paper was just the beginning. The rest of the story was out there somewhere. It might be in knowing my parents as individuals with their own separate dreams and histories, well before I arrived.

Whoa! How could I know my parents before I was born—before they were married? Wasn't that impossible? Especially now. Who was left to tell their story?

Overwhelmed by the research necessary to adequately answer those questions, I didn't do anything, didn't tell anyone—not one word of the story on blue paper. Packing it quietly and safely away along with my own suspicions and fears, I would control my parents' story… until *I* was ready. Or so I thought.

Part I

Chapter 1

Mouse as Spirit

Two years later, Mother's story returned on its own. I climbed the ladder against the wall in the deserted barn at The Last House on Park Street to sit in the open doorway of the hayloft one last time. I inhaled the balmy June air, the scent of the pine forest that we, the Cutter children, planted between the river and Park Street, how many Arbor Days ago? We had such glorious freedom in the summers, taking our time, following the cow paths across the pasture on our way to King's Island. I could still feel the silt of the Mississippi River bottom between my toes. I could smell the thick, hot air of those joyous afternoons, when we all waded out to the sandbar under the bowing elm branches, where my father anchored his beloved Seabee all summer long.

I gazed across the wide gravel driveway to the apartment above the garage. Looking into the sunlit room I recalled the summer of 1954, when that beautiful young Hungarian refugee painted his mysterious watercolor portrait of the Cutter children. Below me was the interstitial land, the piece of ground between the garage and the barn. The kids owned that piece of real estate every summer, for our father's price of a few clear agates. On that weedy overgrown plot, we built Shanty Town when the geese flew north in the spring and dismantled our town as the geese flew south for the winter. Shanty Town shaped our lives in ways we could never have imagined, but our parents knew exactly what they were doing.

I tried to shake off the impending loss, knowing it will all be gone tomorrow. The property will be torched to make room for a housing development. What an intense fire it will take to burn down the home where my father grew up, where my mother cooked and knitted and every year baked hundreds of Valentine cookies for our classmates. She worked well past midnight, hunched over the kitchen table, squeezing each name in pink powdered sugar through the pastry tube onto the heart-shaped sugar cookies. In the living room of that house, Mika Ogata, our Japanese exchange student, unpacked his bags that June day in 1956, when he arrived to present his transforming, enduring gifts of peace.

Imagine the heat, the incense and vibrant colors that fire will produce, the aroma of four generations of love and care in the walls of our home, of the barn where I sat. At that moment a fat grey mouse skittered across the floor and plunked head-first into the oat bin. Following his path, I noticed an old wooden trunk that must have been forgotten in the moving. I lifted the heavy lid and discovered parts of the Cutter kids' Halloween costumes from more than forty years ago, all sprinkled with rat and mouse droppings. A pair of Grandma Cutter's high-top button shoes, camouflaged in splotches of fragrant mold, rested on top of a mouse-chewed antique black-beaded velvet evening jacket—a complete witch's costume.

At the bottom of the trunk, I spotted a black notebook. Shaking off oat husks and bits of straw, I decided it couldn't be anything important or somebody would have claimed it by now—one day before the fire. I sat down in the doorway and opened the cover.

What luck! It was my father's World War II journal stuffed with a dozen postcards and letters some with mouse-nibbled onion skin envelopes dating from 1938 to 1940 complete with 6-cent stamps in the corners. None of the letters offered any clues about my parents' early years together and, at first glance, the book appeared to be mostly flight training notations from his years at Pensacola Naval Academy.

Holding the journal close, I climbed down the ladder. It might be insignificant, but it was more than I had yesterday, more of my father than I'd had for over twenty years. It was at the very least something he held in his hands and carried with him, in some way it was a part of his story. However battered and torn, my father's journal electrified my interest in Mother's mysterious story on blue paper.

Were my childhood memories of that house and the people who passed through there nothing more than wistfulness? Could my memories have been too good to be true?

As I drove down the driveway with my father's journal on the seat beside me, I said goodbye to the blessed trees in the yard. I had assumed they would stand forever—the oldest elm with the girls' swing still dangling from a high branch. My favorite tree was a fifty-year old cedar, the first base on our family's front-yard softball field.

At the end of the driveway, was a small grove of pine trees where Mother hid Easter eggs in the low branches, to be fair to the little kids. What was always obvious was my mother's sense of justice, the care and confidence she magnanimously bestowed, like DNA, on all her children.

A good example of Mother's parenting skills was the Christmas I was thirteen and feeling stupid, irrationally annoyed, awkward, in other words, behaving like a typical adolescent. Sometimes I wanted to be invisible, hide behind the living room door and watch them playing with Christmas presents, fighting over the last candy in the stockings. Mother knew just how to return me to the flow.

Still wearing her church dress and sensible heels, she slid the standing rib roast into the oven and called me to the kitchen.

"Charlie? How would you like to come set the dining room table for dinner? You do such a nice job and you could use Grandma's silver." She raised her voice above all the racket in the living room. "And," she added temptingly, "you could use those China plates you get such a kick out of." Then, as if she'd just thought of it, she grabbed my arm and led me to the dining room. "How 'bout using the porcelain dancing children for the centerpiece? That is, if you like." Wow! The porcelain dancing children *and* Grandma Cutter's China.

The China plates were ancient and delicate with a low-fired yellow crackle glaze. Painted around the edge of each plate was the scene of an enthroned, fat, half-naked Chinese Emperor, being carried by servants, in a parade led by elephants, draped in red blankets and golden tassels.

In our house, setting the table was a privilege, usually reserved for Mother's expertise. She could create a beautiful, memorable scene out of one flower and some ribbon. Mother loved setting the table, especially on the "big" days—birthdays, New Year's Day, Easter, Christmas and, of course, Arbor Day.

Mother reached deep into the back of the dining room buffet and produced two wooden boxes. Sitting on the floor beside me, she carefully unfolded the purple velvet wrapping and placed the figurines in my hands—a happy dancing boy, playing the tambourine and dressed in a floppy summer hat and light blue shorts. The barefoot girl wore a long, flowing, yellow dress and a flower garland in her hair, with ribbons draped in curls over her shoulders.

Those dancing children were as fragile and rare as Grandma Cutter's dishes and most people might well have considered the likelihood of chipped or shattered China. But Mother was never afraid of *things* getting broken, it was broken spirits she worried about the most. Of that fact, I am sure.

Ten years after I discovered my father's journal, in December of 1994, while sorting a pile of used books to be donated to the hospital fundraiser, I picked up that tattered black book once again. All those years I spent working and raising my own four children, I had only half, or less, of my life's story to share with them and through those years, I'd felt a lingering longing for something I could never satisfy or even identify. Maybe now was the time to examine more of my father's story.

A few old letters addressed to The Secretary of The Coronado Dance Band, Last House on Park Street, floated to the carpet. The return addresses read: Eugene Bird. He was a professional saxophone player and friend of my father.

Saving the letters for later, I flipped through the typed, worn pages of my father's journal, quickly scanning for any references to my mother. The first entry, dated January 4, 1939, begins after his graduation from University of Minnesota Law School, as he enters Officer's Candidate School in Pensacola, Florida.

> The first day of flying this year marks the end of a twelve day
> vacation. The left wing flew in the morning which meant a
> seven fifteen muster and my cleaning detail had the duty.

Disappointing again. Nothing personal, nothing revealing, mostly flight school jargon, math problems, radio and weather exam notes, Navy rules and regulations, and all the writing faded and difficult to read. For the second time, I abandoned the journal and returned to the letters from Eugene Bird. He and my father had been friends since boyhood. I learned that they created the Coronado Dance Band, when they were in high school, as a way to earn money entertaining summer visitors in small resorts along the shores of Lake Nisswa in northern Minnesota.

I hadn't seen Eugene since my father's funeral. He'd be eighty years old if he was even alive. The years and my resources were passing so quickly. Soon there would be no one left to offer insight. Act quickly. It wasn't much I needed, just a few answers to fill in pieces of the puzzle.

Simple questions like what was most important to my father? Why, after the war, did he at times seem unreachable and profoundly sad, then erupt in anger? But most important to me now were the suspicions my mother described in her story of Bridget and Peter. Could my father be alive, somewhere on this earth? Would he even have considered leaving his wife and eight children?

The moment had arrived. I summoned courage, telling myself that if I didn't follow this story, no one else would. On New Year's Eve, traditionally an evening for bold game-changing decisions, I made some phone calls.

It was 10 degrees below zero New Year's Day 1995. Trudging through a snow bank toward a tidy Minneapolis bungalow, I saw the kitchen door open, steam escaped, and within seconds there he was, the assistant to the Secretary of The Coronado Dance Band, my father's best friend.

"Charlie," he called through a frosty cloud. Eugene Bird greeted me with a warm hug. Hearing the name my father gave me, transported me back to our yard in Anoka, under the shade of the oak trees. It was August, 1949, 90 degrees, 100% humidity.

I was five years old, barefoot, wearing blue and white striped seersucker shorts and sitting on my father's lap. My legs dangled through the arm of the metal lawn chair and with one ear up against his chest, I felt the vibration of my father's voice through his khaki work shirt. The smell of sweat mingled with oil and gas from his work down on the flat. He'd been repairing the irrigator just moments before his friends drove into the yard and climbed out of Eugene Bird's red sports car.

Sy, Chalky and Eugene exchanged backslaps and handshakes with my father and then settled into the metal chairs under the ancient oak trees. Those men often stopped by for a Sunday afternoon visit.

Mother came through the porch door, carrying a wicker tray laden with the usual hot summer day men's refreshments, cold beer in frosty Pilsner glasses along with pickled herring and Nabisco Hi-Ho Crackers. Looking through the bubbles in my father's glass, I watched the distorted faces of his friends laughing and rocking back and forth in the metal chairs. That moment could have lasted ten years and I would have been content. There I was, in the center, listening to old jokes from familiar, friendly voices. My father told them that I was quite clever for a five-year-old.

"Ah hah," Chalky laughed, puffing his cigar and blowing loopy smoke rings to the tops of the oak trees. "So what is it she can do?" he asked. I wondered too.

My father said, "Oh she's quite a little monkey. Here," he said lifting me up. "Show them how you can turn a somersault right on this chair." I was proud, as I performed, turning completely upside down and back to my father's lap, but during the turn, my leg got caught in the arm of the chair.

I didn't feel it, but Sy was alarmed. "Oh my, I think I heard something crack."

"Yup," Eugene agreed, coming over to look at my leg. "Yes, indeed I think she's gone and broken her leg," he said, cautiously tapping my shin bone. Off we went in a parade to the local hospital on Ferry Street. Eugene parked his red car by the curb, and the men waited, like sentinels, until my father rolled the high-backed, wooden wheelchair out onto the hospital porch. *Clever little monkey*, his friends wrote on my cast.

Forty-five years later, that clever little monkey was stomping snow off her boots in Eugene's kitchen doorway and following him into his warm living room.

Eugene at nearly 80, was handsome, cute even, energetic and crisp in a white dress shirt, black pressed pants and canary yellow cardigan. As I followed him into the living room, I noticed that he looked almost the same as the last time I'd seen him, thirty-five years ago, though maybe a little sadder. Or was it melancholy? Don't let it be confusion.

Settled into matching chairs, on either side of a coffee table, I told him about finding my father's journal. "There were letters in that journal from you to Dad," I said, "planning gigs for the Irish dance band. That sounded like fun. Was it? Did my dad like it?" Trying not to sound too desperate, but I was. Desperate to extract some tidbit, any little nugget about my father's life. At that moment, I believed Eugene Bird was my only chance.

There was a long pause before Eugene spoke again.

"Your father played the piccolo, the flute and the fiddle too," Gene said, smiling, looking down at the floor. Well, that was something, wasn't it? I waited through another quiet space while Eugene seemed to be thinking of what to say next.

I'd never heard my father play the music of any of those instruments, but I was embarrassed to admit it. Maybe I hadn't been paying attention. Eugene explained that The Coronado Dance Band was named for a Minnesota dance hall, frequented by Eugene and my dad and having no connection to the North Island Naval Base in Coronado, California, where my father was first assigned as a Navy officer. What an odd coincidence.

Eugene poured coffee into China cups, as he told me how much he admired my grandparents, how he'd spent his childhood playing in the yard, dancing in the living room and playing tennis on the court at my grandparents' house at the end of Park Street.

"We were friends, your father and I," he said. "All our lives … roommates at the University." Eugene began to warm up. "Very close," he continued. "Studied together, took our meals together at Mrs. Bryan's Tea Shop, five dollars a month. Imagine that, Charlie. And … in those days roommates even shared a bed! We went home to Anoka together for all our breaks. Very close, … yes." His eyes filled with tears and focused softly distant—miles beyond Minneapolis and years from this moment.

I watched Eugene's face and imagined his worry-free rides home with my father, the laughter and stimulating conversations they must have had about college classes, football games, girls and summer band gigs.

"You must have known him really well," I said, hoping to prod more memories. I'd settle for anything because I knew precious little about my father's childhood. Eugene stared at a spot on the rug between his sharply polished black shoes. He seemed to be weighing his memories. Then he glanced sideways at me, trying to anticipate my reaction, as if he was about to divulge a long-held secret.

"Did you know, Charlie?" he began, looking me straight in the eye. "Your father never wanted to be a lawyer?"

Maybe Gene had dementia. My ears throbbed, then hummed. My face warmed.

What could be sadder than my father spending his whole, short life working at something he didn't like, wearing deep dents in his shoes where his big toe pressed down while he walked to court, to the bank, and post office and paced the courthouse hallway waiting for a verdict? I could have cried, if I'd let myself. That was my temptation. It might have been the end of this conversation.

My father was a frugal man. He had two pairs of work shoes. I knew about the worn impressions inside his size 12 shoes because I polished those shoes every Sunday night. Plain Oxfords—one pair, dark brown, the other maroon. I held those shoes tight for the buffing by putting two fingers into the cups where his big toes worked.

He must have hated the daily routine. Shaving and putting on a starched collar, suit and tie, working till dark and on weekends, taking phone calls and appointments at home, trading legal fees for potatoes and rutabagas, parsnips and carrots all thrown into the cellar by poor dirt farmers in the middle of the night. All that for something he never wanted to do?

How could I not have noticed? Why would he do it? That is not the way we were raised—not one of his eight children. We learned early on to dream big, because he taught us, anything was possible with hard work and, of course, proper purpose.

As far as I knew, my father never participated in anything he had not carefully orchestrated for his total amusement and enjoyment, all outcomes unfolding exactly as he intended. I wish I'd known such an important fact (if it was a fact); it might have helped solve a few puzzles of my own.

Gene leaned closer to me and patted my arm.

"He wanted to be an engineer, Charlie," he explained, trying to soften the effects of his disclosure. "He dreamed of inventions and exploration. But that first year of University, his father had been elected Judge and your grandparents felt strongly that Darrah should take over the family law firm. I think it was very difficult for him. In fact, it was. He changed that year."

"How, how did he change?" I asked.

"Well, after the Christmas break, he was more serious, less music, more library. I don't have to tell you how important flying became … after that. Did he ever tell you the story of how he started flying?"

With a smile, Gene spoke happily, recalling his childhood.

"I'll never forget," he said, "it was a typical Minnesota August day, you know, humid, calm. Sweet, sweet air though, like it always was just after the second mowing of alfalfa. He and I were nine years old, playing marbles on the dirt road, there on Park Street, between your grandparents' house and the field. A little yellow biplane landed in a cloud of alfalfa dust right in the center of the field. Seemed it came out of nowhere. Pilot climbed out and hollered at us, 'Anyone wanna learn to fly?' Imagine that. Your dad yelled, 'I do.' He left his marbles in the road, ran across the field and jumped in the plane, just like that. I stood at the edge of the field, watched him go … up over the phone lines. His first flying lesson and he was hooked, thrilled, addicted. That was the beginning, oh dear, yes, that was the beginning."

Gene's eyes watered and his chin quivered. I couldn't believe the clarity of his memories. He's had a long life, a career with his music, a fifty-year marriage. Strange how some memories attach—maybe fiercely tethered to neurons, either by frequent reflection or the constant flow of love. In Eugene's case, it might be both.

"You know Mary Helen," he said, calling me by my mother's name, "I could have said 'I do,' and gone instead, but I didn't and that was the beginning." In that instant, I think Eugene believed he was apologizing to my mother. She would have known exactly what to say. The China cup in his lap rattled in its saucer. Placing it gently on the table, he dropped his face in his hands, and seemed to fall completely into the memories of all that was ignited on that August day in the alfalfa field, when those two boys, so young and innocent, left their game of marbles on the dirt road and one went flying, setting his course. The other observed.

I drove home after work with my father, on that same dirt road. In 1956 I started working after school as a "go-fer" and file clerk at Cutter & Babcock Attorney's at Law on East Main Street downtown Anoka. Dad was excited about having his children "learn the business," but when Leedsie was old enough, he just wasn't interested in working at the office. He said it was because he had to milk our cow Beulah every afternoon promptly at 4:30 or she could get engorged and we would have no milk, butter, cream or ice cream.

Dad asked my sister, Acey, to work in the office when she was 13, but she had her eye on a more interesting and forbidden opportunity, working as a carhop at Bimbo's drive-in across the alfalfa field right on Highway 10. Acey was the brave one. She didn't mind taking chances.

For most kids, the office work would have been really boring. For one thing the whole building smelled musty like old books and the wood floors creaked with every step. But maybe worst of all was filing documents in the basement, also used as the coffee-break room. There were no windows in the basement and the thick concrete walls next to the file cabinets were cold and held years of odors—stale cigarette smoke and coffee cooking to a dark crust on the hot plate.

Even so, I took the safe route, working every day after school for 18 cents an hour and driving home with my father at 5 o'clock or after his last client. Most days in the summers we went home for lunch together at The Last House on Park Street.

It was customary for me to wait for my father in the front office. I'd sit on the long oak bench, under the two mounted deer heads that hung on the wall; their blue-gray glass eyes were fixed on the hallway leading to his office. At Christmas time he rigged up red lights on the deer's noses.

Even though I was expected to conduct myself in a business-like fashion, the front office was comfortable territory for me. I knew everyone who came in. I knew my father's clients, people like Howie, the Jewish owner of the junk yard, and others that some lawyers in town were not interested in representing.

I knew the names of the husbands and children of the legal typists and the secretaries who worked in the front office. I knew all the loyal employees, who worked way in the back office and down in the basement, researching, typing and proofing every description of every piece of land in the county. Those women proof-read every mortgage, satisfaction of mortgage, deed, contract for deed, quit claim deed, every mechanic's lien and every death decree—all the ingredients of an abstract of title. The employees of the abstract company were the same women or the daughters of women who had worked at 316 East Main Street for my grandfather, Leeds Cutter I. Frances, Maxine, Doris, Evelyn, Arlene, Marlys and Vivian were part of our extended family.

Seldom did my father talk to me in the car as he drove slowly down Main Street over the Rum River Bridge to Park Street and home, contemplating what? That's what I could never figure out. I studied his profile and wanted to cry at his sadness. He was quiet—staring through the windshield, thinking about work, maybe; or was he bracing for all that awaited him at home. The year Mother was pregnant with our eighth baby, my two-year-old sister, Oscar, was always screaming her head off because she bumped into the corner of the coffee table again and again. The little kids fighting and climbing on top of the bookcase.

From the driveway, even before we'd get to the rose garden, you could hear my nine-year-old brother yelling at everyone because someone knocked his erector set over, again. You couldn't count all the mosquito bites, fat wood ticks and cases of poison ivy in the summer. Every year the Christmas tree tipped over, bubble lights shattered and oozed on the carpet. Every single year. Two times Dad had to come home from work because of a howling chimney fire when someone put too much wrapping paper in the fireplace all at once.

I think my father was puzzled by the big kids gradually growing out of his control, stretching outside his visions for them. Acey aspired to be a carhop at Bimbos, and Leedsie suddenly preferred the public skating rink with a warming house that reeked of creosote and rocked with hockey-playing, leather-jacketed "thugs."

Hard for my father to understand why his children would enjoy those things more than working for him at the office or skating with him on the river next to a bonfire he'd built especially for them on Willow Island. His life must have felt increasingly more complicated, as his brood matured.

And now Eugene, his best friend, is telling me, *your father never wanted to be a lawyer. He wanted to be an engineer.* All of which flooded my head with even more questions. Did my father *want* to live by the river in his parents' house? Did he *want* to have eight children? Or was he doing what he really loved when he died, as the well-intentioned folks assured us at his funeral?

"There's not a day in my life I don't miss your father," Eugene mumbled tearfully. "If he had never learned to fly, his life would have been so different," he said, wiping the tears from his face. "I take responsibility for everything that happened. Full responsibility. He took chances with that flying," Eugene's voice trailed off, "sometimes he had to, I guess." Eugene had spent all these years with regret, and actually believing he might have had some control over my father's decisions, or his fate.

I walked across the room and gave him a hug.

"Oh, it wasn't your fault," I told him. "He did what he wanted to do. Didn't he?"

"I don't know… I really don't." Gene lifted his face. "He could have done anything in the world. He was brilliant and resourceful. But … I think once he was up in the air, he just wanted to fly. You know? Intent on that. He used to say that he felt more connected to the earth when he was in the air."

Of course I could imagine that was true. Especially since my father required all of his children get their pilot's license before they could drive a car. From a distance of ten thousand feet up, in a small plane, big things appear miniature and even junkyards are well-organized, everything seems peaceful and manageable. From the air, the big picture is an intentional, well-planned tapestry.

"If I were you, Charlie," Eugene said, wiping his nose with a white hankie. "I'd take a close look at that journal you found. Really close. Read *all* the letters and study *every* entry. Every detail. Make sense of it. Might just help you understand a few things. You hear?"

On my one-hour drive home from Minneapolis to Northfield, I began to appreciate the value of the two artifacts from the past, the messages from my parents over space and time.

Before long, I would learn the truth and beauty of the profound Buddhist saying: *If you tug on anything at all, you'll find it connected to everything else in the universe.*

I had discovered something to savor about my father—an undying friendship and an insight into his life that might explain some of the choices he made. I needed to find out more, but it's true that we only uncover the amount we can absorb at any given time. In addition, three of my children began moving their books and clothes and cherished childhood collections permanently out of our house, as two headed for graduate school and the third to teach in Central America. That was about all I could handle.

At the same time, my husband, Mike, and I had restored a hundred-year-old log house and were operating a bed and breakfast. We offered four-course dinners and early morning breakfasts. During the day I worked as a guardian *ad litem* for the County and as Prevention and Intervention Program Coordinator for High-Risk Youth at Rice County Community Corrections.

I was irretrievably drawn to the anger, frustration, and cause of a group of exceptionally talented adolescents. The goal of The Northfield Union of Youth was to create a youth-run youth center with a mission, "to bring power and voice to youth and to create a caring community."

With reckless abandon and an unmistakable affinity, I jumped aboard their train. It was my attention to the needs of unheard adolescents that fulfilled my craving for the truth about my own childhood, but only temporarily.

Chapter 2

Take What Comes by Your Hand

Finally my opportunity arrived. In 2005, my 61st year, I returned to college with a self-designed degree concentration titled, Writing the Narrative: Creative Writing and the Science of Social Relationships. Still, it wasn't until I began an assignment to write a story using time-shifting that I remembered Eugene Bird's advice. Once again I picked up my father's journal, this time carefully scrutinizing every page, each entry. When all the elements came together, even the most minute, hand-written details in the margins resulted in revelations.

Truths emerged in unexpected places, and I began to see and believe that everything in my world is connected to everything else and that the past and the future are intimately entwined, just waiting for me to make the connections. I began *tugging*.

At the same time, my youngest sister, Eightball Sarah Doll, told me that Mother had left a locked trunk filled with letters written by her and my father before and during World War II. A potential gold mine. Mother instructed Eightball not to open trunk until after she died.

"If you like, I'll send you a package of war letters," Eightball offered.

I didn't request anything specific. I was so grateful for any material that I didn't even think to be fussy. "I promise I'll take good care of whatever you send." Regardless of what Eightball sent, soon I would see their own handwriting in letters that were important enough to be locked away.

"Why do you think she didn't want you to see the letters?" I asked my sister.

"I suppose, those memories were too difficult, for one reason or another. And," she added matter-of-factly, "my guess is that Mom didn't want to discuss them. There's a ton of letters there!"

It was during the conversation with my sister that I had my first doubts about pursuing this project. What if there was something volatile, too personal or incriminating in Mother's trunk of letters, something I'd rather not know. Otherwise why would she have instructed my sister to leave the trunk locked until after her death?

After some consideration, I remembered a bit of relevant advice from my fourth grade year at St. Stephen's Catholic School.

I didn't have many friends, primarily because I was a skinny kid and lived in the country—neither was popular at the time. But two popular girls, Kathleen and Rachel, paid attention to me, and I liked both of them. They were chunky girls, there was no denying that and they were intriguing.

Kathleen told me she was part Cherokee. With beautiful white teeth and black silky hair, she also had the distinction of wearing a bra way before anyone else in fourth grade. Kathleen played the piano like an artist-angel with long dark fingers, white smooth fingernails and amazingly clear, healthy cuticles.

I noticed cuticles, maybe more than the average fourth-grader because once a month, my mother gathered her hand-care supplies and sat me down across the coffee table in the living room. After I'd soaked one hand in warm soapy water, she would take my hand and place it on a folded white towel, motioning for me to put the other hand in the water.

Using her light wood cuticle board, with the beveled edge, she gently pushed the softened skin back on each nail, exposing just the right amount of *moon*, explaining, as she sculpted, how much moon should be exposed for the perfect health of the nail. Then switching to her metal nail file, Mother shaped each nail, rounded—not pointed—for optimum nail strength. She finished the ritual with a soft, efficient buffing and a final pat of approval.

Rachel was big-boned and had pretty swirls and patterns of soft black hair on her arms and face. She carried me around the playground like a baby doll, which seemed a strange desire, but interesting. Rachel was an artist, too. She won a contest with her detailed drawing of Pope Pius the XII. One day on the playground Rachel and Kathleen challenged me to be the judge of which one of them was the fattest.

Tapping her finger on the collar of my white blouse, Kathleen ordered, "You have to report the answer to us tomorrow at the 2 o'clock recess, right here by the swing set."

Rachel added, with her big arms folded across her chest, "If you don't, we won't play with you … ever again."

My older brother and sister usually offered good advice. Leedsie stopped playing the piano and said, "Just tell them the truth. They already know anyway." And, he resumed playing his favorite boogie-woogie.

Sticking her face out our bedroom door, Acey gave me her standard impatient response, "It's all in the timing." Then she slammed the door in my face.

Nestled deep into her chair in the living room, Mother was knitting. On the floor in front of her, the little kids were constructing a house out of a cardboard box. Her latest knitting project was a dark brown sweater for my father. She frowned as she concentrated on a four-inch yellow band across the chest of the sweater. Inside the band was a complex design of four brown derby hats, perfectly centered over a yellow and brown border of waves. The overall effect was strange and gave the impression of the formal looking hats dancing on the edge of a brown sea.

Sometimes, my mother was complicated. I hesitated asking her advice because she frequently answered questions with confusing adages: Apples don't fall from the trees, was her favorite; Never ask a man in trouble for help; A stitch in time saves nine; Don't wait for the other shoe to drop; A dog who brings a bone will carry one away.

In spite of the risk, I asked Mother for help. She lay her knitting carefully in her lap, folded her hands over the brown yarn and said, "Take what comes by your hand." That was it, *take what comes by your hand.* She picked up her knitting and carried on.

Carefully looking at my hands—the palms with all the lines running east to west, north and south and the fronts with healthy cuticles and rounded nails—and I suddenly knew the solution. The next day at recess I instructed Rachel and Kathleen, "Take one hand in the other, bend your fingers backward, now look at the dimples and whoever has the deepest dimples is the fattest one."

Taking what came by my hand and with intention, I opened my father's journal. The town where my parents and I grew up, Anoka, was situated between two rivers, the Rum and the Mississippi. A Dakota word or a part of the word: *A-no-ka-tan-han* means on both sides, from both sides. There was also a tradition, among the Chippewa, that the main river commanded its tributaries to flow toward it. *An-o-key* means, they are commanded to flow, or commanding someone to carry a message, or complete an errand.

The letters, from Eightball, arrived Fed-Ex next-day air with an added bonus of my father's Navy Reports. The reports outlined exactly where he was during the course of World War II and *what he was made of,* at least in the view of the U.S. Navy.

With all my new resources, I began the process, the incredible 70-year journey through the ancestral artifacts in my possession, exploring the entire matrix of my parents' journey together, the choices they made, including the exact moment I joined their story.

As the name Anoka is translated, *to carry a message and complete an errand,* I would "review without passion" their posthumous contributions, beginning the most fascinating adventure of my lifetime, reporting our combined story *from both sides of the river* through space and time.

Part II

A life not examined, is a life not worth living. ~Socrates

Chapter 3

Year of the Tiger

Spring, 1938: University of Minnesota, Leeds Darrah Cutter II graduated from Law School, and in October of that year he began one year of flight training in Officer Candidate School (OCS), Pensacola, Florida.

During this time, Mary Helen and Darrah have commenced the courting ritual. At least Mary Helen sounds like she's flirting in her first letter since Darrah entered OCS. Or, is she following up on some previous sign of interest from him? She grew up with Darrah's sister but, according to her accounts, he had never considered her a serious long-term candidate for his affections. Mary Helen was a tomboy. When she wasn't with Darrah's sister Fritzi, she preferred the company of her older brothers Rob and Stub, referring to them frequently as "the boys." She also liked tennis, golf and dancing, seldom mentioning domestic chores—sewing, knitting or cooking—among her favorite activities.

At nineteen, Mary Helen looked like the typical long legged, lean all-American Irish lassie with shoulder length wavy dark hair pulled back to show a thin, smiling face, solid well shaped nose and deep-set complex eyes.

The photo I have shows her face, playfully tilted to the left, her right hand in motion and her hips just slightly turned as if she was caught in the middle of a dance outside in the yard. She looks professional in a white wide-sleeved blouse with a long black silk ribbon tied neatly under the collar and a matching white skirt that ends just above her white anklets and saddle shoes. Mary Helen appears to know exactly what she's doing. I can almost hear her singing, as she often did in the car on the way to town,

Rachel, Rachel I've been thinking what a fine thing it would be if all the boys in all the world were lined up halfway 'cross the sea.

The handwriting and the message, in this, her first letter, exemplify her photo—fluid and playful with lyrical dramatic dancing loops on all her Ds, possibly inspired by his name, Darrah.

Dear Darrah,

Feminine or not I think that uniforms are really inspirin. Undoubtedly the natives of Florida say the cold weather is "most unusual." Don't they? However, I do think Minnesota winters are probably going to hit a new low this year. I've been steadily cold since the last of October and I'm afraid I'll be that way until May.

You would have been more bored than you were on our shopping tour in Fort Francis if you'd been with us in Minneapolis last Saturday. Your mother, Fritzi, Mary and I went down and shopped for a dress for your mother. We all enjoyed tramping in and out of each and every one of the salons of fashion, but I just thought to myself that you would have been considering it all entirely a waste of time.

Did you start flying yet? Really I think there'd be nothing more ideal than sailing boats, riding horses and all the other various methods provided for your amusement (not to mention my letters) unless it would be to work the way you do—learning to fly.

I do hope they provide ample facilities for cribbage and that at least one of the boys can offer competition enough for you so that you won't be skunked every game by me when you get back. Quite a long way to put it, when I just mean that I still think I'm good at cribbage.

Good night, Mary Helen

Darrah left Anoka in October and it sounds like he might be back in May. I think Mary Helen is trying to impress him by using a southern accent, "inspirin." She wants him to know that she's not a silly, unsophisticated country girl. After all, she has been shopping with his sisters and his mother in the Minneapolis "salons of fashion." I can feel the planned redundancy, her need to remind him of her intelligence, as she mentions her acumen at cribbage.

Even though Mary Helen graduated early from high school as valedictorian, her parents cannot afford to send all six children to college. So, they decided that her older brother Charles had the most potential, and Mary Helen, with some longing for school herself, helps support that effort by working at the telephone company and also at the local radio station writing soap operas.

December 22, 1938: On the same day Mary Helen mails that first flirtatious letter, another event occurs that will profoundly impact the lives of Mary Helen, Darrah and all of their children.

Across the Pacific, eight-thousand miles away, in the mountains of northern Japan, about 400 miles north of Hiroshima, in the land of the rising sun, an auspicious birth takes place. In Yamagata Prefecture, a boy, the first son is born to a Buddhist Priest, Ryohan and his wife, Hama Ogata. The birth is important to the Ogata family, especially the grandfather, who is delighted because the family needs a boy to keep the temple tradition.

Ryodo Ogata is wrapped up tightly in white linens at the Sagae City hospital and carried home to the courtyard of his father's temple. Heavy snowflakes fall and mound gently near the base of bamboo plantings along the temple wall. Delicate snowballs have formed on the branches of the persimmon and cherry trees beside the tea house at the front gate of the temple precinct. Snow quilts the shrine and the stone statue of Buddha in the cemetery behind the temple as Ryodo's parents stand proudly, holding their child, at the top of the wide polished stairs at the entrance to the temple. They know this son, this baby boy, will one day assume the duties, the sacred legacy of his father, his grandfather, and his great-grandfather as High Priest of Yoshunin Temple, Soto denomination, Sagae City, Yamagata Prefecture, Japan.

Ryohan celebrates the birth of his son with a short poem written in calligraphy, which included the line: "A baby boy's cry went through the clear morning sky." It's the only verse Ryodo remembers; the calligraphy has since been lost.

The baby boy, however, is stricken with pneumonia three times, once at six months old, again at one year and once more at one and a half. The third time the doctor gave up on him—abandoned him. But his grandfather does not give up. He reads a special Sutra which is believed to have magical power.

Japanese Horoscope—From the Year of the Tiger 1938: "No one knows exactly, but for sure it was a long time ago or even earlier that the Lord High Creator put the whole universe in order. It was a tall order, getting it all to work together. The Lord High Creator had what it took, plus patience and time. For sure to this very day all of us creatures are finding out new and wonderful things, which the Lord High Creator thought up a long time ago. Prediction: The Tiger Spirit represents great terrestrial power. This universal symbol strands over all life and earth. There will be times of short tempers, possible conflict, plus narrow mindedness. The Spirit will assist deep thinkers and careful planners to save the day. This is a time of greater focus. May you have a year of hope, love and salvation."

This horoscope not only defines the life Ryodo Ogata will live, it also characterizes the relationship that Mary Helen White and Darrah Cutter initiated in 1938 the year of the Tiger.

Chapter 4

Flying Philosopher

January 24, 1939: United States Naval Air Base, Pensacola, Florida.

Leeds Darrah Cutter's journal.

> Why wouldn't it be a good idea to keep that small notebook
> in the pocket of my flight jacket for jotting down the random
> ideas that occur to me during the day, as a result of the varied
> stimuli that I come in contact with? For example, write up an
> article for Larry on why we are down here. There was that
> hopeless story in the last issue of <u>Colliers</u> where the handsome,
> young hero, a Pensacola graduate took up flying for the good
> of his soul. It cleaned him of any unpleasantness that may have
> left him a fouled feeling. But there is little of that exhilarating,
> wholesome feeling that such writers would have us find in the
> cockpits of our ships, with too much wind in your face for
> normal lung function, bare business, like metal surroundings,
> a mixed smell that comes of wax, gasoline, oil, salt water,
> dope and paint, a tangled mess of overalls, scarf, life jacket,
> parachute straps and safety belt. The spiritual element is nil.

The first entry in Darrah's journal indicates a desire, a method, for organization. Maybe that's because his first Report on the Fitness of Officers rates his qualities as mostly average, not exceptional. "He is alert, intelligent and interested in the service. Is of good character and has a frank, agreeable personality." But he received no score at all for neatness of person.

Darrah's evenings at the start of OCS sound lonely. He plays pool or attends the station show, but primarily his journal reveals hours and hours of studying and helping the Desk Officer with legal matters on the base. He is an unparalleled bookworm and he knows it. One morning he reports having gone to bed with none other than his carburetor manual, and falling asleep before removing his uniform—a serious infraction, or what, in the military, is referred to as a "down."

From The Year of the Tiger (January 28, 1938 – February 15, 1939): Earth is listed as the dominate element of this period of The Tiger Year Spirit. Winds in all forms are in the realm of The Tiger influence.

Tuesday: This morning there was 23-knot wind and rain. There wasn't a plane that turned over during flight training, which included spins, spirals and attempted power landings. We marched to ground school—in raincoats and water-proof cap covers—with a swishing after beat to the thumping of our feet. The grades were "up," and the ignition exam was passed with a three point seven.

Darrah's social life seems to be more encouraging, as he celebrates his "ups," or good scores, with squadron buddies and a game of hearts, followed by a station movie, which he says, "killed the night." He then critiques the movie and rewrites the ending, adding another character to suit his tastes.

Following is Darrah's critique. It is a revision that is more than mildly foretelling.

The main character had found that his present life was too complicated, too much uncertainty of events and of human relations. Economics and moral values were conflicting and uncertain. He sought a solution in the simpler life, as that concept had been portrayed to him through an article he'd recently read, "The Simple Life." But to wind it all up well, let him get things just as mixed up when he gets to that simpler place. He doesn't understand the codes of the natives and they don't understand him. Things are just as bad, no better and no worse, than they were before. Try to create the impression that all such difficulties spring from a source within the individual. To bring that out, it might be well to have another character, one of the type who gets along on a superlative scale in the original setting, and who, on a visit, gets along equally well there.

February 6, 1939
Dear Darrah,

Friday nite eight girls, including Fritz and Mary and I, went to see Robert Taylor emote at the Green Theatre and as I care not for him the plot must have been quite adequate because I enjoyed it. Then we went down to the Grill and proceeded to wear out our welcome with "Franklin D. Roosevelt Jones." Saturday nite Fritzi had a dinner party out at the Cutter *ménage* and we all gabbled around and reminisced after a fashion. Sunday we were at Weavers for breakfast at ten. Don't smile like that. Ten o'clock is a nice time to eat breakfast. Your father went down to see the fights in Minneapolis Friday nite and the fellow that he and I favored, won.

Your family was worried because you didn't write Friday but I, because of your admonition, refrained from saying, "He is well and happy, at least so he said in the letter I received." Counting last week as one and this as two, you owe me a letter next week. No? I shan't betray you to your family or even Fritz.

Mary Helen

Their relationship seems to remain a secret from Darrah's parents and his sisters. I wonder why they choose to keep it a secret. I suspect the main reason is because Mary Helen is Catholic and that could be a serious issue for his very Methodist family and for her family, as well. Mary Helen's restraint is surprising. I know that Fritzi is her best friend at this time in her life because Fritzi is a military wife. Her husband, Fred, is serving in the army.

March 6, 1939: Darrah is now a twenty-five-year-old Aviation Cadet filled with hope and anticipation of great success at the Navy flight academy.

> Captain Kier reported to the squadron as an instructor today.
> He too forsakes the law business to fly while he is young
> enough.

But not all of Darrah's flight school experiences are as comforting as the presence of an instructor who made a similar professional choice. The frightening adjustments of crosswind approaches and learning to cut the gun and weather-cock into the wind, learning the hard way that the slightest movement of the controls would spoil the landing, which is the reality of his early and daunting experiences in Officer Candidate School.

Wednesday twenty-sixth of April, 1939:
It's an odd sensation to go by a soaring bird. The bird appears almost certainly to be going backwards.

The Birds Flew By—Going Backwards
The shadow of another plane
Coming into mine
The ground, forgetful of our dimension
Portrays an accident
With its thoughts of crumpled wings
And torn fabric
Twisted spans and spilled oil
That we aloft can laugh at

It was the old story of spinning in. Squadron One is the only squadron, I yet know of, where the student is permitted, or required rather, to do violent maneuvers close to the water. When I recall some of the flipper turns that I made under five-hundred feet, I wonder that more did not spin in. I got my tenth hour instruction today and did more poorly on it than I did on my seventh. That old trouble of holding up a wing or doing too tight a turn haunted me all hour and worried my instructor to death.

Did my father want to be a writer? I'd never heard about his writing, ever. And, I wonder at the prescience, the insight of his journal entry relating to inherent danger, necessary risks all culminating in the unexpected find of a poem. It seems to have been written "while aloft," because the penciled lines are zigzagged up and down the page, resembling his flight pattern in gusty, unpredictable winds.

Monday, April 10, 1939
A clear and windy day.
This week we started our first gunnery in ground school, shooting the machine guns, single shot and by bursts of ten, this morning. With cotton in our ears, we waited our turns on the canopied platforms and performed with varying degrees of ineptitude. Watching through the sights, the bullets kick up a continuous stream of sand that shifts away from the target and

back, as you notice it too late, and then swing the gun too far back.

One of our class has earned himself the nickname, or prefix rather of Killer Hogan by his contempt for the (ground) traffic. He is a short, stocky, happy lad with heavy features, deep set eyes, thick lips and high cheek bones. The sport of kidding him has undoubtedly done more to enhance his reputation than any antics of his, but there it is and he is stuck with it, to his serene unconcern.

The next journal entry is typed with any errors assiduously crossed out with a series of capital XXX's.

March 7, 1939
Generalizations on 15 Hours in Squadron One

Fifteen hours isn't much on which to base accurate conclusions, but for a matter of humor or to check up on later, here goes. The whole business of primary flying seems to come down to learning to isolate particular sensations, select relevant stimuli from irrelevant stimuli, and associate certain forms of response with those. This association must be so close, or become so close that a conscious thought process is not required.

Flying an airplane, or riding in one, involves a great number of sensations, some of which the student has never experienced before, and some he has. Fewer than the number that he has experienced is the number to which he has had to attach any consequences in the past.

Predominate among these sensations is the feeling accompanying a shift of weight that occurs when the ship is not completely balanced in flight and a slip or skid occurs. The rider in an aircraft is affected in the same way as is the little black ball in the bank indicator.

However, in this generation of automobiles, we have come to associate this feeling of the skid with the performance of a normal turn, and it is difficult for the student to even realize that the sensation exists, never before has he paid attention to it.

It is an interesting corollary to this that a student can detect a slight slip much more easily than a slight skid. Recognition of the shift of weight is rendered more difficult by the tenseness of the muscles particularly of the leg. When a student realizes that relaxation will enable him to feel skips and slips it becomes much easier for him to relax. Relaxation then is not merely an academic condition achieved by long familiarity with flight, and has significance other than denoting a skilled performer.

> *Blue cloud in the night*
> *Below the moon by star lit light*
> *A paler hue than days deep blue*
> *A nearer thing that's farther*
> *The skeleton of fire*
> *That herald of the storm*
> *Betrays the tumbled mountains of mist gray white*
> *By lightning's light*
> *Swift and blinding bright*
> *The ghostly blue is gone*
> *And the anger of the air is there*
> *That shuts me from the stars*
> *And dins into my ears.*

Following this poem, the next entry is accompanied by two penciled drawings of a design for a shiftable fuselage.

Perhaps this idle thought has not been recorded here as yet. But it occurred to me that a tailless plane might be balanced by making a fuselage that could be shifted about to cause a corresponding shift in the center of gravity and thereby keep that center of gravity under the center of lift, or in such a position as to create force moments that would change the angle of attack. The circumstance that defeats the idea is probably the fact, as shown by some charts that I have seen, that at negative angles of attack the center of pressure leaves the airfoil.

September, 1939
Tuesday night was night flying for squadron four, so I missed out on the second rehearsal of the local symphony, which, by

the way, the yeoman in the office spelled *symphahty* when he put the telephone announcement on my hook, whether by way of humor or ignorance, I don't know.

The night before graduation in Pensacola, Darrah finishes night maneuvers and returns to the base carrying his briefcase, as usual, filled with his personal papers and articles he's drafting. Through the huge open windows of the dining hall, he hears an orchestra and the cavernous sounds of a sing-along as his classmates join in their final chorus of the Navy theme. Standing alone on the sidewalk, he hums along.

Anchors aweigh, my boys, anchors aweigh
Farewell to college joys, we sail at break of day-ay-ay-ay
Through our last night on shore, drink to the foam,
Until we meet once more,
Here's wishing you a happy voyage home.

Once again, flying trumps music. Darrah misses orchestra rehearsal in favor of flying. I can't tell if that is a matter of preference or duty?

The year of training is complete and the new cadets receive their orders and disperse, some unhappily stationed in Hawaii. Perhaps they are unhappy because of the distance from home, rather than any real knowledge or fear of war. The other Navy aviators are assigned to North Island near San Diego, California. Darrah is in the latter group, taking a short leave home before reporting for duty.

Near the end of journal entries, before Darrah leaves for San Diego, two months before he becomes engaged to my mother, he writes (in pencil) a brief but revealing story synopsis. With my heart forcing blood to my brain, I read this in disbelief—without blinking, breathing or swallowing. At first I did not want to expose this story outline. But I promised myself to "review without passion," and that is my intention.

Cynic on modern attitude toward romance: Plot to involve male who has outstanding capabilities in several fields but who goes only so far in each and stops either of his own volition or by failure induced by lack of interest. His shortcoming will be a lack of social adaptability. Character number 2, the girlfriend, made it look like a conventional perfect mating romance, but he comes to his senses and prances off into the woods—Canadian preferably—to trap or prospect, if an excuse be needed. Might bring in another love affair early, and get in a dig through fickleness.

Darrah begins to describe the Canadian setting for his story.

Now from the top of the rock, north of the lonely roadway, was a wilderness of stone, brush and small trees. Forbidding to one who did not know it. There were…

Another draft interrupted, as was my mother's story of Bridget and Peter.

Chapter 5

Crossing the Rubicon

October 27, 1939
A handshake and a few words from the Captain, Audrey Fitch, who has since been promoted to Rear Admiral, and we were off in all directions, all madly engaged in the last minute of loading our cars to get away. I took the eastern route from Pensacola to home and drove almost straight through, arriving in Minnesota to find the great grey geese feeding in the cornfield near the southern border cinching the feeling that I was home.

After a two-week visit, I left for San Diego, apprehensive and knowing full well that I was stepping into something new and unfamiliar. I reported two days early, on the fifteenth of November 1939, and started flying on the seventeenth.

Ah! The grey geese feeding in the cornfield. The cornfield I will one day know well, too. The field where I will help my eldest brother, Leedsie, milk his cow Beulah. The place where my siblings and I will clump together by the grove of pine trees at the end of our driveway, waiting at dawn with our parents, holding our pieces of smoked glass in front of our eyes, as we watch the eclipse of the sun. That cornfield will someday be an alfalfa field and I will drive the Ford tractor, wearing a bikini. I will spread manure from one end of the field to the other while I sing <u>Wake Up Little Suzie</u> and <u>A Restless Wind</u>.

My father loved geese; they fly in formation and mate for life. I've noticed they tuck their feet tight to their feathered bellies until they descend low over the water, making their final approach, like an airplane, dropping their paddles just before landing. Geese stick their delicate necks out during flight, steadfastly soaring into new adventures.

The last photo of Darrah before he reports for naval duty introduces a 25-year-old officer, looking a lot like a young Prince Charles. It's hard to tell from this photo, but Darrah has a prominent nose. He's standing outside his parents' home, in the driveway, a spot I know intimately, just between the fireplace chimney and the porch window, and below the upstairs window that will eventually serve as the nursery for many of his babies. He stands on the spot where I will plant giant red canna lilies and orange and yellow marigolds for my 4-H home improvement project, when I am thirteen.

Yes, he's handsome, confident, fit and tanned from a year in Florida. Smartly, radiantly decked in his dress whites, including white shoes, white cap with black visor and Navy insignia. He's holding the ceremonial sword in its black sheath at his left side, the sword we will all use to cut our twenty-first birthday cakes. I can tell he wants to smile for this picture, but probably considered the photo serious business—the last before he departs for North Island Navy Base in San Diego, California.

In November of 1939 Darrah receives a nudging letter from his mother reminding him that Fritzi's friend, Mary Helen White, is living in San Diego.

"Why don't you give her a call?" his mother suggests. Mary Helen worked temporarily as a soap opera writer and program director for a San Diego radio station. There it is again, the secret kept. Darrah's mother isn't aware that the two have already advanced a relationship on their own.

The Navy Ensign asks the hometown girl out for the evening. As a child, when I heard about their first date, that was all I ever dreamed of—exactly what I wanted for myself.

I imagined an outdoor, candle-lit restaurant under a vine-covered arbor, salty ocean breezes and rustling palm trees, shrimp cocktail with chilled red dipping sauce served in doubled-layered crystal bowls with ice in the bottom glass. The café probably smelled of freshly laundered tablecloths and brilliant white napkins dried in the warm California sun. Of course there would be a single red rose on each table. Mother told me about their first real date and her initial reservations.

"He carried a briefcase, even in high school and I'd always believed he'd thought me young and silly. We played tennis in the afternoon, and in the evening we went to dinner and a movie at the Officer's Club on the base, then back to my apartment where we drank tea, played cribbage and mostly talked about our differences."

And there were plenty of those. Darrah was a Republican-Methodist. His maternal grandparents were both Irish: The Dohertys and the Darrahs. His father was English.

Mary Helen was 100% pure Irish, Catholic and Democrat. Her maternal grandparents, Mary Ellen Carmody and Milo Conroy, emigrated from County Cork and her father was also the son of County Cork immigrants. Darrah loved the country, the unexplored, the wild wilderness. She thrived in the city. She said, "I never expected to hear from him again. He returned to the base and called at 4 a.m. to say, 'Good almost morning,'" she told me. "He called an hour later to ask if I'd accompany him to breakfast."

After the completion of her temporary assignment in San Diego, Mary

Helen returned to St. Cloud, Minnesota to live with her six siblings and her parents. Donald Francis White was a laconic, frugal school teacher, fired once because of his pacifist opinions. Her mother, Anna Conroy White, worked all her life in prayer and sacrifice to earn the status of membership in the Third Order of St. Francis of Assisi. Typical for the order, Grandma owned her own full-length brown wool, hooded burial robe, complete with a white braided belt and an over-sized brown wood rosary.

The crucifix on Grandma's rosary had a secret door with a tiny glass window on the back. Inside the sliding glass door was a relic, a frayed piece of brown fabric from the *actual* robe of St. Francis. Grandma kept her robe, neatly folded and carefully wrapped with moth balls in white tissue paper inside a gray Dayton's box under her bed, where anyone could easily find it in case she suddenly died.

I frequently stayed overnight with my grandparents in St. Cloud. Every night, Grandma rubbed her hands and mine with Jergens lotion. She turned off the marble and bronze table lamp beside her bed, and we knelt on the floor by her bed with our heads bowed down on the nubs of her white chenille bedspread. In the dark of my grandparent's bedroom, lulled by the incense of Grandpa's cherry pipe tobacco, floating in from the living room, Grandma and I recited her favorite prayer, *The Memorium.*

> *Remember Oh most gracious Virgin Mary that never was it known that anyone who fled to thy protection, implored thy help or sought thy intercession was left unaided. Inspired by this confidence we fly unto thee oh Virgin of Virgins our Mother. To thee we come, before thee we stand, sinful and sorrowful. Oh Mother of the word incarnate despise not our petitions, but in thy mercy, hear and answer us. A-men.*

Mary Helen's father never owned a car and believed that mirrors were reserved for the vain. He built a shrine to The Blessed Virgin Mary in his St. Cloud neighborhood. The four-foot stone walls enclosing the shrine were sculpted like waves surrounding and protecting the life-sized concrete statue of Mary. Blue morning glories adorned the walls and Mary, with her head bowed and her eyes closed, stood on a cloud in her blue and white gown. A white veil covered her head and her hands were folded in serene supplication.

The floor of the grotto was a stone mosaic intentionally designed with the pointy edges of the stones facing upward, so that when we knelt on the sharp stones to pray the Rosary, our suffering was to remind us of those worse off—the soldiers, the poor, the sick, the dying, the poor souls in purgatory and especially the Russians. On those stones, we prayed:

> *O my Jesus, forgive us our sins, save us from the fires of hell. Lead all souls to heaven especially those most in need of thy mercy.*

December 4, 1939
Dear Darrah,

What does VP 12 mean? I've been meaning to ask because I hate to write anything I don't understand.

Mother and Dad had their wedding anniversary last Sunday and I had the picture made for them and one for you as I promised. So I am sending it to you. They think it looks human, but if you don't agree I shall pay the return postage.

I expected your mother up today, but the Dohertys were there, so she didn't come. The reason I didn't write last nite was that I thought she'd probably bring your picture with her. But she didn't come and I don't have the picture yet. Goodness me! I seem to stay on the same subject a long time. However, I do have a solution. You have your picture taken there and send it to me. Please do! Promise? And also now I have a locket, so will you send me a small one to put in it? I think it's about as large as a dollar. Please hon, I don't want a picture of Tyrone Power. If I did I'd get it out of any old movie magazine. It's you I want. I think Darrah is much superior. That, of course, is a personal opinion and to be credited as such.

I'm so disappointed that you won't be coming home for Christmas. How long will it be before you do come home?

Good nite, dear

Love Mary Helen

Yes, this courtship is taking off. Mary Helen is talking about wedding anniversaries, personal photos to *wear on her sleeve*, promises, and finally a locket with a photo inside—safe and secure as the holy tabernacle itself.

The familiar shortcut for honey, "hon," and "good nite, dear," all sound like commitment and anticipation of a long, caring life together.

Dear Darrah,

Your letter came this morning and I'm so glad you're well. I was worried because it's been such a long time since you've written.

Judy and Stub were in Anoka last weekend and I do believe that your family is going to Fritzi's. It'd be the grandest Christmas ever, if you could manage to come, but that's silly, isn't it? It's funny. I can't imagine missing anyone the way I do you. Why is it?

There's a thousand things I want to tell you and I can't seem to write them all. Like the grand place I found for a mystery story. It's an old house built way back on the end of a dark street. There are winding paths with arched fences along the way and weird, weather beaten signs giving directions such as, "Keep Out," "Turn to the Right," "Private Property," and all that sort of thing. Then there are queer wooden "igs" all over and wooden crows and old wash tubs filled with sand and tin can tops fastened on long poles. I wish you could see it. It's really spooky.

I'm a success! I made a cake today and permit me to brag—it was good. Honest it was, at least all the family said so. Am I so bad? Even though, I admit, I'm not one of the seven best cooks

I finished the sweater I started to knit for Uncle Earl. But I must confess. It's a bit large. In fact several sizes too large. Ah me! P'raps another time I will be more successful.

A lady from Cold Spring asked me to go to Katherine Cornell's play with her. Aren't I lucky? I wish it were you, though, that I was going with. I think crazy things like that all the time. Crazy, because they're so impossible. But I'll write and tell you about it and that will be a little bit the same. Won't it?

About the picture. I don't need a picture to remember you. Of course, we'll wait for the snapshots. It'd just be so nice. And I won't have you making deprecating statements about yourself. If you change one little bit (except to write oftener), I shant like it at all. I'm really serious, too. I like you just as you are.

We're going to have some voice recordings made at the radio station. They're going to give each of us a disc although I don't know what good mine will do me. I don't have a phonograph but the boys at the studio say I can play it there. Just kidding me, as usual I suppose.

When I called your house last week your dad answered and I never heard anyone sound so much like another person. You sound almost exactly alike. I've been so lonesome for you ever since.

I'll get over it though. I suppose I'll have to, if you don't come home soon. I'll be furious if you don't hope that I keep on being lonesome. I most likely will. Just trying to be a Pollyanna, I guess, saying I'll get over it.

Be sure to come home before you change your mind about loving me.

I've had a headache and cold all day so I'm going to try to fight off the flu with lemonade.

Good nite, dear

Love, Mary Helen

December 20, 1939
Dear Darrah,

I've never been so completely happy as I was (and am) when I opened your gift today. It's simply lovely—both in itself and in its symbolism. I immediately put it on and all the girls at the office asked what and where and who. I naturally made the most of a grand opportunity to display my knowledge of the Navy by explaining in detail—at least insofar as you've explained to me. I'm still terribly thrilled and pleased and will undoubtedly continue to be so. Thank you millions of times, dear, for a most perfect gift. It means such a great deal.

In spite of their obvious differences, they have arrived at a new stage. Mary Helen receives Darrah's "wings," courtesy of the U.S. mail, as a prelude to engagement. The Bob Crosby Band, playing a song from their new album, is featured at the St. Cloud radio station. Mary Helen stops parading her Christmas present to listen to the words of the song, Day In, Day Out. As months pass, she and Darrah continue, and even cement, their courtship.

December 22, 1939
Dear Darrah,

Merry Christmas! Is it Christmas today? I hope so. I did try to time this properly. Where are you going to have Christmas dinner? You should see me—I wish I could see you—with these wings. I'm so proud of them. They're the very best present I've ever had. As for waiting for you, I don't think I'll ever change my mind about that. How much longer before you'll be here? Don't make it too long dear. This has been an awfully long month.

We bought our turkey tonite. It was grand fun, going around looking at everything. Christmas is a lovely time. Everyone seems to enjoy being alive and everything is so beautiful. I love it. What I'm trying to say, seems to be, that you've made me very happy, changed Christmas this year, which looked dreary, into a lovely holiday. I'm really not doing a very good job of expressing myself but you must know what I mean. Don't you?

Good nite dear.

Love, Mary Helen

I can feel Mary Helen's infatuation literally taking wing, with utter joy and love, but I can also see her toe in the waters of protest, referring to "an awfully long month." I recognize her ecstasy about Christmas. That emotion and the childlike anticipation were constants in my life with her. But the war is raging in Europe and Mary Helen must be feeling some conflict because of her upbringing and her father's powerful moral courage and convictions in the name of peace. Grandpa White was sentenced to complete 250 hours of community service for publicly expressing his pacifist philosophy. To pay his debt to society, after retirement, he volunteered at the St. Cloud Reformatory teaching inmates how to read and write.

Sagae City, Yamagata Prefecture, Japan
   December 22, 1939: Ryodo Ogata's first birthday, celebrated in the heart of his grandfather's snow covered temple in Sagae City. The one-year-old recently survived his second serious bout of pneumonia, so there is a double celebration.

Traditionally, all the people who attended the marriage ceremony of his parents are invited to the temple to pray and to celebrate Ryodo's first birthday. Ojisan (Grandpa) Ogata, assisted by Ryodo's father, sounds the gong at the top step of the temple. Then kneeling in front of the altar he reads a special sutra honoring his grandson with prayers for good health, harmony or *wa*, and a long life as the future Buddhist priest.

At the same moment, the North Island Navy base in San Diego is welcoming the new naval aviators, including Leeds Darrah Cutter II. As they arrive on base, there is an eerie and heightened sense of urgency, an uneasy, unspoken feeling that peacetime might be running out for the United States.

December 27, 1939
Dear Darrah,

Are you all right? I'm going to quit going to movies if I can't stop letting those newsreels and war pictures scare me. They used to be such an impersonal matter—thought it was horrible, murdering and all that, but nothing concrete about it at all. You are perfectly well and everything, aren't you?

Mr. Eastman died Christmas Eve. It said in his obituary that he was a nephew of Captain Cutter of Anoka. What relative of yours was he? Or wasn't he? I think everyone sincerely misses Mr. Eastman. He really was a wonderful man. It must be nice to die like that—with everyone saying kind things while you're alive and after you're gone, too.

Christmas was grand. We got a book that you'd like, I think, "Quizzes and Answers." It's fun, but I only guess right on about one out of each set of twenty-five. Maybe I can memorize it though, then you'll be proud of me, because there's about two thousand hard (hard for me anyway) questions in it.

Do you think you'll come home before my hair turns white? I wear reading glasses now and have taken to worrying (because of you only) so the white-hair stage is merely a step away. Honey, I miss you so much!

Love, Mary Helen

Mary Helen writes with a completely new and biased opinion regarding the signs of impending war and how it could affect her. Her thoughts are shifting from love and beauty to fears of loss and death. In another of her letters around this period she asks Darrah, "Ah me! Why wasn't it the grocer's boy? At least I'd see him occasionally. That's pure nonsense. It couldn't be the grocer's boy, nor even the butcher boy, because neither of them is you."

I recognize her reference to "hair turning white." It comes back again when I am twelve years old and my father does not return from a fishing trip on the day she expected him. It's exciting to discover little treasures like that, the genesis of their secret code.

But as 1939 comes to an end, Mary Helen has every reason to suspect trouble brewing in the Pacific region. She must be questioning her allegiance, and her loyalties.

I can imagine the White household during that holiday season in St. Cloud. I can smell Grandma's traditional Irish stew bubbling, deepening in flavor and filling their house with the scents of glazed onions and earthy carrots, potatoes soaked in beef stock and rich brown gravy, served in wide bowls with clumps of Irish soda bread resting on the wide edges of the bowls. I can hear the emotional and repetitive dinner table conversations in that house, where her father must be expressing his strong feelings against the war.

And as the New Year begins in 1940, my grandfather, along with all Americans, can feel war tensions increasing. Both the Navy and the War Department have circuitously tightened security. The civilian firms manufacturing airplanes for the armed services are directed to keep as many facts as possible quiet because of foreign spies.

At the same time, at the North Island Navy base, where Darrah is training, everyone is aware that a war is going on. The real question is: Can the United States possibly avoid becoming part of the conflict?

The 1940 New Year's Message by Rear Admiral Towers holds a note of hope, peace and irony.

> With many nations of the world at war, we must not leave undone any honorable effort to remain at peace. Our security lies in our strength, and our strength depends upon vigilance and preparedness. The awareness of every nation to the fact that ours is the most efficient Naval Aviation in the world is of great value to our Commander-in-Chief in his efforts to

maintain peace. It is our duty to keep to that standard, and it is up to every man to contribute the best he possesses. I know you will do it.

Nonetheless, war is in the air and *on* the air. Since Mary Helen is working at a radio station in St. Cloud, she is not unaware.

Chapter 6

Qualified For Promotion

May 21, 1940 – September 30, 1940: The Navy Report on the Fitness of Officers evaluating Ensign United States Naval Reserve, Leeds D. Cutter, describes Darrah's official status as Commander Patrol Squadron Twelve, specialty in tactics and gunnery, primary and advanced. His commanding officer (C.O.) scores Darrah as "above average," up from "average" on the previous report, advanced to the "exceptional" category of all military requirements, which include: intelligence, judgment, initiative, force, leadership, moral courage, cooperation, loyalty, perseverance, reactions in emergencies, endurance, industry, military bearing of person and dress.

With the exception of the last one (military bearing of person and dress), I recognize every one of the Navy's requirements as a quality, not only expected, but demanded of me as I grew up. I can see, too, why my father required that his children learn to fly before they could have a driver's license. He believed, as the Navy taught him, that flying builds endurance, leadership, sound reactions in emergencies and judgment and, he added, self-confidence.

His commanding officer's remarks on this report:

Ensign Cutter is of excellent personal and military character. He is quiet, pleasant and cheerful. He performs his duties in an efficient manner and is inclined to reason things out before attempting any course of action. As assistant engineering officer his work has been very satisfactory. He is a consistent pilot and is considered well qualified for promotion when due.

December 7, 1940: The Anoka County Herald: "The marriage of Miss Mary Helen White, daughter of Mr. and Mrs. Donald Francis White, 315 Fourth Avenue South, St. Cloud, and Ensign Leeds Darrah Cutter, son of Mr. and Mrs. Leeds Hancock Cutter of this city, was duly solemnized at Holy Angels Catholic Church, St. Cloud, Saturday, December 7, at 2 o'clock with Rev. T. Leo Keavenly officiating."

Unbeknownst to the newlyweds, that same day the Navy Department announces that Navy Secretary Frank Knox wrote to the Speaker of the House. Secretary Knox recommended legislation authorizing the Navy to expend $300,000,000 to improve the aircraft defense of existing vessels of the Navy, stating that it was anticipated the entire program would extend over a period of five or six years.

Following their modest 34 guest wedding, Mary Helen and Darrah leave for their honeymoon to Little Rock, New Orleans, and Dallas, Texas.

The newlyweds begin a joyful, playful, extended honeymoon under the palm trees in Coronado on "B" Street, dancing to the Jimmy Dorsey tune, I Hear a Rhapsody. But at the same time, Darrah's assignment begins a subtle, ominous shift to more gunnery training, including a patrol plane expansion program in advance of a total reassignment.

His C.O. has upgraded Darrah's designation as "distinctly above average," and includes these remarks:

> Ensign Cutter has demonstrated an impressive capacity for attention to detail, is loyal and cheerful. He is an excellent patrol plane navigator, well qualified for promotion when due.

My mother told me that the year and a half she spent in Coronado was the happiest of her life. That is until September of 1941, when my father was assigned to Pearl Harbor. She lived alone in Coronado preparing to have their first baby, nicknamed 3.2, due in November.

She begins the following letter during a long and difficult labor for a breech birth at Mercy Hospital in Coronado. Writing letters of this sort must have been common for couples during the war. Grandma White is with her daughter during the birth.

November 4, 1941
Darling,

3.2 and I are getting too lonesome, so he has decided that I will come and meet him today. We are both in beautiful health and better spirits. Trust you feel the same. I know he's a boy because he's just like you. He started to get up at 4:15 a.m. and I am still trying to complete the job.

After Mary Helen's quick introduction, Grandma White takes over writing the letter.

Dear Darrah,

Mary Helen gave me this, and asked me to finish it for her. We are now at Mercy Hospital. Dr. Booth came after us, and brought us over on the ferry at 6:00 a.m. I am sitting in her room now with her. We don't know just when they will be taking her to the delivery room. She is such a brave little darling. I'm sure you would be proud of her. She misses you so much, but is glad for you to be spared this ordeal.

Your mother went up to Biggs last Friday, stayed in Long Beach that night then went on up. We sent her a wire at 4:00 a.m. She would not have gone but thought she would get back in time, and it would be better then than afterward, as Mary Helen did not welcome the idea of both of us being gone when she was in the hospital. I write more on this later.

Well Darrah, it is noon and Leeds Darrah III, otherwise known as three-two, has arrived, plump and pretty 7-1/2 #. Mary Helen is fine, so is 3.2, and sends her love.

Love, Mother White

November 8, 1941
Darling,

This is the fourth day of our son's life. Your two letters written prior to his bow to this world came today and your radiogram came last night. Dearest, you are the most thoughtful person in the world and I love you the very best. As for living situations, I am not at all interested in living in Waikiki. In fact for me there is one person living in Honolulu and if I never see anyone except you and 3.2 darling, I can think of it only—as close to being in heaven. I love you so very, very much. We can be glad 3.2 was upside down, he came out with a beautiful head. Dr. Booth said he was a W.P.A. worker, came out sitting down.

All my love, Mary Helen

Mary Helen cradles her baby, as she waits by the window on "B" Street, listening to the radio day and night, hoping for any clues about Darrah's whereabouts and the war. Her days are filled with worry about her husband and learning about her baby, feeding him and rocking him to sleep, writing letters to her husband and planning a trip—a one-year wedding anniversary reunion in Pearl Harbor.

November 11, 1941
Dearest,

Now the President is propounding something or other in regard to this silly war. I don't know why he's mad at anybody. I'm not. He and

Eleanor should have a baby. That'd make him be all over being mad at those people.

Today 3.2 is one week old and tomorrow his daddy will be 27 years old. I hope when he's 27 that he will be half as wonderful as his daddy. I love you so much. Must have my bath now. I'll write again tomorrow and everyday from now on.

Love MH

It's a sad thing to know that 3.2's daddy will not live to see his son's 27th birthday. Sadder still: 3.2 will not live to see it himself.

At this time, one month before the Japanese bombed Pearl Harbor, I can tell by her letter that Mary Helen is receiving mail from Darrah, but the bulk of those letters have not survived the years of trunk life upstairs in the barn. Or, did she not save them as diligently as he preserved her letters?

Both Mary Helen and Darrah are aware of F.D.R.'s feelings regarding war, and as a result they may take some comfort in hearing these words:

> I have seen war. I have seen war on land and sea. I have seen blood running from the wounded. I have seen men coughing out their gassed lungs. I have seen the dead in the mud. I have seen cities destroyed. I have seen two hundred limping exhausted men come out of line—the survivors of a regiment of one thousand that went forward forty-eight hours before. I have seen children starving. I have seen the agony of mothers and wives. I hate war.

November 1941 from the Journal:
Without any polls, it is safe to hazard a number of motives for being here. We are learning to do something that not everyone knows how to do, yet. The good old eagerness of the human being to get ahead of his fellows. We want to show those fellows in college who topped us that they cannot do everything. The simplest of psychologies of course and erroneous in the manner of all simple psychologies in that it allows us to regard the result as a sole cause. Not so simple.

There is, too, in many of us the desire to tempt the dangerous just for the self-satisfaction of getting away with it, not for any

hope of exciting admiration or envy in others. A career in the
Navy? Well hardly it doesn't take much of an intellect to look
ahead and wonder where the money is going to come from—
unless of course we do get into a war… etc.

Hmmm, "Tempting the dangerous," he said. "Just for the self satisfaction."

I remember what Gene Bird told me about my father taking chances,
another fact or question I'll have to face. To be fair, maybe it is entirely
human to tempt the dangerous but is it wise to prod it?

He's practicing bombing formation maneuvers in Pearl Harbor and I
wonder if my father questions his choice—flying for the Navy. His doubts
and fears are safely recorded in his journal, eliminating the need to share
any anxieties with his young, worried bride.

The next day he receives bad news in a radiogram from Coronado, where
Mary Helen and Leeds III wait for Darrah to come back on leave. She has
been hoping against hope for an anniversary trip to Pearl Harbor herself,
although by this time, U.S. peace negotiations with Japan were coming to
an end.

The following entry is the first and only mention of my mother or any
family members in my father's journal, which was, at first reading, disappointing but maybe not surprising considering his work ethic. He expected
that all tasks be "completed in a business-like fashion." After careful scru-
tiny of his journal, I understood his diligent efforts to keep his personal and
professional lives on separate pages. So it was reassuring to see a spillover,
a mixing of oil and water in this next entry.

November 25, 1941 from the Journal:
I am distraught. Telegram from MH today. Navy will not
allow her to come to Pearl Harbor as we planned. Our first
anniversary and my only opportunity to see 3.2 since his birth.
No explanation forthcoming.

November 30, 1941
Darling,

The war news is so bad today that I feel almost despondent and despair-
ing that you will ever come home in the next ten years. I thought that
they had to give you a leave sometime or another during the year.

Leeds and I need you to come back home and we don't like it a bit that you're gone for so long and that we never get a chance to see you. I yap enough to make you glad that you're stuck out there but then if you'd come home, I'd quit. Can't Pat Akerman do anything for you in the way of leaving there or getting me out there? I wish I could come even if I had to take Leeds home and leave him with Mother. Honey, make 'em do something about this and soon.

All my love, MH

Late that November, U.S. peace negotiations with Japan have come to an end. Overall, the political situation feels dubious and unsettled.

December 7, 1941, begins in San Diego like most other Sundays. For Mary Helen it is a sad day because she will celebrate her first wedding anniversary without her husband.

"Am I acting like a spoiled child?" she asks herself as she pushes 3.2 in the baby buggy to the Sacred Heart Catholic Church for Sunday Mass. Along the way, she sees other couples playing golf, fathers mowing lawns or playing on the porch with their children.

"How nice it would be 3.2., if your daddy was here to go fishing or just loaf around on the front porch reading the Sunday paper. Don't you agree, Darling?"

At Mass, Father Stick places Holy Communion on her tongue, and Mary Helen bows her head and holds her baby tight. The priest ends Mass with a prayer.

Lord guard and guide the men who fly
Control their minds with instinct fit
What time, adventuring, they quit
The firm security of land;
Grant steadfast eye and skillful hand.
Aloft in solitudes of space,
Uphold them with Thy saving grace.
O God, protect the men who fly
Thru lonely ways beneath the sky. A-men.

For Mary Helen, there is no obvious portent of doom, no ominous black cloud hanging over the city or the North Island base. Nothing warning citizens or military personnel of a threat to their familiar world.

Mary Helen walks back to the house on "B" Street, hoping that God *will* protect the men who fly, especially the one she married on this day one year ago. At 11 o'clock a.m., she turns the radio on in the kitchen, while she bathes 3.2. in cool water, before putting him in the cradle for his morning nap.

Due to the three-hour time difference, Darrah's journal ends abruptly as he describes the same moments on December 7th in Pearl Harbor. The morning is calm, quiet and humid; the sky is blue with small patches of clouds, an ordinary morning, unusual only in that all the battleships are in port at once. At 7:55 a.m. the "Prep" flag went up at bases and aboard ships, as usual. Men stand by to hoist the colors as the Bos'n pipe or the strains of the National Anthem give the signal.

At 8 a.m., Darrah is just finishing breakfast when he hears an air defense siren, followed rapidly by an explosion in the direction of the battleships moored offshore.

Still in civilian clothes, Darrah runs from his quarters to the hangars, checking his assigned aircraft. Another explosion an hour later and sheer chaos breaks loose across the island. The sounds of anti-aircraft guns in full action, shrapnel and debris flying and black smoke everywhere, finally force him down into an emergency bunker where he watches the black clouds of low-flying Japanese Zeros. The surprise, day-long bombing raid ultimately killed 2,403 people, destroyed 188 planes and 8 battleships, crippling the Pacific Fleet.

In San Diego, and all across the United States, radio announcers are on the air: "We interrupt this broadcast to bring you a special news bulletin. Pearl Harbor has been attacked by the Japanese."

Mary Helen listens, with her hands over her ears, and her head down on the kitchen table, crying as President Roosevelt solemnly addresses Congress in words which will be repeated for many years.

Yesterday, December 7, 1941, a date that will live in infamy—the United States was suddenly and deliberately attacked by the Naval and Air Forces of the Empire of Japan. The areas of attack were Pearl Harbor, Malaya, Hong Kong, Guam, Philippine Islands, Wake and Midway. No matter how long it may take us to overcome this premeditated invasion, the American people in their righteous might will win through to absolute victory. Hostilities exist. There is no blinking at the fact that our people, our territory and our interests are in grave danger. With confidence in our armed forces, with the unbounding determination of our people, we will gain the inevitable triumph, so help us God.

Mary Helen shudders and cries, rocking her body back and forth beside the radio. Her mantra is, "So help us God, so help *him* God. Bring him back, bring him back. Please God, bring him back."

Navy personnel on North Island are bombarded with demands from wives and families for news of troops assigned to Pearl Harbor. Within 24 hours, Mary Helen receives a radiogram: Cutter okay stop letter enroute stop. With some resignation, Mary Helen plans her son's baptism and begins to think of home.

After the destruction and chaos, Darrah stays in Pearl Harbor for a few months before his secret assignment to a carrier (or flattop) near Midway Island, where the tide turns for the U.S. and Japan's naval commander Yamamoto, is outsmarted in one of the most decisive naval battles in U.S. history.

In his latest report, Darrah is described as a Naval Aviator with additional duties as Engineering Officer. In the bracket of: present address of either wife or next of kin, the address of "315 4th Avenue S., St. Cloud, Minn." is typed in opposite "Wife." No *name* of "wife" or any room for identification of children exists on this Navy form.

Darrah's employment is now listed as, "after December 7, 1941, operations of war."

He receives a score of 4 out of 4. Comments by C.O.:

> Lt. Cutter is an outstanding officer and naval aviator. He is intelligent, forceful in a quiet manner, cooperative, loyal, industrious, courteous and of pleasing personality. He can be relied upon to perform well on independent missions, using good judgment and initiative. His work as squadron engineer officer has been outstanding. He reacts well under war conditions. Heartily recommended for promotion when due.

In comparison with other officers of his rank Darrah was designated as Outstanding—the highest rank given.

As Darrah leads a bombing squadron during the battle of Midway Island, Mary Helen is inconsolably lonely. She worries and waits for his safe return, even though I think she is unaware of the complex job her husband is performing or the real dangers. Her thoughts about taking 3.2 and leaving Coronado are turning into plans. She caresses her baby's temple and sings her hopes through lullabies, singing probably more to herself than to her baby.

You go to sleep now, my angel baby
Don't you worry now, my angel baby
Your daddy loves you so
You know he's coming home
When the war is done, my angel baby
La, la, la, la, la, la, my angel baby

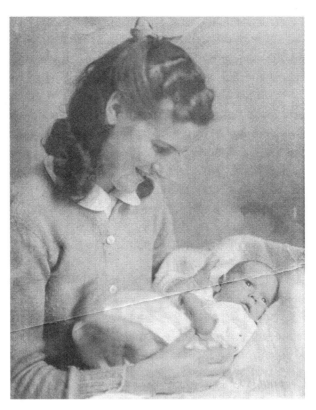

A good soldier has few choices but to be loyal and "stay the course." Domestic matters are a low priority, regardless of how distracting, physically, economically, and mentally they become to the important and delicate matters of flying and bombing missions. So, the skill of compartmentalizing becomes a necessity of war for all good soldiers.

It's been two weeks since Mary Helen has heard anything from Darrah and he has not received her letter explaining her decision to leave Coronado. She packs 3.2. into the car and begins the five-day road trip to Minnesota, stopping at Biggs to visit her friend Lyde. With all the confusion of war and lack of information, critical mail is either intercepted or lost in the shuffle.

The following plea is mailed, probably from an aircraft carrier somewhere out at sea between Pearl Harbor and Midway Island. Darrah has been on patrol for months, has not seen Mary Helen for almost a whole year and still has not met his baby boy.

August 3, 1942
Dear Mother and Dad,

I have been very lax about writing lately. But the only way I've found to keep my spirits at a livable level is to think only of today's and tomorrow's duties and drive all else from my head. This attitude is not conducive to writing letters.

Now I am so worried about MH that I am beside myself. As long as she was at Lyde's I felt all right but now I don't know where she is. The last letter, I got it yesterday was mailed on the sixteenth and she was then at Weeds. But they were leaving. Wils was going into the army. And I got a letter mailed to her in Biggs, forwarded to Weeds, forwarded to some address in Coronado—then forwarded to me out here. And I don't know what to do.

I know that MH has been very upset about this whole business—and she shouldn't be alone. Still I don't want to write to her and tell her to go back to Minnesota. She wouldn't—or might not understand— I might get the opportunity to go back tomorrow—and I may not for years.

The job that I have is not one that will earn me the privilege of leave in the states. I am practically a ground officer—tied down to a desk. If it weren't for the fact that a few more months of flying patrol would leave me nearly deaf, I should bend all efforts to get rid of this job.

As it is I have done all that I can, without offending the skipper, to get transferred to a squadron with another type of plane so that I would be taking a more active part in things. I've wanted to fly the four-motor planes anyway.

I wish I could get MH out here. Those pictures that I had taken were all mailed to MH at Biggs. She will—if she ever gets them—send some to you.

The film came today. Thanks much, and I am eager to get to town to see them. Maybe tomorrow or the next day.

This is really a weary war—in this area at any rate. Anything you can write to me about MH and how she's getting along, will be a help. And please keep in close touch with her.

Yours, Darrah

He must have been relieved to read that Mary Helen and 3.2 have safely returned to St. Cloud to live once again with her parents, her brothers and sisters. In a letter to Darrah, she tells him of her social activities, baby showers she's attended, winning prizes at bridge and she expresses a formidable insecurity as a joke, but I wonder how real her concern is, after such an extended separation. "I'm getting awfully lucky at bridge, but afraid my luck will break soon and you will desert me for one of those grass-skirted girls in Hawaii. You won't, will you?"

She is becoming more desperate and outspoken about the war too, angry at the Japanese and saying so, voicing her suspicion that her mail is being censored and not delivered, frustrated at my father's absence and all this emotional stress, well before his real physical injuries occur.

February 20, 1942
There's nothing else to tell you, except the baby is adorable, and that he and I wish that you'd go to town on your next shore leave and have a photo taken, and send it to us. Why don't you do something about the fact that you aren't getting your mail? I'm writing to you and if they don't object to my expressing rather weird opinions and completely unflattering ones about the Japanese, then you should be getting it

even it it's censored. Why don't you come back to Coronado? If you did I'd come to see you. Might even come live with you for a while. Only if you promise to not be ornery.

Whew! I'm feeling like she needs a deep breath. I want her to take a deep breath. If only she knew what he was doing, and what he had to do. If only she realized how impossible it must be to divide his intelligence between human and Navy, his loyalties between family and country, and in that process, maintain his moral courage to carry out the dictates of his conscience and convictions, *fearlessly and without thought.*

As I read her letter, I feel protective and defensive. I remember a few more times than I like, stalling around my dinner, watching the noodles get hard and brittle and the sauce cold, while I waited for my father to come home at night—late from work again, knowing Mother would not be happy. He'd have to eat alone, and she would not speak as she stood, with her back to him, laboriously reheating his dinner at the stove. Then, painfully placing his plate on the table before she silently left the room to "bathe the babies."

I waited on those nights, "played" with my food, when I could feel the tension building. Every fifteen minutes, I moved my placemat down the table, one chair at a time until, when he finally arrived and wearily dropped his briefcase on the floor, I was sitting to the right of his place at the end of the table. I couldn't bear for him to eat alone in a cold kitchen when it was dark outside. Was he being ornery then?

And, what if he responds to her desires that he get back to Coronado, how will that affect the job he's doing for the Navy and his country? How must this stress affect his safety?

Chapter 7

Heart and Soul

April 1942
Darling,

Today is a new and different day as is to be expected. But at any rate, it is raining and this is only the second time that it has rained since spring began officially last week. Your dad has again reversed his decision and is going to Chicago tomorrow. I don't yet know whether by train or plane. I rather hope that he takes the plane because it is so much faster and he hasn't been so well the last few days so I think that a good rest will do him no end of good. He will no doubt say this noon whether he is going to take the plane or the train. Maybe he'll be in time for me to add that bit of news to this epistle.

The baby is rapidly developing an intelligent, or at least semi-intelligent, attitude toward things in general. This morning he actually picked up his string of beads and tried to separate them. He's rather stupid at times I fear. Dr. Lippert says that I expect too much of him and that he's unusually quick for a baby his age, also that he's exceptionally strong. You can take his word or mine, depending on whom you think has the better chance of being right.

I'm going to take your Dad down to meet the plane to Chicago in the morning. I do hope that he has a restful trip.

What happened to George Paxton after he was wounded? Did he come back to the States or couldn't he get here, and what has happened to the Turners? I do wish I knew where everyone is. Spring makes me restless. This not doing much of anything makes me even more restless. I wish I knew what to do to overcome it. It would make me much easier in my mind if I knew when and where it is all going to end but then I guess that it would make everyone easier if we knew.

All my love always, MH

Softening her tone, Mary Helen recounts humorous details of Leedsie's development at almost six months old.

In the last paragraph, she unravels a litany of people injured, people missing, people she loves. Thankfully she seems to love no one more than the recipient of her letter. I wonder how many servicemen received "Dear John" letters and how close Mary Helen will come to feeling similarly discouraged and hopeless.

There is a foretelling statement in her letter too, as she briefly mentions Darrah's father and a trip he is planning. Even though in the spring of 1942, the diagnosis of acute leukemia has not yet been made, Darrah's father, Judge Leeds Hancock Cutter I, will die suddenly, on November 12, 1942—Darrah's 28th birthday. How much can the human spirit tolerate and still concentrate on strategies of defense and offense.

> **April 1, 1942 through August 21, 1942** Navy Officer's Report: Lieutenant Commander, U.S.N.R. Leeds D. Cutter requests next duty to be "Any squadron of 4-engine planes, anywhere within the Continental Limits of U.S."
>
> Lt. Cutter is an outstanding officer and military character in all respects. He is quiet, pleasant, aggressive, efficient, loyal, and cooperative, with keen sense of responsibility and ability to carry out projects to completion once commenced. This officer is one of the best reserve officers I have contacted to date.

As the year 1942 continues, the United States seems to gain self confidence. The Navy has recovered from Pearl Harbor, and is in the offensive mode. In June the Navy carried the war away from American shores straight to the heart of the enemy, and in a decisive three-day Battle of Midway Island, killed a large percentage of the Japanese pilots, sank to the bottom four Japanese carriers, and destroyed 258 aircraft.

From Spring of 1942 until just before Christmas, I find no written communication between Mary Helen and Darrah, but they must have finally met during that period because Mary Helen's Christmas thank you includes a hint of a second pregnancy and two possibilities for a girl's name Eleanor and Eleanor Ann. The name of Eleanor baffles me completely. It looks as if my father was home in November, perhaps for the funeral of his father and then gone back to the war again before Christmas. Grieving, during war time, like nylon stockings, must have been considered an unnecessary luxury.

December 1942

Darling,

You're an angel again! As always your gifts were much too gorgeous for me but they certainly made me feel like all the most loved women in the world. It is certainly and without a doubt the most beautiful nightgown I, or for that matter anyone, has ever owned. It's long enough. I've never had one that covered that long expanse of legs of mine before. Can't you see me being very lush and chi-chi in either that with my yummy bed jacket or the too wonderful robe? And, now, as if that weren't more beauty than I can take in—these slips. I don't know which I like better. The one with eyelet business on the top and bottom, looks like my blue suit, and the one with the little embroidery flowers, looks like a Valentine.

I'm so glad you went to Church this morning. Did you mind? It really made Christmas much less lonely for me, thinking that you'd gone. Thank you for that too, love.

Maud sent Leeds a yellow knit suit. Tex and Charles sent him a pink teddy bear with a bell around his neck. You and I (Santa) gave him a set of musical boxes (Eleanor and Eleanor Ann gave him the same thing).

I hope, dear, that you've had your package by now. It wasn't so good, but I'll never seem to obtain your knack for selecting wonderful and thoughtful gifts.

Thank you so much, darling, for being you and for having married me. That means more to me than any other thing I've ever known to happen. And of all miracles it's the one I can never quite understand but I thank God every day that it's true.

All my love always, MH

July 28, 1943: Acey or Mary Ellen, (not Eleanor or Eleanor Ann) is born. I don't know where the name Eleanor came from. The name Acey resulted from my parent's wish to name this child Anne Conroy, after Mother's mother, but at the time of her birth my great grandmother, Mary Ellen Carmody, died and it was customary to name the next child after the deceased relative. So they gave her the nickname using the Anne Conroy initials.

I can't tell when my father was transferred but the following letter from him to his mother was mailed with a return address of: Lt. Commander L.D. Cutter, U.S. Naval Torpedo Testing Range, Montauk, Long Island.

August 1 Sunday: Acey's first day at home
Dear Mom

I wasn't so good on my promise to write Wednesday. That was the only day I took off and having been awake most of Tuesday nite slept when I should have written. Work picked up at the station a little too—we had an airplane for a week and lost it. I had to run an investigation and I managed to waste a lot of time on it. The new pilots coming out of flight school don't have much experience.

Tuesday night we woke up about midnite—had gone calling that evening on the neighbors and didn't go to bed before eleven. MH didn't feel well and it wasn't just the cramps. We called the doctor at 0200 and he came and said "nothing doing until noon or about." He gave MH a shot in the arm to quiet her so she could sleep—but there was no sleeping—and at four we started to get ready to go to the hospital as fast as we could—we hadn't even packed a bag—between pains MH told me what to get for her and I put it into the bag. I would try to find everything. We got off about four thirty. I'd only been there, South Hampton, once—in the daylight and going the other way—the directions the doc gave me were very meager. But we got there without a hitch. I'd called the doctor again at four and asked him if what had happened was a sure sign and he'd said "no" but for us to go down if we wanted to—but he'd advise waiting until daylight. MH decided we shouldn't. We had a few minutes to spare I guess but not many. The nurse called the doctor as soon as we got there.

I saw MH at six and the baby at six ten—both looked very well and healthy. MH got pretty tired of the hospital—it was crowded—we got her into a semi-private room with Mrs. Pepses who is the daughter of Mr. Stravkopoupos, who owns a soda fountain and a lunch store here in town. That was nice but it was an inside room—i.e., on the court that encloses the ambulance entrance. She got pretty tired of it—so she persuaded the doctors and me that she should come home today.

We made the trip with no casualty and the new family unit is installed awaiting the Navy's shipment of her clothes, beds, etc.

She just first yelled now—when Mrs. White gave her a bottle of water—midway between feeding times. MH looks swell, eats well, and we have her in bed—it's only ten feet to the bathroom and she's promised to stay in bed—it's much more pleasant here in this big bedroom looking on the green yard and the ocean—if there's no complications we'll all be happier.

The baby is a pretty one with lots of darkish hair—MH says it will be light, there are patches of very blonde hair—she has very long fingers and extremely long toes. Her head is more squarely shaped than Leeds' was (MH says) she does have fat cheeks and a big frame. She gained a little—and eats very well and is spoiled already—she quits yelling if she's held.

Love, Darrah

Montauk, Long Island: It is while they are living in this bright and cheery place, looking out on a wide green lawn and the ocean beyond that my parents begin sailing and sport fishing and putting down roots, albeit it shallow ones.

Their house is a large gray-shingled Cape Cod, lovely with many big bedrooms, porches and room for entertaining. Help with housekeeping and childcare is not hard to find. And that seems to be a very fortunate circumstance, as Darrah is only temporarily based ashore as Aircraft Maintenance Supervisor, where he distinguishes himself. According to his C.O.:

> Lt. Cdr. Cutter's personal and military character is excellent. He has performed the duties as officer in charge of Montauk Aviation Detachment in a very satisfactory manner. He is considered suitable material for eventual appointment to permanent commission in the regular navy. This officer possesses those qualities which are necessary for the satisfactory completion of technical testing and installation of aviation equipment. He is industrious and persevering and dependable. He is eligible for promotion. In comparison with other officers of his rank and approximate length of service this officer is designated beyond outstanding. He is excellent.

Based on their history, I can't imagine that either Mary Helen or Darrah would seriously entertain the possibility of a career in the Navy, although he must feel some satisfaction in meeting the high standard of achievement necessary for an appointment of permanent commission in the regular Navy.

Even though Darrah could be called at any time to fly overseas and be gone for extended periods at a time, the Montauk assignment provides something resembling a stable home life, friends and dinner together every night.

Here I go again;
I hear those trumpets blow again;

The next baby arrives thirteen months later.

Darrah's Navy report during this period includes the following comments from his C.O.:

> With his operational and maintenance experience, combined with his personal abilities and an imperturbable nature, this officer would be a valuable asset to any aviation organization. He is highly recommended for promotion.

The Navy is not magnanimous with their compliments. They give nothing away. In determining deficiencies or weaknesses, the Commanding Officers base their ratings strictly on professional qualifications and demeanor. I am most interested in the word "imperturbable" because I don't think my father's personal communications exemplify an unflappable or serene personality. I am grateful to discover his humanity, and particularly his tender, honest communication with his mother. I've always believed that a man's integrity as a husband is predictive based on the strength of the relationship he sustained with his mother.

September 2, 1944
Dear Mom,

Wonder if you got my telegram? I wasn't sure anything would catch up to you—rodeo-ing out there all over the state of Colorado. We almost missed Charlie too—MH was so afraid of another false alarm that she waited too long. I ran out of gas and had to borrow a car enroute—but made it to the hospital in one half hour from leaving home (about 32 miles). Charlie arrived seventeen minutes later—the doc was there and waiting—we'd called him and he didn't have far to go. That was a busy day. I had flown to Washington in the morning and didn't get home until seven. We left for the hospital at nine.

The baby is fat and very dark complected—black hair and lots of it. MH seems to be doing well—she's strong—but somewhat worn out. She's had sieges of labor pains for the last six weeks.

They (the Navy) are planning to move my unit and consolidate it with another fifty miles away—rather a senseless move—but I guess they are going through with it—so that will be one more move for us before going to sea. This time we go either to Newport or Quosset. Love to you and Mary from Leedsie, Acey, Charlie, MH and Darrah. P.S., a boy and two girls now in the family. Should we stop there?

What a gift! My heart raced when I found these two letters from my father to his mother describing the births of Acey and me. Not only is it heartening that my father respected his mother enough to share his confidences, but now I know—he is genuinely proud of his children. He wasn't just having babies because my mother was Catholic.

For seven years, in Minnesota, I worked with adolescent girls in a mother-daughter program, Women's Edition, sponsored by Rice County Community Corrections. Most of the girls referred to the program, lived in foster care and were products of divorce—and most had absent fathers.

I was moved by the wisdom of those young girls. Every year they chose the topics to be discussed in the program, and every year they wanted to talk about the subject of absent fathers. One year, in an attempt to improve the program, I asked each girl privately, "If you could have anything in the world, what would you want?" Every single girl said the same thing, "I'd like to sit across the table from my father, just for fifteen minutes."

As I listened to them, I thought, *Wow! I'd like that, too.* "What would you say?" I asked, thinking these are angry girls. Their dads *chose* to leave them and once physically gone, *chose* to ignore them. They probably want an opportunity to spew and rage at their fathers, to tell them how miserable and impossible they had made their lives. I could imagine their invectives: *Why did ya bother havin' me anyway? I don't wanna hear about your new wife, your new kids, just send some money to my mom! Deadbeat. Loser. Sorry excuse for a human being.*

But, the girls surprised me. "I'd like to hear him say just one thing. 'I'm proud of you.' That's it. I don't want to hear 'You're pretty,' or 'You're smart,' just 'I'm proud of you.' Then he can go." Those girls' desires were no different from mine, but I couldn't make their dreams or mine come true. Sometimes we just have to imagine.

After Eightball Sarah Doll entrusted my parents' stack of war letters, I took them protectively with me to our winter home in Kino Bay, Mexico, where I would have plenty of time to sort by date and briefly read each letter to determine its relevance to my story.

Not once in 45 years had I ever doubted my father's affection for me, but I had nothing tangible to convince myself, beyond my imagination and my memories. I also understand how rewriting history becomes necessary for survival. On that day overlooking the Sea of Cortez in Kino Bay, sitting at a makeshift desk of an upside-down paper basket and a dusty old trunk, I discovered proof of my father's interest in my life, his pride in the color of my skin, my hair and even the fact that I was chubby—that I was born!! It was written by him for me to find someday, far into the future—my information, my validation. He was *not* aloof, disengaged or disinterested in the births and lives—and particularly the names—of his children.

My search to learn more about my parents drew me virtually and literally into their everyday lives in Montauk, Long Island in 1944. The war in the Pacific is raging, but I am safely here now. I am Charlie Anne Conroy Cutter and I am two weeks old, asleep in the antique walnut cradle in the small bedroom at the top of the stairs.

The maple leaves are turning gold to orange and blood red in our peaceful yard sloping down toward the Atlantic. I can feel and smell the drying, sun-roasting leaves crunching under my parents' bare feet. Late on a crisp autumn evening the smell of babies' baths and my mother's Yardley oil linger outside my bedroom and float down the stairs to the hallway. There's a mingling of lavender with the sweet scent of the maple wood fire in the living room. They're listening to The Tommy Dorsey orchestra on the record player, as Bing Crosby sings, *I'll be seeing you in all the old familiar places.*

My parents are dancing barefoot in the dark, their long Irish toes just barely touching, during their waltz. My mother, dressed in one of her "chi-chi" satin slips in the light of the fireplace, is saying goodbye once more. They whisper polite and dignified vows to write often; he promises again and again that he *will* return. She cries and wonders how she will do it all without him. This war could become more difficult, much more dangerous than before. They will be discouraged, distraught, even, God forbid—*ornery.*

My father wonders to himself if he and my mother will make it through this war. He knows what's coming next, and he cannot tell her. He must be loyal and unswerving in allegiance, fidelity, faithfulness and constancy, all with reference to a cause and a higher authority—the Navy. But by Christmas he had his orders and soon, as they feared, out to sea he went with an unknown assignment and a dire new rank: Commander of Bombing Squadron Seventeen.

My heart aches as I read his words and feel his desperation to be connected to his fledgling family, his need for the basic human sustenance and daily assurance. The lack of control he has to remedy his situation resonates loudly and clearly in his next letter. The Navy trains their men to be disciplined and conditioned. In the Navy, you learn to WAIT. But can you expect that same patience of the spouses?

December 30, 1944
Dearest,

No mail today—I'm discouraged about the postal system in these United States, if I don't hear from you soon I shall be distraught.

Today was payday, but through some mistake in the records they did not get my flight pay credited. I should get that straightened out before next pay day. Since the C.O. on the station here did not get my orders signed until Friday, I won't be able to make the new allotments until Friday. They tell me that they won't take effect on January's pay so that the first check you get for the increased allotment will be one March. I'll send you cash in the meantime.

I am very, very lonesome for you darling, my arms are empty every night and my bed is cold. I don't even look at the various girls around and about anymore because I can't see you, with whom to compare them—it always made me so happy to see that you were more lovely.

How are Leedsie, Acey and Charlie Anne doing?

Tomorrow we have no classes—Gates and I are going fishing—I guess. He's borrowed the equipment. I'll write what, if anything, we catch.

How does the house look now? How is it working? Do you get along all right? Have you any help? Honey I do wish I was there with you.

I love you forever and ever and ever and five days and five nights.

Love Darrah

One Hundred and Fifty Hours Remaining

Wednesday, 3 January 1945
Dearest,

This was a long day—and another with no mail. Maybe that's part of the toughening up program—to keep the letters from your loved ones away in order to see to what depths despair can drive you.

I do hope that everything at home is all right. Did the allotment check come through? Did you get the refrigerator? A stove? Does the furnace continue to work? Honey there are so many things that go round and hang in my head that I would like to know. What do Leeds and Acey do? Does Charlie creep yet? Do you fix yourself meals? Are you well?

Oh darling, how will I ever stand the interminable stretch of sea duty—that hasn't started yet. The meals have improved a little—but not too much.

We are still studying—on the ground—the new and intricate devices that have been invented for finding and destroying the enemy, be he in submarines, surface ships or aircraft. We are a people clever with machines. Not until after next week do we begin to use the aircraft here—then 150 hours of flying and we are through. I am counting the days.

There are some boys just back from PBM duty in the Pacific who are here going thru the course preparatory to going out again. I haven't had a chance to talk to them yet. Apparently the Navy is trying a new rotational system—crew for crew instead of squadron for squadron.

Please honey let me know that everything is well.

I love you forever and ever and ever and five days and five nights.

Love, Darrah

Tell Leedsie the Widenloaf story for me—or can he tell you?

January 10, 1945

Dearest,

Today was a pretty good day. Everything went right. My link trainer flights were well and smoothly done. I worked out a navigational problem that had been bothering me for 3 days. I just seemed to be able to think and act more clearly and quickly. Tonite I felt so fresh that I challenged all present to a bowling match and beat Goldblange, who took me up on it. It was the first time I had bowled since some time in 1941, when you and I went in San Diego. They have some alleys here on the station. They are good alleys but you have to fight your way thru a mob of enlisted men to get to an alley. But I shall go again, I think.

You see what put me in such good form and made it stop raining around here were the two letters I got from you this morning. I was getting pretty much in the dumps—having gotten only one letter since I'd been here—you could probably tell by my last letter.

You didn't, my love forever, answer my many questions I've asked you from time to time. So tonight I sent a telegram. I have to get this income tax thing in—it needs your signature and to make it out, I have to know how much we paid this year. I think we made 3 payments of about $40 each but I'm not sure of the amount, so I asked you to send a form, get it from Mother, sign it in the proper place and mail it and the dope from our check stubs—on what we paid. I hope you did before this gets to you. If not, there might still be time. Did you find the iron? Did Emmet send the rest of the stuff? Did you write about the rain coat or iron? Did you notify the allotment Bureau of a change of address? We might have a check mailed to Montauk after the station closes. Do you still love me? Even now?

Honey, I don't live without you very well, I do need you every minute.

I have some bad news—I got a letter from Dan—written by Eliza. (These must be Navy/Coronado friends of my parents.) He was in a Jacksonville hospital—but will be moved by the 15th of Jan. He lost his right leg above the knee. Eliza had been with him for a week. I shall write to him tonight. They certainly hit a rough turn in luck.

I'm sending two money orders, I know you don't need them—but I thought you might want to buy a new hat or something—and I have enough to manage on and cover the balance of the income tax too, I think.

Let me know that you have received them. I worry about them until I hear.

You have accomplished a lot—I am proud of you. I'd like to know our phone number and street address.

I love you forever and ever and ever and for five days and five nights.

Hug all three kids for me. Love, Darrah

There are no letters between January 1945 and July 1945. It is at this time that fire bombing missions are taking place over Tokyo and other Japanese cities and my father is an active participant, as commander of Bombing Squadron Seventeen. There is a pattern in their missing letters. Long absences of written communication usually indicates a reunion—and thank God for that. It appears my parents reunited sometime in the spring of 1945. Then my father was back to the bombing missions over Asia—counting down the few hours remaining in his tour of duty. Less than fifty hours remain, when a letter posted from a Navy hospital, written on official Navy stationary, arrives addressed to Mary Helen Cutter: next of kin.

Chapter 8

An Officer and a Gentleman

3 July, 1945
Dearest,

George Fraser is writing this for me. My 3000 hours of good luck gave out and I made a forced landing in a rice paddy. I got out with minor cuts, sprains and a pair of burned hands. It will be a couple or three weeks before I can handle a pencil.

The corpsmen in sick bay are taking good care of me. I have about a dozen taking care of me. I would much rather be under your care and sharing it with the three kids.

I haven't received any mail since leaving Hawaii, which was about a month ago.

I suppose it is chasing me all over the ocean.

Tell Mother I will get her out a letter in a day or so.

Love, Darrah

Dear Mrs. Cutter,

First, please don't worry too much. Doc and I have worked together since he was in VP-24. We practically lived together during the days he was in Headquarters Squadron, Fleet Air Wing Two, so it isn't really a stranger that is writing this letter.

I have seen your picture so many times and have heard Doc mention you and the kids many times in our talks together so I feel I know you fairly well.

I am on a ship near here and will watch close over him and do what I can to help him while he is laid up.

His letter to you covers the situation very well and needs no further explanation. His injuries are as he described and he is receiving the best in medical attention.

His mail should be coming through in the very near future and I know he will be more than happy when it does arrive.

I'll help with the letter to his mother probably this afternoon or tomorrow morning.

Again I ask, please don't worry, he is coming along fine.

Yours, George Fraser G.R. Fraser Lieut. USNRVPB-17. c/o F.P.O. S.F. Cal

My father was Commander of Patrol Bombing Squadron Seventeen in the South Pacific, when his plane lost power over China and he made a forced landing. The enemy had infiltrated the Navy base and filled the aircraft gas tanks with water.

The report issued by his C.O. follows:

Cutter is an outstanding officer and a gentleman. He is a very effective squadron commander of the highest type. He is a highly popular leader. On 30 June 1945, while flying a Martin "Mariner" seaplane over land, his engines suddenly failed (water in fuel). A forced landing in a rice paddy was instantly necessary. By his great courage and skill Cutter put the heavily loaded and fast-moving plane on the ground in such a manner as to save the lives of 17 of the 24 occupants. Although he suffered serious injuries from burns of the face, ears, arms and hands, he has shown great fortitude during convalescence and has retained fully his zeal for his responsibilities. He therefore has not been relieved of command of his squadron, and I believe he will be conducting flight operations actively against the Japs again with the same high skill as before and within a very short time.

As he dictated his letters to the Chaplin aboard the hospital ship, my father intentionally minimized his injuries. Maybe my mother knew anyway, but it's not hard to discern that she is not amused. The following letter is written in a backhand so forceful that I expect the tip from her fountain pen will snap at any moment from the strain, fly from the page and crack my front tooth completely off. Her exclamation marks scream with terror and fury. The frills and flirtations are as far gone as any hopes of Darrah's complete and healthy return.

Darling, (or are you?)

You, my friend, are an unmitigated lug. So you want to finish your tour of duty! Fine way to carry on and then try to get sympathy from my already overtaxed mentality.

You are deserving of none and will get same. Ken Jensen called from Milwaukee tonight and said it took him some traveling and time to get home. He has 30 days and then goes to a place near Detroit and expects instructor duty someplace. He said you are a wonderful skipper and everyone was grateful to you for your handling of the ship when you crashed.

I can hear you when you read this, "what in _____ ____and how can I get out of here any faster etc." But, honey, there simply must be someone who is capable of caring for that squadron and, believe it or not, while I think you are, no doubt, better than they could find anywhere else, I also jolly well think that the sooner you quit trying to fool me into believing that they can get along without everyone else, but that they have to keep you, my sweet, the happier we'll both be.

Another item while we're on the subject of what I'm annoyed at—sort of halfway annoyed and halfway amused—if you say one word more about how I simply must save money, so help me Henry, I will do something I will no doubt regret. I just won't be nagged, as you should know by now.

It boils down to this. Jenson is home. Bud Guy is on his way, as are three other planes in his squadron—he has 37 points and is a "high point man," so let's have no more stuff about wanting to be home, but hope to make it Christmas, or some other idiotic time, or else get on the ball and get here. I won't waste my perfectly good energy on living in Anoka, unless you intend to snap into it and get here. Fred isn't able to come, which is a disappointment, but at least Fritz knows he's anxious to come, as she is to have him. He shows it.

Marge DeLong Smith brought her little boy out tonite and we roasted wieners in the fireplace outside. It's warm here in the daytime, but really cold at night. Marge's husband is out of the service. Ann DeLong is to be married a week from tomorrow. Her fiancé is also out of the service. Allan Chambers is only working part time. Silly to say,

I wish you were here now because, if you don't, I don't either.

Love MH

P.S. I'm terribly tired and am practically sorry for this before I send it but, damn—I do get fed up with stuff and nonsense from time to time. Don't blame Jenson because I was ornery before he called.

Oh, what we have surrendered in our loss of handwritten correspondence. I can see and feel my mother's anger and fear as she forms her letters, her words. The D's in Darling, Detroit and Don't stand alone as mighty defiant statements. If my father's burns weren't blistering enough, there's some added fuel. She is not going to do this job alone.

Another ghost-written letter by George Fraser on U.S. Navy stationary adds some dimension to my mother's state of mind. Aside from the fact that she wants her husband, out of the hospital, well and home, she is pregnant with their fourth child.

14 July, 1945
Dearest,

The Chaplin is still ghosting for me. Everything is on the mend and now I just have to wait it out.

Fred has been over to see me twice and said that in his letters from Fritzi, you were golfing together quite frequently. I wish I could join you. I swear I'll both golf and dance when I get back.

I mailed a box of shells to you, and I'd like to know if you've received them.

I've dreamed that you and I were walking together on and on in the deep grass along the river, where the wild daisies grow. All was calm and serene. We had no troubles or separations ahead. The elm trees with limbs bowed down till the leaves touched the water as it boiled over the sand bar. Through this arch across the mild river on the green slopes and valleys opposite, we could see a cavalcade of stalwart young men and tall women, led by our own Leedsie, Acey, Dorthie Anne, Charles Hancock and the other unborn and unnamed. I know we have faith enough in each other and our future will be so justified.

Let me know if Leedsie liked his new bedtime story as well as the others.

Still believe I'll be home on schedule.

Love, Darrah

August 6, 1945: 11 a.m. in Tokyo: U.S. President Harry S. Truman autho-rizes the dropping of the atomic bomb on Hiroshima.

Written August 3, 1945 but postmarked **August 6, 1945** at 6 p.m. Pacific time: a painstaking letter from Lt. Commander Leeds D. Cutter to his mother and mailed from the Navy hospital. He has been in the hospital for over a month and I wonder after reading the following letter, whether he knew, before he mailed it, that the bomb had indeed been dropped on Japan that day.

Dear Mom

These shots every four hours make the time go by faster. I just get cooled off from one when its time for another. That's the only consola-tion about the things though, unless of course these grafts are all suc-cessful. Then I'll believe it was worth it. No mail has come through for some time. Since I've been out here I've only received two let-ters from you and two from M.H. There must be a lot along the way somewhere.

The doctor isn't going to look at my hands until Monday so we won't know about the grafts until then.

I lost everything I owned, and had with me in the crash. The accident was so bad that I haven't mourned much about the loss of personal property. The Navy reimbursed me for a portion. But I had my articles that I prized highly, and can't replace.

I get more sure everyday that I will be able to get out of the Navy, one way or another, shortly after the tour is over—whether the war is over or not—which it will be.

Hope that Mary (his sister) got the package.

Love, Darrah

August 9, 1945: U.S. drops the atom bomb on Nagasaki and on August 14 at 4 p.m. Pacific time, President Truman announces that Tokyo accepted the Allied terms with no "qualifications" and that the Allied forces have been ordered to cease firing. Japan surrenders unconditionally on September 2, 1945, two days after my first birthday.

The damage of the war worldwide is staggering: 61 million people— mostly civilians lost their lives. In Japan, the stench of sewer gas, rotting garbage, and the acrid smell of ashes and scorched debris pervade the air everywhere in the country. Most of the vulnerable wood framed, tiled-roofed houses of the Japanese people are replaced by damp, dark concrete buildings.

The U.S. began the occupation of Japan in September of 1945 when General MacArthur became, except in name, dictator of Japan, demilita-rizing and demobilization of the former imperial forces was completed by early 1946.

The winter of 1946, occupying forces took over all steam-heated build-ings and the Japanese were out in the cold. Thousands of people lived in railroad stations and public parks. By the next summer, new homes were built with a standardized dimension of 216 square feet, which required 2400 board-feet of material.

All the Japanese heard from the Americans was democracy, democracy, democracy. All the Japanese cared about was food. MacArthur sent a tele-gram asking government to send food. They refused, and he sent another telegram, "Send me food or send me bullets." They sent 870,000 tons of food, but fish was no longer available in the Japanese diet because the fish-ing fleets had been too badly damaged by the war.

Emperor Hirohito was reduced to being a symbol of unity for Japan. The Japanese people began to see him in person outside the Imperial Palace, at hospital openings, schools, mines, industrial plants; he broke ground for public buildings. He was guided around as he muttered, *"Ah-so, ah-so."* People began referring to the once solitary, impenetrable, aloof leader as *"Ah-so-san,"* taking him to their hearts. They saw in their emperor some-thing of their own conquered selves, also forced to do what was alien to him.

At the start of the occupation, Ryodo Ogata was seven years old and had just entered second grade in Sagae City public school. The American occu-pation forces gave him the name "Mike," which he continues to use today.

As a result of the war, United States emerged as the world's leading military and economic power. Geopolitical boundaries changed radically, with the Soviet Union controlling most of Eastern Europe. The strained relations between the U.S. and Soviet Union set the stage for the Cold War, which would define global politics and individual families for decades to come.

In his last letter to his mother, my father sounds broken, doubtful and weary of the job he has completed and even more skeptical of the "task" he is about to undertake.

September 10, 1945
Dear Mom,

Mail has been pretty good lately. Today I received your 30 August letter. Got another yesterday too.

I'm stopping in Manila temporarily—held up here by weather. My squadron is scattered all over the west Pacific. I should get them together up north soon. Fred isn't here and as far as I can find out, hasn't been. I haven't seen him since 1 August.

Don't worry about my being on duty. As long as I can't come home I'm better off on duty than sitting around "recuperating." Anyway I'm recuperated already—no kidding. Both hands are usable—only a little tender on the backs. There are no other signs of burns. The other burns were very slight and didn't deserve mention anyway—didn't even put dressings on them. The only reason the scars bothered me was that in sleeping on them I kept them from healing. They are ok now though. The docs say further grafts are unnecessary.

They have sent a dispatch requesting a relief for me so I may get home for Christmas. Overall transportation back is terrible—it's apt to take six weeks to get to the west coast or more.

I'd like to take a short "vacation" with M.H, when I get back. But I don't know as I can afford it. She and I have a big job ahead. We've just been camping on a more or less temporary basis—expensive as it was—for nearly four years.

To adjust ourselves to less income, a permanent circle of friends, which will have to develop, and life continually together, is going to be a task that will require care.

M.H. is a very wonderful girl and I know she and I can make a go of it. Living together for us is still more of an adventure than an actuality.

I'm going to wish I had cold weather clothes next week.

See you soon, Love Darrah

I am most interested in his phrase, *life continually together*, because I know he is intentional in his choice of words and it's hard for me to imagine living together as a *task*, unless of course, he really believed it might be. He might be right about needing *cold weather clothes.*

Mother's birthday is October 22, and my father has made it home to discover that she is not there. *The war hero returns to an empty house.* How was that scenario possible or even conceivable?

October 22, 1945
Dearest,

Happy Birthday!

I wrapped the gift that Leedsie and Charlie Anne and I got for you at home this noon and had no ink or pen with which to prepare a card. You'll know the present, it's wrapped in green paper—all that White's had. I have another present here that I can't send. I'm mailing the package with this.

I was bitterly disappointed when I found that you couldn't get home when we planned, and I'd missed my letters. I suppose I showed that in my phone conversations—but I just couldn't sound happy about it. It is so terribly lonesome without you. Charlie is doing fine and Mary says she's glad to keep her.

I feel sick every time I think that it will be two weeks before I see you—a letter might help.

Love, Darrah

My father makes it home sometime in October of 1945, when mother is seven months pregnant. But oddly enough, it's her birthday and she is not there and won't be for two weeks. It's not clear whether he's missed a letter or phone call from her, or whether she took Acey and left town without informing him.

This letter reminded me of times when my mother just got in the car and left, by herself. We watched at the living room window as the car flew down the driveway, past the rose garden, past the grove of plum trees, disappearing in a pouf of dust out onto Park Street ... and gone. She'd be gone for an absolutely frightening amount of time—maybe an hour or more sometimes. Leedsie, Acey and I sat silently on the stairs in the dark hallway waiting to hear the tires crunching on the driveway gravel. Then, when we couldn't wait any longer, one of us would pick up the phone and ask the operator to please connect us with our father at his office. Dad would come home from work and Mother magically returned. That was the order of events.

On the other hand, and to be fair, a critical transition is about to occur. My father referred to his trepidations in the most recent letter to his mother. My mother has been "in charge" for five years and will now have an equal partner for the first time in her married life. She must be wondering, what will change, what will improve, how will they manage with less income and more children, and what will the compromises be. She may consciously or subconsciously need a breath of fresh air before beginning the *task* of continually living together.

Part III

The Last House on Park Street

From my father's letter to my mother dated July 14, 1945:

> Through the arch, across the mild river, on the green slopes and
> valleys opposite, we could see a cavalcade of stalwart young men
> and tall women, led by our own Leedsie, Acey, Dorthie Anne,
> Charles Hancock and the other unborn and unnamed. I know we
> have faith enough in each other, and our future will be so justified.

World War II ended September 2, 1945. My parents are finally reunited
in November 1946. They moved with Leedsie, Acey and me back to my
father's hometown of Anoka to live in the house where he grew up. We
will play softball in the yard where he planted trees, across the street from
where his first airplane ride, at age nine, took him up over the alfalfa field,
and beyond the Mississippi River.

Once my parents retired from "camping," they probably surprised themselves at how skilled they were as parents. Doing what came naturally to
both of them, resulted in a future that would justify their journey.

How do you raise children, intentionally? From my perspective, the
Lieutenant Commander and the writer of soap operas combined their talents to inspire a healthy sense of humor, and a love of nature, adventure,
and exploration. From the beginning, we were endowed with "a voice," and
the freedom to grow, take risks, and empower ourselves.

Make mistakes here, while we can guide you, fall here, where we can catch you and learn from your fall.

All doors to learning opened wide before us, from shooting a bulls-eye and flying an airplane, to swimming, art classes, dancing, respecting history and the environment and building community. All people were equal, every moment, every detail mattered. Remember: there must always be a purpose.

Chapter 9

Circle of Kneading

January 11, 1946: My father rushed Mother to the hospital in Minneapolis to have our fourth baby. It was a snowy, blustery, howling night. I was two and a half, but the wonder of that night is embedded in my brain, as my very first memory—all because of a gift I will not forget.

Without my parents home to bathe us and read to us, I would normally have been colder, lonelier, but this night was different. It might seem unlikely that a two and a half year old could remember a winter evening so clearly but I've examined the situation from all sides, and believe it or not, it is true.

As always, when a new baby was born, Grandma White boarded the Greyhound bus from St. Cloud to Anoka to take care of us. She never missed a birth, starting with Leedsie's in San Diego to Acey's and mine in New York and this, the first one in Minnesota.

The fire in the living room crackled and the scent of oak wood floated into the kitchen where I sat at the table on top of a phone book, tied securely to my chair with a dish towel. Grandma worked at the table in front of me, making dough for rolls. Parker House dinner rolls were her specialty. She began by mixing warm milk with yeast and sugar in a huge Red Wing pottery bowl. Then quickly mixing it together with her finger, she added melted butter and eggs and stirred the batter with a big wooden spoon that she carried in her over-sized, hand-stitched leather purse. That bag held all her belongings, her prayer book, a glow-in-the-dark rosary, Jergens lotion and her mending. It was her *Gohly Bag.*

Grandma added flour and dumped the dough onto the table, sending clouds of flour in every direction. Each time she made rolls, I watched with particular attention to the kneading of the sticky uncontrollable mass, she magically transformed into soft, compliant, silky dough. I studied the pattern of her hands, shifting so quickly, folding the dough, then pressing her palms down, making a duck face. Quickly giving the dough a quarter turn, adding a flourish of flour, so efficient and skilled, that I could never keep track of which step came first or last, in the circle of kneading.

The sweet, yeasty waves filled me more completely than anything I could eat. Grandma cut and rolled three equal, but separate, portions of dough into tight, seamless golf balls and slapped them altogether, with a pinch and a twist to make one roll with three knobs. She repeated the process until she had two dozen rolls. Then brushing the crowns of each knob with an egg and water mix, she "set them up to rise." That was her line, "set them up to rise," like the Parker House rolls were the most special kind of treasure she'd ever seen. She told me she was a baker. I was awestruck by her power to create.

On that near-blizzard night, Grandma Cutter, Vivienne Rose, blew through the porch door on a gust of snow and wind. Dusting the snow off, she carried her dark blue overnight suitcase into the kitchen and set it right on the table where Grandma White was making rolls, sending puffs of flour up over the table. If you were watching through the steamy kitchen window that night, you could probably tell that Grandma Cutter had lived in that house once and was perfectly comfortable putting her suitcase right in the middle of Grandma White's dusting of flour.

The kitchen was peaceful, warm and safe, the night complete with both Grandmas—the Methodist and the Catholic, the Democrat and the Republican—chatting companionably in the same house, knowing their way around. That was the memorable gift. It must be instinctive, to feel comfort in the presence of grandmas, who love you unconditionally. They wondered what we would have, a boy or a girl.

Apparently, the name my parents discussed was Charles Hancock, which meant my name would change to Dorthie Anne. Hard to imagine how my life would have turned out if I'd been named Dorthie instead of Charlie. Dull, I suspect. It wouldn't matter to my parents whether the new baby was a boy or a girl, because all the girls got boys' names anyway. "Time for another boy," the grandmas agreed.

Grandma Cutter opened her suitcase with a big mirror on the cover.

Inside was pink silk lining and little pockets on the sides, bulging with boxes and bottles of medicine for her heart. Reaching deep into one of the pockets, she lifted out a tiny plastic box and handed it to me. Inside were two little Scotty dogs, made of stone, one white and one black, each with a magnet on the bottom.

Leaning down so close to me I could smell her neck washed in rose water, she arranged the doggies to demonstrate how they kiss, and how they run away from each other. Grandma had a pair of doggies for Acey too. How smart she was to bring presents for the big kids when a new little kid was coming home soon.

The two Grandmas carried their bags into the living room. And later, standing in the doorway, I watched my grandmas sitting and visiting together in the Queen Anne chairs by the fire, one embroidering an elaborate colorful tapestry for an antique footstool, and the other darning stockings.

It was the last time I would see Grandma Cutter. She had a heart attack and died that winter.

The new baby's name was changed again. My father named him Andrew Shinski Bulgarian Prime Minister, and I kept my name. The score was now boys 2, girls 2. In that house on the Mississippi River, my parents had four more children.

Our next baby was a girl, Milo, born two years later on January 6, the Epiphany, a Holy Day of obligation. Milo was born, and the three kings from the Orient followed a star to find the baby Jesus in the manger and present gifts of gold, frankincense and myrrh.

Milo fit perfectly into our family: girls 3, boys 2. It was the summer after Milo was born that Mom and Dad began the tradition of hiring a professional photographer to take our photos. From then on, the Gene Garrett Studios from Nicollet Avenue, Minneapolis, arrived every summer to take "candid" shots of my father's dream-cavalcade unfolding.

Mother especially liked outdoor photos and she insisted on fresh haircuts for everyone and new dresses for the girls. In the black and white picture of all three girls together, you can see that Mother placed a quilt, handmade by Grandma Cutter, in the grass in the front yard at a spot closest to home base on our softball field. It was as if she wanted to record forever that all the girls were certainly capable of hitting a homerun.

Acey and I are sitting up looking lady-like and right above the camera at the photographer. Behind us, you can see some of the pine trees my father planted when he was little. And just beyond that little grove, is Park Street. More distant is the alfalfa field where my father had his first airplane ride. Farther still on the horizon, although you can barely see it, is the Catholic Cemetery on Highway 10 where my great grandparents Mary Ellen and Milo Carmody are buried.

Acey is wearing a new dress with a white blouse top and a Scottish plaid skirt. You can still see the fold marks on the sleeves of her blouse. Just before Acey sat down on the quilt, Mother unfolded the new dress from the white tissue paper, lifted it out of the Dayton's box, and pulled it down over her head. Acey looks completely relaxed. Her hair is silky light brown and falls into perfect gentle curls, just so, under her ears, and her bangs are very straight.

I'm over on the left with crooked bangs. Mother couldn't find her good scissors, so she tried to cut my bangs even, with her pinking shears, while Gene Garrett set up his camera. I can still feel the crisp, scratchy fabric of my new ruffled dress. It's decorated with baby lambs kicking up their little hooves, as they run through a rose garden all over the bodice and skirt. You might notice I'm missing a front tooth, because I knocked it out on the side of the playpen when I was two. Mother told me I swallowed it. Acey said I would never, ever get a new tooth in that space.

"Just get used to it," she told me with her usual authority. "It's probably growing inside your stomach."

My missing front tooth wasn't my biggest worry that day. Six month-old Milo is crawling between us on the quilt, looking as innocent and delicate as a Gerber Baby dressed in a wide-collared ruffled pinafore. But just before he snapped the photo, Mr. Garrett threw a red rubber ball in the air to get Milo's attention. Unfortunately the ball landed on my dress and at just the moment he snapped the picture, Milo reached into my lap for the ball, grabbed it and pulled my dress up. I tried to stop her by grabbing her hand. At the same time I'm following instructions, smiling nicely for Mr. Garrett so we can get this over with. I felt cool air rising higher and higher up my legs and prayed to The Blessed Virgin Mary that the picture would not turn out.

Chapter 10

Sesson

Sesson joined our household that year, for three days a week, and God knows Mother needed help. Sesson was a beautiful Danish woman, gentle, big-bosomed and after a full day at our house, she smelled sweetly of sweat. She was totally devoted and loyal to my mother and her need for naps, line-dried and ironed sheets, fresh cleaned chickens, and in times of crisis, lunches of nice little B.L.T.s.

"Just between you, me and the fencepost," Sesson told me, "I came over from Denmark in the bottom of a boat." She taught me how to tie my shoes when I was five, so I could properly attend kindergarten. She demonstrated how to pick the pin-feathers out of Mrs. Schenk's chickens, which were delivered to the pantry door once a week with their throats slit and their heads and feet still dangling down. I also learned how to efficiently hang clothes on the line, under the crab apple trees, next to the garage. Sesson and I each carried a wicker basket of wet laundry, mostly sheets, out the pantry door, over the driveway into the grass under the line.

"Always wanna keep a pin in your mouth," she instructed with a wooden pin in her mouth. "Then take the corner of the sheet and pin it to the line. Holding that one, pin the next sheet over the corner of the last, then pin the two together. You see? You can hang two sheets with only three pins." Sesson inhaled deeply and smiled. "Ahhh, nothing in the world smells or feels better than clothes dried on the line."

Sesson drove Chevys only and arrived promptly at The Last House on Park Street at 8 a.m. Monday, Wednesday and Friday. Each day at 5 p.m., she returned home to her family in the country. Sesson was attentive, watching our activities, inside and out. Sometimes she could see where we were going from the dining room windows, where she ironed endless shirts and sheets on the Mangle ironing machine.

She warned us, "I have eyes in the back of my head, so I know where you're going and just what you're taking with you." Sesson did not "tell on us," unless it was a matter of life or death.

Chapter 11

War around the Edges

My father never talked about the war, but sometimes I'd see him sitting motionless in his maroon Plymouth, long after coming home from work. With my back up against the fireplace, I would draw the sheer curtain slowly open, just enough to peek out—but not enough so he'd know I was there.

Leading Mother from the kitchen to the window, I whispered, "Look at him, looking out over the river. See that? See? He doesn't move. His fedora doesn't move, almost like he's not even breathing, like he's made of stone in a game of statue maker. He just waits there, Mom. Waiting till the sun goes completely down, on the other side of the river. Why does he do that? He does it a lot." Mother looked puzzled, as she stood beside me, looking out into the car parked too long in the driveway.

"I don't know for sure," she whispered. "He might be thinking of his parents. They were very close and they both died so young … and suddenly. Or," she said, twisting the hem of her apron, "he might be thinking of the war."

I didn't know much about the war, except that we were not allowed to look at my father's Navy yearbooks. They were kept on the very top shelf of the bookcase in the living room, neatly stacked next to the skin disease book.

Mother told us the simple version, the one we were allowed to tell in school on Hero Day. Dad crash-landed his plane during the war with the Japanese. "He was the skipper," she said, "and responsible for his crew. He went back into that burning plane to carry his seventeen crew members out and saved their lives. He was a hero."

I tried to imagine my father with flames on his face and his ears burning, while he pulled and tugged and dragged those men from the plane, trying to breathe through the smoke. His hands were red, too, with little white streams running through them. After he returned from the war, he couldn't wear his wedding ring.

The scars on my father's face, his neck and hands were obvious. Mostly, I noticed the ones on his ears where I could imagine the whole history of the war, without ever looking at his yearbooks. His ears turned purple in the winter when they were cold, or when he was angry, and then little white ripples ran through the purple skin in all directions like a web of teeny streams. I saw those white ripples for the first time when his forty-drawer agate collection fell over on top of him. All the agates he'd sorted by color and clarity, year and location, polished and saved since he was four years old, bounced, scattered and cracked, mingling all the years together, covering the floor of the shop.

"Damn!" he yelled from the floor, surrounded by his precious collection. His ears turned purple and I ran to the house to tell Mom that Dad swore.

Sometimes we didn't know what was happening with our father. It was the invisible scars that were most frightening. He would be quiet for days and then suddenly erupt in anger over what seemed like nothing.

Acey and I argued about who got to hold the baby. The one who wasn't rocking the baby had to put the books away or dust the banister in the hallway, or help set the table.

"You get out! It's my turn," Acey snarled, trying to take baby Milo from my arms.

"No, you get out, it's my turn. Leave me alone or I'm telling."

"Oh, yeah?" she countered, clawing my arms with her fingernails. "Well, yack, yack, yack, yack."

Right back at her, only louder, I hollered, "Yack, yack, yack, yourself." We could have gone on for hours, if our father hadn't suddenly appeared, coins rattling angrily in his pockets. His ears turned purple, while he furiously led us by *our* ears to the bathroom, where he washed our mouths out with Ivory soap, 99-100% pure.

"Don't you ever let me hear you making those noises again!" He shouted, as he cleansed our mouths. Years later, I learned that the Anti-aircraft Artillery (AAA), nicknamed ack-ack because of the sound it makes while firing, is weaponry specifically designed to shoot airplanes down.

How strange my father must have felt on so many Christmas mornings when at least one of his children proudly presented Mother with her present. The perfume cost mere pennies from Smith's 5 & Dime, and that was probably charged to our parents' account.

To a child, the bottle was irresistible—clear die-cut glass shaped precisely like a bomb with a red plastic cap in the shape of a big, fat bullet. Atom Bomb perfume, by Jergens. You could smell it, the war was in our house, all around the edges.

Chapter 12

Ma Barker's Gang

A week after Mother's Day, the year I was finishing first grade, we were preparing for the birth of our next baby, number six. Mother was upstairs, resting. Dad made his usual Saturday morning breakfast. Standing by the stove with a sturdy wooden spoon, he stirred oatmeal, or fricasseed butterfly wings, as he called it. His recipe for oatmeal never changed: 4 cups water to 4 cups oatmeal. We all grew up believing that oatmeal was like squares of hard-rock Christmas candy, so solid and impervious, the milk splashed off.

"You know, Children," he said as he drove the huge wooden spoon through the mucky oatmeal, "every sixth child born is Chinese." Each pregnancy seemed to be more difficult than the one before. Mother required more sleep and sometimes she'd just outright faint, in the middle of the hall floor. If Sesson wasn't there, and Leedsie, Acey and I decided things were too difficult to handle, we'd pick up the phone and ask the operator to connect us to Dad's office. He'd rush home and help Mother upstairs to bed.

During those years, Dad ran for Anoka County Attorney and Mother campaigned by his side, wearing her navy blue satin maternity dress with the over-sized rhinestone buttons. At the same time, The Last House on Park Street was undergoing yearly renovations—a downstairs bathroom, a new master bedroom, a library, a sun porch and more bedrooms for children. A steady stream of carpenters, plumbers, wall paper hangers arrived daily and became part of our family, because Mother integrated them into our daily lives. It wasn't unusual for her to ask Wally, the carpenter, to baby sit, while she ran to the store or to get a haircut.

Before summer arrived, the count was girls 3, boys 3. Dad named our *Chinese* baby, Marcus Aurelius Mad Russian. There was no telling what inexplicable name Dad would come up with, nothing was ordinary, especially not our father. And, there would be more names because he dreamed of having an entire softball team.

It was two years later, just before the downtown Memorial Day parade, when our father told us the story of the infamous Midwest outlaws, Ma Barker and her juvenile delinquent sons, Herman, Lloyd, Arthur and Fred. Every year as the school year wound to a close, Dad revealed a new and tantalizing mystery with the hope that we, the Cutter kids, might participate in the solution over the summer months.

Most of my father's challenges involved using searching techniques and commandments that the Native Americans might have followed 100 years earlier on this very same land.

#1. Walk around small trees, never on them, never cut them down;

#2. Never dig in the mounds because they are sacred;

#3. Always check tree trunks and limbs for unusual or fresh cuts;

#4. Pay close attention to the seasons and the in-between seasons, so you will always know when something is out of place;

#5. Close your eyes and *smell* the time of year;

#6. Never leave any garbage behind and pick up what you find;

#7. Finally do not disturb the birds or animals in the woods, walk softly by putting your toe down first, followed gently by your heel and learn to listen to the ground. Lie down, keep your ear to the earth.

This current mystery had the potential to be the most exciting ever. It might have been because my father was County Attorney that he cared so much about the Barker gang crimes. Whatever the reason, Leedsie, Acey and I sat at the table waiting for our Saturday morning oatmeal, while Dad explained the history of the infamous outlaws.

For almost thirty years, Ma Barker and her boys stole money and kidnapped people in several states, mostly Kansas. But the cases most interesting to my father were the December 16, 1932, robbery of the Third Northwestern Bank in Minneapolis, where the Barker gang made off with $81,000 in cash and $185,000 in bonds, killing two policemen in the process. The other local case was the 1933 kidnapping of William Hamm, founder of the Hamm's brewery in St. Paul. Hamm was later released after the family paid a $100,000 ransom.

Another Barker gang robbery was the payroll at the St. Paul Stockyards National Bank, where they killed another policeman. The FBI (or G-Men) killed Ma and Fred Barker in a raid. My father had our attention even before he got to the summer challenge.

"Intriguing part of all this," he explained, building the plot, "is part of the money from those two local robberies has never been found. However, there was some talk of Lloyd Barker burying money in the rural Anoka area, since they traveled these parts on their way to the lakes up north." He scratched his chin as he stirred the cereal. "Always wondered if that stash could be right here in our woods." He told us that one of the brothers, Arthur, was trying to escape Alcatraz, when he got killed by the G-men.

"The only surviving brother," Dad said, carving our cereal out of the pan and into bowls, "was Lloyd. And oddly enough, he was an Army cook in a prisoner-of-war camp right here in Minnesota at Fort Custer. Ironically, the guy received a good conduct medal and an honorable discharge. Amazing, isn't it."

Leedsie said, "Then maybe Lloyd came and got the money."

"Nope," Dad said. "In 1949, Lloyd's wife killed him. Money's never been found, never entered circulation. Not yet. But I suspect someone knows its whereabouts. Wouldn't be at all surprised," he said, "if that money turned up right here on this property."

I knew this could be the most important summer of my whole life and of all the bad luck, it was the summer my parents decided to send me to Bemidji. Our seventh baby was on the way, and Mother had already fainted twice. This pregnancy was a tough one and she ended up staying in bed most of the day. The dust hadn't even settled from the last remodeling job and we needed another bathroom upstairs. On top of that, Mother's sister, Nelly, called for help with her three little blond babies way up there in the land of Paul Bunyan and Babe the Blue Ox.

To tell the truth, I think Mother needed a break from all those kids.

Someone had to go to Bemidji and they promised it would only be until the baby was born. Mother convinced my father that I was the most likely candidate, but Dad did not want me to miss the Fourth of July, almost his favorite holiday of the entire year, second only to Arbor Day.

My father abhorred the idea of his children leaving home, ever, for any reason. Mother explained that she needed Acey to help with the little kids and I was just the right age to help my aunt. Imagining everything I would miss, the Fourth of July, cap guns with boxes of caps at the ends of our beds when we woke up. We always went to see the fireworks at the Anoka County Fairgrounds. Add to that, the possibility of the Barker gang's money hidden somewhere in our woods. I wanted to hide myself, under the sofa until they decided to send someone else to Aunt Nelly and Uncle Leo's.

Chapter 13

Prayers and Sins in Bemidji

My biggest worry was not for me as much as it was for the safety and welfare of the new baby. I thought I should be home to help my parents choose the right name. A name can affect a baby and the choices that child makes for the rest its life. No one else seemed concerned, but I felt a responsibility to the new baby, especially if it's a boy. No, I was certain; this would be a very bad summer for me to be away.

Uncle Leo drove down the driveway, through the familiar scent of the blossoming wild plum trees, toward Park Street and I watched out the back window of his old Ford. My brothers and sisters waved from the porch steps, holding their stick and twine horses, just like serious G-men, ready to begin the search for Ma Barker's money. I cried until I threw up, but Uncle Leo just kept driving up north. The best thing I could do now was pray for our next baby to be a girl.

The first day in Bemidji, Aunt Nelly asked me to pull her three blue-eyed children in their brand new Radio Flyer wagon.

"Take them around the block, but be careful when you turn corners," she warned me in a loud voice as if I didn't understand English. As I headed out the driveway with the wagon full of children, my aunt pointed out all the dangers of wagon pulling.

"Most important!" she cautioned, following beside me. "Pay attention to the turns, because the wagon could tip over and the children could all fall out onto the sidewalk and get badly hurt, seriously bruised and cut, even crack their heads wide open. So, do you hear me, Charlie? Be careful."

It was a simple enough job, pulling three children in a wagon down a flat, treeless sidewalk, past houses all exactly the same, each with a table lamp, each with clear plastic covers on the lampshades. The lamps were placed exactly in the center of the picture windows.

I counted the houses so I wouldn't get lost and when I got to end of the street, I turned the corner and the wagon tipped over. The children fell out and screamed until Aunt Nelly came running from her house in the middle of the block.

"Oh my heavens! I told you that's what would happen," she clucked victoriously as she ran toward us. "And it did. Didn't it?" My aunt's face turned red. "That is a perfect example of a mortal sin."

"First of all," she said holding up one, shaking finger at a time, "what you did was wrong. Secondly," she said, holding up two fingers, "you knew it was wrong because I told you so. Then, number three, and this is the big one, Charlie. *You did it anyway.* You did it anyway; right there, that is the difference between a venial sin and a mortal sin. Therefore, what you have done is this. You have destroyed some of God's sanctifying grace that was resting in your soul and now you have to go to confession. You must try to get that grace back where it belongs." Finally my aunt picked up the children, lined them up in the wagon and called over her shoulder, as she headed down the sidewalk.

"I'm going back to the house to call the priest immediately." And that was my first confession in Bemidji, but not my last. I knew the difference between a mortal sin and a venial sin but if I had to go to confession every time I made a mistake, there'd be no time left in the day to change the baby's diapers.

One time, when I was only five years old, I went with Mom to Knodt's grocery store to pick up a few things. While she shopped, I took a package of Wrigley's Juicy Fruit gum and put it in my pocket. On the way home, Mom called out, "Who's got Juicy Fruit gum?" You can smell Juicy Fruit gum a mile away.

I said, "I do."

"Where do you get that?" she asked as she pulled the car over the side of the road. We weren't allowed to have candy or gum or pop, except on special occasions. We weren't allowed to steal either.

"On the shelf, right before you go out the door at Knodt's," I confessed. Mother turned the car around and took me back to Knodt's. On the ride back to the store, Mom told me that the Knodts have to buy all their groceries and even a 5-cent package of gum is very important to them.

"Now, you take that gum back in there and tell Mrs. Knodt, you're sorry."

My parents believed in restorative justice long before it was a popular tool at the Department of Corrections.

The second night in Bemidji we had hot dogs and potato salad on paper plates in the breezeway. I'd never heard of a breezeway, but it's a space between the house and garage with just a roof over it, no walls. In the middle of the floor of the breezeway is a picnic table with a plastic yellow and white checked tablecloth and bottles of ketchup, mustard and sweet pickle relish lined up around a plastic holder for paper napkins. The breezeway table stays set up with supplies, ready to go, all summer long in Bemidji. No surprises. I wanted to go home. The phone on the kitchen wall rang.

Uncle Leo called out to the breezeway, "Charlie, it's for you. … Your dad." He'd called to make sure I was okay. I lied and told him I was. I think that was the first time anyone ever called me on the telephone.

"Did Leedsie and Acey find Ma Barker's money yet?" I asked. I could picture them happily digging holes under the gooseberry bushes. They would fill in the holes and move deeper in the woods under the big oak trees, looking for clues everywhere they went and covering their paths, carefully so no one could follow. Oh, I wanted to be with them. They'd never know how hopeless and useless it feels to be so far away from where you belong.

"Nope, not yet," Dad said. "I suspect it'll take all summer to comb those woods. But don't worry we'll have you back here by the Fourth." I could tell he missed me, not half as much as I missed being home. I tried not to cry.

"You be a good girl and a help to your Aunt, hear?" He told me he was working on a really big surprise. "Might just be ready by the time you get home."

"What will you name the baby, Dad?" I closed my eyes, crossed my fingers, and hoped his answer wouldn't be the name he and mother talked about earlier, a name I couldn't even pronounce. It was so important to me—the name of our baby. For months I prayed to Jesus, Mary and Joseph for one regular name in our family. I even prayed to my patron saint, Anne, mother of The Blessed Virgin Mary.

Why not? I wondered. *Why couldn't they consider simple, normal names, for example names like the children I pulled in the wagon in Bemidji, Mary, James and Peter. Maybe they don't realize how difficult it is to have Cutter for a last name, not to mention girls with boys' names and boys with just plain crazy names. Didn't they know how the bullies on Park Street chased me with snakes and fake guns, yelling, 'Hey Cutter, Cutter, cut the butter? Whatcha gonna name yur next one? Cookie?' Not to mention, Charlie, which the bullies said was a boy's name. Even Ma Barker gave her boys regular names.*

At the other end of the phone line, my father was steadfast. "Same name," he said. I cringed and shut my eyes, while he uttered the dreaded name. He said it out loud again.

"If it's a boy, it's Zeolodus." He said it so happily, gleefully even, like the name was music. Zeolodus was the name of an ancient ancestor, but what a cruel name for a baby. I just couldn't let it happen. I continued praying, on my knees by my bed in Bemidji, for a girl. *"Please Jesus, Mary and Joseph, please bring us a girl. Get The Holy Ghost to help if you have to but we really need another girl and I'll help take care of her, so will Acey, we promise. I'll wash her diapers and rock her in the glider, please."*

During the first week in Bemidji, I was beyond lonesome, so homesick that even a trip to see Paul Bunyan didn't cheer me up. Uncle Leo arranged for the 30-foot-tall wooden statue of Paul Bunyan to talk to me. Mr. Bunyan wore a blue plaid shirt and blue work pants with red wooden suspenders. The toes of his lumberman boots were four feet tall. His voice came out of big wooden moving lips, that sounded like two fat boards clapping together. With one hand on the head of Babe the Blue Ox, Paul Bunyan waved the other hand and his wooden eyeballs rolled down and looked right at me.

"Well, well." His words thundered through the amusement park. "Looky here folks, what we have coming through the gate right now." Grown-ups and children with pink and green cotton candy turned to look at me walking under the Welcome Gate.

Mr. Bunyan said, "It looks like Charlie Cutter from Anoka came all the way to Bemidji to meet Babe here."

"Wow, how did he know that?" I asked Uncle Leo.

"Paul Bunyan knows everything," he said. I didn't want to get into a conversation with Paul Bunyan while people stared from the top of the Ferris wheel swinging in their baskets, so I didn't ask if he might know if we were going to get a girl or a boy.

Taking the kids for a wagon ride on a cement sidewalk didn't really compare with searching for Ma Barker's money in the woods. Things started looking up the second week, though, when I met a girl named Suzanne. She was nothing like my friend Lolly at home, but she'd have to do. I told her about Lolly, hoping Suzanne would take the hint. I told how Lolly liked to make forts and tree houses with us and didn't mind getting dirty, even playing with our pigs in their pen or feeding a baby lamb out of a baby bottle in the basement.

"For example," I told her, "Lolly would love to look for Ma Barker's money." She was the perfect friend and every day I spent in Bemidji, I appreciated Lolly more and more, especially her happy freckled face. I even missed the orange and yellow plaid ribbons on her pony tail.

Suzanne was a nice girl—the *only* girl my age within three blocks. She said, "I'll play in the dirt with you and I'd look for Ma Barker's money too. I know where there's a sandbox and a tree we can climb." So we became friends, but not for long.

Just as it seemed I could make it till the new baby was born, I committed another mortal sin. When the toilet at my aunt's house plugged up, Aunt Nelly asked me how much toilet paper I used. I didn't know. We didn't keep track of, or even talk about, stuff like that at our house.

"What do you mean?" I asked.

"How many squares did you use?" She demanded, clapping one palm on top of the other. "One? Two? Six or Ten?"

"I didn't count them," I told her, trying to figure out how anyone would know. You just take what you need.

"Well, you see?" Holding a long strip of toilet paper in my face, Aunt Nelly counted out five tear lines. I'd never noticed tear lines in toilet paper before. "This is something you should know certainly by the time you reach the age of reason, which you did last year, when you received your First Holy Communion and went to Confession for the first time." She took a deep impatient breath, rolled her eyes and continued, "Using more than five squares *is* a sin."

It was beginning to feel as though I couldn't escape sinning in Bemidji. You just never know what experience is going to stick in your brain for fifty-four years—maybe longer, could be all the way through your stay in the nursing home when you're really, really old. But, every single time I go to the bathroom, I do consider, *what actually is the sin of using six or more squares of toilet paper?*

Two days after Suzanne introduced me to a maple tree perfect for climbing, we were eating hamburgers and Red Dot potato chips in the breezeway, when Aunt Nelly said I could no longer be friends with Suzanne.

"Why?" A potato chip stuck sideways in my throat and I cried, knowing there would be nothing left without a friend, a tree and some dirt.

"Well, it's simple." My aunt said, looking at me as if I should have figured it out all by myself. "Suzanne is not Catholic," she said, while Uncle Leo nodded in agreement. That was that. Or so they thought.

The next day I met Suzanne in a small grassy space between our houses. I was almost crying when I told her, "My aunt says I can't play with you because you're not Catholic."

Suzanne wrinkled up her nose, like something smelled really bad. "What's that?"

"Well, it doesn't matter so much that you understand everything about it, Suzanne. Being Catholic is a kind of club, like a girls-only club. But when you're a Catholic you pray and suffer for all the people who aren't in the club, so they will join the club. Or, you pray for Catholics who died and went down to purgatory where it's not as hot as it is in hell. The good part of purgatory is they can get out and go straight on up to heaven, if they get enough prayers."

"There's really only one bad part about being Catholic. The mass on Holy Thursday is really long and you hafta eat fish on Friday, or you can have poached eggs, or tomato sauce with bread chunks floating in it. And that's not as bad as it sounds."

"So, I have an idea and if you help me, we can still play together. Will you help me, Suzanne?"

She nodded and followed behind me through the grassy spot.

"Do you *want* to be a Catholic, Suzanne? Cuz that's an important part of this whole thing."

She nodded again. "Yah, I do."

"I mean do you *really* want to be Catholic?"

"Really, I do," Suzanne said, adding a smile to her answer.

"Do you have a hose at your house?" I asked. "That's all I need to baptize you."

"Yah, we have a hose."

"Okay, let's go." When I was ready, I told Suzanne to plug her nose.

After all, baptism was the easiest of all the sacraments. I learned it from The Baltimore Catechism the year I reached the age of reason. There are three kinds of baptism: by water, desire, or blood. My plan was to use a combination of water and desire and that's why I asked Suzanne if she was really sure she wanted to be a Catholic, which would satisfy the desire part.

With Suzanne holding her nose, bowing down in front of me, I held the hose, running cold water over her head. "I baptize you in the name of the Father, the Son and the Holy Ghost. There, now you're Catholic, Suzanne and we can play together, plus now you can go to heaven." And since Suzanne was a Catholic, I asked if she would help me pray for a girl baby.

On the third of July, Dad called to tell me that mother was in the hospital having the baby.

"Can I come home now? Please, Dad?"

"Not quite yet, but I'll call back as soon as the baby arrives. Pretty quick now, you'll be home." I prayed longer and louder that night. *Please God bring us a girl baby. Think how embarrassed you'd be with a name like Zeolodus? You'd always be the last one called on to go out for recess. You'd never get picked for anyone's team. No one would talk to you because they couldn't pronounce your name. Please dear God.*

Finally, Dad called on the Fourth of July to tell me the baby was born the night before. *Maybe the baby was born right while I was praying. Wouldn't that be something?* I was afraid to ask, but I did anyway.

"Is it a boy or a girl?"

"It's a girl, he said. "She has lots of black hair. She's very pretty and very strong, just like your mother." Uhhh what a relief. My prayers were answered.

"Praying really does work, doesn't it, Dad. I prayed and prayed for a girl." I was completely happy and satisfied with the power of prayer.

"What *did* you name her?" I asked.

"Oscar," he said.

If that wasn't bad enough, my Aunt Nelly was waiting at the picnic table for me and she did not look amused. By this time, under my breath, I had started calling her, Nervous Nelly, because she was. But I could handle anything now; soon I would be going home. Back to the place where I belonged, to shoot a new cap gun and help find Ma Barker's money.

"I understand that you baptized Suzanne." Aunt Nelly began with soft voice, attempting to control her anger. She didn't want to commit a sin herself, especially when there was so little time left. She tapped her fingernails on the plastic tablecloth. Her voice was gradually rising, and I was puzzled.

"Why did you baptize Elizabeth?" Why wouldn't she be happy?

"I solved a problem and got a new Catholic. What's wrong with that?" I asked.

Her head started bobbing up and down, the arteries in her neck bulged, and she finally lost it, so completely. Aunt Nelly yelled loud enough for all the neighbors on both sides of the street to hear.

"SUZANNE'S FATHER IS THE METHODIST MINISTER!"

As for Ma Barker's money, Leedsie, Acey and Andrew Shinski did not find it that summer, but believe it or not, the next summer as we began building our forts in the gooseberry woods, we happened upon some significant clues.

Following Native American commandment #3, we discovered something unusual under an oak tree near the fence line by the cow path. Leedsie saw it first and called to Acey and me. "Here, quick, take a look at this." We stood together wordlessly staring at the sight immediately in front of us, under the fattest limb of the tree. First a pile of fresh dirt then a hole that had not been there the summer before; it was sharply cut, five feet long, four feet wide and four feet deep. Directly above the hole about six feet over our heads, dangling from a thick rope was an enormous pulley.

We could not speak. We could not even run to the house. We fell on the dirt pile and stared at each other. We stared at the heavy metal pulley over our heads, as it stirred slightly in the breeze. We looked again and again at the very precise hole.

Chapter 14

Swimming Lessons

My parents were simultaneously over-protective and open-minded. Dad wanted to home-school all his children, shield us in every way from unsavory elements and the possibility of contracting polio. Mother overruled him. He taught us archery, gun safety and target practice, against her better judgment.

Dad obsessed over the polio epidemic and the dangers of flies in the house and swimming in the river. "No eating from open food containers in public places." But we could eat all the hamburgers and potato salad served four days a year at the Anoka County Fair in the 4-H food booth.

We were never allowed to go the movie theatre, even the year *Quo Vadis* was showing downtown and all the kids at St. Stephen's Catholic school were released to attend. The Cutter kids remained in school, at their desks.

At the time there was no public pool in Anoka and knowing how to swim was important to our parents. So the summer I was committing sins in Bemidji, Dad hired Mr. Lightner to build a 60 x 18 foot swimming pool out of concrete blocks. That was the surprise he'd promised, when I talked to him on my aunt's telephone. It wasn't a fancy or even particularly attractive pool but it was sensible, safe and nicely positioned between a row of wild plum trees near the driveway and a grove of apple trees just before the open field of burdock.

Summer days at 5 p.m., rain or shine, Sy Jablonski, our swimming coach, arrived with his own children for swimming lessons. Several other children, belonging to friends of my parents came regularly for swimming lessons.

For years we took swimming lessons from Sy at the Rice Street beach on the Mississippi River. But, since no one had any idea what caused polio, Dad wanted to eliminate every possible source.

Sy had been a swimmer for the University of Minnesota Gophers. Every day after work, he parked his dark green Chevy at the end of our driveway, under the plum trees so it would be shaded and cool at the end of lessons. After changing into his trunks, Sy would dive into the deep end of our pool. He'd swim along the bottom, then up to the surface, entertaining us with what he called, *The Mississippi Crawl*.

It was a stroke similar to the crawl, but instead of cupping his hands to pull the water back, he made little sweeping motions with his hands in front of his face, as if he was pushing nasty river debris off to the sides. Then standing on the wall at the shallow end of the pool, Sy blew his whistle to begin swimming lessons with forty laps—no stopping, no complaining about unheated or cloudy water.

Sy tolerated no excuses: being tired, hungry or having a better place to go did not impress him. After his warm-up show, swimming lessons proceeded in a business-like fashion and ended at 6:30 sharp. Oscar started swimming when she was one year old and by the time she was three, she swam the entire 60-foot length of the pool with an audience of thirty people applauding. No one cheered louder than Sy Jablonski, our patron saint of swimming. He loved swimming and he taught us to love it, too.

Chapter 15

Cow Paths

Our summer days by the river were unusually ordinary and exceptionally rewarding from our stick and twine horses to our self-designed agenda. We did not wake up in the morning asking our parents, "What are we going to do today?" We had our own transcendent purpose.

The cow paths across our property were an early and dependable road map for us. Acey and I would close our eyes, stretch our arms out to the side, and pretending we were blind, see how long we could stay on the path without falling.

We walked those trails from Mr. Porter's milking shed to King's Island most days of the summer, until one Saturday morning in June.

The lilacs and wild plums were blooming, scenting the entire yard, when Mr. Porter came over in his overalls and torn straw hat to see Dad, and he looked serious. I was afraid we would be forbidden to walk behind the cows. Mr. Porter was gentle hermit-bachelor. He took care of his mother in a house that was as old as ours. His parents homesteaded and farmed the land where Mr. Porter lived. His grandparents were among the first to arrive in the Anoka settlement in 1853, coincidentally, the same year as the first cow appeared in town.

When Dad came out into the yard, Mr. Porter tipped his hat and spoke, in a voice softer than the swishing of a cow's tail. "You know, Mr. Cutter, don't mind if the kids want to walk the cow paths with us on occasion, but I do have one request. Prefer they don't come to the milking shed or make any noise near bouts at milking time. The only thing I wanna hear is the sound of milk hitting the side of the pail. You understand that don't you?"

My father shook Mr. Porter's hand and said, "Yes Sir. I'll tell them. Nice to see you, Sir."

"Find a way to explore, respectfully," he told us. On that point my parents always agreed.

Twice a day at 7 a.m. and 5 p.m., Mr. Porter and his hired man, Mr. Doherty, walked across Park Street in the direction of the river, down a winding dirt lane shaded by 100-year-old oak trees to the milking shed that separated our properties. They each milked ten cows and then they began their daily pilgrimage along the cow path.

We tried hard, we really did, to stay away, but one summer morning, Leedsie, Acey and I pretended we were G-men, creeping slowly and silently to the rickety slat walls of the milking shed. We wanted a peek at what was so sacred about milking time. Through the open slats, I could smell the sweet air of cows' breath mingled with fresh alfalfa, as the cows stomped through to their stalls. Mr. Porter gently called each heifer by name, as he patted them on their hind legs. Rose, Petunia, Lily, Blossom, Daisy, Violet, Begonia. You could tell how much he loved his cows by the way he said their names.

Even without looking, I could see Mr. Porter milking his cows. The streams of milk hit the side of the bucket with alternating beats. Mr. Porter's head would be resting in that soft warm spot of the cow's upper thigh.

The three of us waited in our separate tree houses high over the cow path. We watched as the two men, released the cows from the shed. The men followed behind the all-girl parade of big-eyed Jerseys, always led by Petunia, the eldest. Using their tails, the cows swatted flies off their backs and marched along noisily chewing their cuds.

Leedsie whispered, "You know they have four stomachs, doncha? And they throw up and eat it all over again—three times."

The rut they walked was narrow and deeply carved from years of marching cows. Passing through Mr. Porter's pasture, they followed their path through the meadow just above the flat along the Mississippi River. The cow path was wide enough for one at a time—no room for partners. That was the way we walked, too.

The parade rolled unencumbered from his property to ours over a field of sandburs and prickly burdock. They meandered through a growing forest of White Pines that we, the Cutter kids, planted on Arbor Day. When Petunia emerged at the end of the forest, she kept walking, following the path over our pasture.

Mr. Porter stayed at the end of the line with his crooked stick, talking gently to his cows, as if they were companionable ladies sitting with him in the shade, enjoying a nice cup of tea and delicate sugar cookies. Mr. Doherty always walked ten steps behind Mr. Porter, nodding and chewing on a stem of grass.

Mr. Doherty barely ever spoke to us. He had a glass eye. If we asked him to, he'd lick his fingers all wet, then he'd reach right in, scoop out his glass eye and hold it in the palm of his hand. It looked like the globe in Sister Jean Marie's second-grade room, only in miniature. I could see oceans and clouds, blue skies even an occasional thunderstorm and flash of lightning in Mr. Doherty's eye. When we were done looking, he popped that eye in and out of his mouth, to get it wet again, and put it back in his head.

If the cows slowed down, Mr. Porter tapped the last one in line, gently with his stick. He followed slowly behind them as they sashayed to their destination. "C'mon now Daisy, stay on the path. Tha'ta girl." The cow path continued past our barns, through gates and over our farm road. His cows stepped high over the fallen elm tree, where we sat to dry off after swimming in the river. They snapped their ears to chase the flies away and lifted their tails to drop steamy cow pies onto the path, without stopping or slowing down. They never tripped or missed a step, almost like they were dancing all the way toward the hill. The closer they got, the faster they walked.

The cow path curved over the final approach. Then leaning sideways into the steep hillside, those big cows walked sideways down the hill to the creek. I was always afraid Petunia would fall, then the rest would follow.

As soon as Petunia entered the creek, Mr. Porter and Mr. Doherty turned around and followed the path back home, until the evening milking.

The cows kept moving forward until their hooves sunk deep into the grey plastic mud of the creek bottom. They slurped water, as they luxuriously made another crossing to their daily resting place in the long, cool grasses and asparagus ferns of King's Island, where the trees look primeval and mysterious.

From the time I was still sucking my thumb, Leedsie, Acey and I built our forts and hideouts in the woods along the cow paths. We used branches and shrubbery for walls; our floors made of moss and wild flowers. The hard mushrooms growing on the sides of old elm trees were our doorbells and light switches. We covered our tracks, like good G-Men, walking backward with broken, leafy branches swiping back and forth across our footsteps.

As the little kids grew, we let them follow us into our days. When Sesson sprayed the house for flies, worried that we all might catch polio, we walked for hours leaving through the garden gate into the pasture, down to the gooseberry woods and across the flat to the river to cool off. Everyone was responsible for finding their own toilet paper—the soft velvety leaves of common mullein.

It was a good day when we found the perfect stones and watched as Leedsie expertly skipped a flat one five, six, seven, eight times on its way over to Willow Island. We climbed on fallen trees balancing with our arms outstretched, daring each other to go farther and farther out into the river, the skill being in knowing when to stop—seconds before the limb cracked off.

We swam in the Mississippi River and swung on twisted monkey vines that hung from forty-foot trees over the creek. Catching a vine, we'd kick off on the side hill, eldest first on the slippery slope. Then swinging high, we followed Leedsie's example and let go at just the right moment, making a heavenly landing in the tall grasses on Kings Island, where Mr. Porter's cows rested leisurely in the shade.

The big kids waited for the little kids to straddle big slippery rocks, wading across to meet us. Technically, none of it was allowed.

In the late afternoon, the big kids carried the little kids, wading back across the creek, beginning our trip home, in time for swimming lessons. We walked along the edge of the river in ankle deep mud with minnows squirming between our toes. And finally the last leg homeward, up the hill through the gooseberry woods slapping mosquitoes all the way.

Sometimes we sat in a line, eldest claiming, "King of the hill," to dry in the sun. When we found wild columbine, we bit the tiny supple tips from the ends of the flowers and sucked the nectar, then ate the whole flower.

We were expected to spend part of our days weeding, picking and selling strawberries at our peach crate stand on the dirt road, in front of the white rail fence around The Last House on Park Street. Our plan was to use the strawberry money to buy a real horse, but our only customer was our father, who stopped on his way home for lunch and dinner.

We jumped over fresh cow pies and threw old ones at each other. You really had to know how to pick the right ones. You could make a big mistake picking up a cow pie that looked dry enough for throwing, but might not be solid all the way through and end up with it on your head.

"It has to do with the weather," Leedsie said, always instructing us about everything related to cows. And, as usual, Acey agreed, "Yup, it's all in the timing."

Leedsie knew everything about cows. Each summer he dished out a new bovine fact sometimes using language that wasn't allowed in, or even near, the house. "Ya know," he said with authority, "if you give a cow purple bubble gum, she can blow purple bubbles out her butt, if she wants to." We believed him because he was the oldest.

Chapter 16

Shanty Town

1953: the first year of Dwight D. Eisenhower's two-term presidency. My father loved Eisenhower. Besides the fact that Eisenhower was a Republican, he had been the very popular and successful Supreme Commander of Allied Forces during World War II. Even though Dad disliked the influence of television, in 1952 he bought a Sylvania floor model, and installed it at the end of the living room. We were allowed to watch the Electoral College cast their votes for either Adlai Stevenson or Dwight D. Eisenhower. After the election, my father turned the TV off and we returned to listening to our favorite radio shows.

It was the summer of my ninth birthday, Leedsie was twelve and Acey ten, when we discovered a power that would affect the choices we made for the rest of our lives. Andrew Shinski was six, Milo, four, Marcus, three, and Oscar just one year old.

Sesson shooed all of us from the house. "Out, out all of you and don't come back until I call you," she ordered, holding the fly spray pump up over her head, as she opened the pantry door for us to exit. Oscar was sleeping in the nursery upstairs.

"Stay away from that river! Current's strong after all that rain. And, don't you be wading in the creek now either, or swinging on those grape vines!"

We followed Leedsie across the driveway over toward the apartment above the garage.

"Now what are we gonna do?" I whined.

Weaving through the sheets on the clothesline and under the ladder by the crab apple tree, past the pile of rocks by the garage, Leedsie suddenly had a brave and radical idea.

"Sesson said, 'no river, no creek.' Let's build a town, right here in the yard, our own town, with our own rules, our own food, and our own school." We each collected broken boards, tar paper, long branches, chicken wire and fence posts. We cleverly planned our buildings so that one wall was the side of the garage, leaving only three more walls, some windows and a door to be constructed.

Leedsie called out, "I'm gonna be the mayor and the judge. So I'll build the courthouse and the city hall." He was a member of The Ramsey Rams 4-H Club and his cow Beulah was his project. That made Leedsie the boss of the alfalfa supply in the barn. He dragged four bales of hay across the pasture to use as benches in his courthouse.

Acey jabbed me in the ribs with a roll of tar paper. "Look out! He's going to make trouble." She was talking about Mr. Skow, the hired man, who was scowling at us from the upstairs window in the apartment over the garage. Mr. Skow never talked to us, he growled and he smelled like a combination of curry powder and dead flower water. His overalls were always dirty, even first thing in the morning. He told Sesson that we were ruining the yard with all our junk. Our building materials—*junk*, he called it.

Following behind Sesson, as she hung sheets on the line, Mr. Skow grumbled, "I'll be telling the Mister 'bout them brats. Don't understand how people can let them kids run 'round like that, actin' like they owned the place."

I lifted a broken, moss-covered piece of plywood out of a tangle of weeds and thistles, thinking it would make a good wall for my house, when I saw Mr. Skow shuffling toward our building site. He stood at the edge of our town and cleared his throat, then he blew his nose by holding one nostril shut and blowing hard on the other side, right on the ground of our town.

He snarled, "What the hell you monsters think yur doin? Makin' a mess as usual. I'm putting a stop ta this damn shanty town, just you wait. Another thing, you kids go through the pasture, ya close the damn gate behind ya!"

Swearing wasn't allowed, or peeing outside, or jumping off the shed roof, or starting fires, or going upstairs to the apartment where Mr. Skow lived.

We were not allowed near his car either. When he first moved into the apartment that summer, he snapped at us, "What are you lookin at?" Then he parked his car under the apple tree right on the grass, where we usually gathered to make plans for the day. No wonder that was the sour apple tree.

Mr. Skow mumbled, as he shuffled away from our building site.

Leedsie said, "Hmmm, shanty town, that's a good name."

Because Acey was the eldest girl, she had the privilege of being *the* teacher and the librarian. She brought books from the top shelf of the book-case in the living room—forbidden material—the skin disease book with real life colored pictures of growths that looked like blue, moldy corn grow-ing out of a man's ear and other unmentionable places. Our father's WWII Navy yearbooks and the stories about Uncle Remus and Aunt Minerva, which was restricted material, until we were thirteen years old.

From our father's desk in the house, Acey confiscated his official notary public stamp to make library cards. She had two pencils and a stack of paper for the school.

Every town needs a newspaper. For the next few summers, I would be the owner of <u>The Shanty Town News</u> and its only reporter. My supplies were a notebook and a pencil with a very good eraser.

Milo was halfway between a little kid and a big kid, so we let her own the grocery store, which meant she had to sneak into the house, get by Sesson and Mother, and find the Nabisco Hi-Ho crackers to sell in the store. Later in the summer she walked to the flat and picked strawberries to sell.

As soon as all our buildings were under construction, Leedsie called a town meeting outside the courthouse. Beulah's head was inside chewing on the benches and her tail swatted flies outside. The rest of us stood by our piles of building supplies. Acey's pet lamb Kiki meandered through our collections nibbling at the few remaining tufts of weeds.

Our mayor spoke, "We're not gonna have any fathers in Shanty Town, cuz we don't have enough boys. If anybody needs help with supplies, let me know and we'll all pitch in. So finish your buildings, then we have to plan a circus to make some money. After that, we'll go for a walk to the river."

"No fathers?" Acey asked. "Well, I guess we could say all the fathers died in the war. Oscar will be everybody's baby. We'll all take care of her."

Andrew Shinski was elected sheriff. He built the jail, but his main job was solving arguments among the town's citizens and keeping a close watch on the activities of Mr. Skow.

Leedsie appointed Marcus Aurelius deputy sheriff and fireman, in charge of helping Andrew and issuing parking tickets for any incorrectly tied stick-and-twine horses.

Fires were not allowed, so we built them very carefully with apple wood twigs and brown needles from the pine cone woods. Leedsie taught us how to start a fire by striking two stones together and Marcus, stood ready with a hose to put the fires out.

After I finished building my combination house and newspaper office, I took my notebook and pencil and crawled way deep into the lilac bushes just outside the living room window. My job as newspaper reporter was to hide in places where I could listen to our parents' private conversations and record every word they said.

Through the open window, I could hear Mother at the upright piano, playing *Moonlight Sonata*. The silky soft curtains billowed up against the back of the piano. It was the perfect spot to watch the driveway and wait for my father's car, when he came home for lunch. He would drive past the rose garden and park in the shade of the oak tree. Then he'd sit there looking at the river for a while before coming in the house.

Dad drove in. The piano music stopped. The screen door on the porch slammed shut. Mom and Dad walked across the driveway on their way down to the pool.

I could hear Sesson in the kitchen, talking to the little kids, while she made their lunch. Waiting for the perfect moment, I ran inside, slid under the sofa in the living room and waited. The little kids ate their lunch and headed back to Shanty Town. When my parents returned from swimming, they went straight to the table on the sun porch and I could hear them perfectly.

Mother said in a low voice, "Mr. Skow has been complaining about the children and Shanty Town, again. He says they'll ruin the yard with all their junk, then he'll have to clean it up."

Sesson served their lunch with tall glasses of iced tea. I could see the tomatoes stuffed with tuna salad. I hoped she added some mint on top.

"Don't worry." My father said reassuringly, "They'll clean it up. That's our deal, all buildings down by Labor Day." Scrunched under the sofa with my pad out in front of me, I wrote down everything they said.

Mother whispered, "Mr. Skow's not to be cooking up there, is he? You know, sometimes I wonder. He smells like food when he comes in for dinner."

"No, absolutely not, no cooking in the apartment," Dad said, putting his fork down with a clang. "You know that's a hazard. That's why he gets his meals here in the house."

"Well, all right, if you're sure and that's clear with him."

"Yes, I'm sure," Dad said. "Don't fuss about it. Any shenanigans and Mr. Skow will have to leave." Mother told Dad about her work on the hospital board and about the people who disagreed with each other. Who she thought was right and who she believed was misguided. I wrote down all the names.

Dad said, "You know on my way home today, I saw a billboard on the highway advertising the housing development planned for Porter's property. That'd make a pretty good backstop on the tennis court, don't you think?" He laughed.

"Oh Darrah, don't let the children hear you," Mother scolded. "You know they'd love to have permission to drag that billboard down Park Street and plant in right here in the yard." It was true, Mr. Yoho, a developer, was planning to build forty or more houses on Mr. Porter's property. There would be sidewalks and street lights instead of cow paths, tar roads instead of dirt roads, curbs and gutters in place of the milking shed and the oak trees surrounding it. We did not want the development.

My parents laughed and I wrote my notes. They pushed their chairs back from the table. He kissed her goodbye and went out the porch door, back to work. She went through the pantry door, over to Shanty Town to fetch the littlest ones for their afternoon naps.

The next day, I watched through a hole in the wall of my newspaper office. Mr. Skow ambled past Shanty Town toward the flat, probably, to fix the leaks in the irrigation pipes. As soon as he was out of sight, I ran next door to the sheriff's office.

"Sheriff, I need your help. I'm going to check out Mr. Skow's apartment for my newspaper story."

Taking his official position seriously, Shinski warned, "We're not sposta go anywhere near that apartment. Mom said." He tried to stare me down, while he tightened his belt and reset his cowboy hat.

"Well, I have to do this. I hafta get a look through the window. I won't go in, okay?"

"All right, then," the sheriff reluctantly gave up. "I'll form a posse and we'll be your lookout. Code'll be G-Man. If I call, you run. And, don't go in!"

With Shinski at the bottom of the apartment steps and his three-year-old deputy Marcus Aurelius staked out in the rock pile, I kept an eye on the pasture and went slowly up the stairs to the apartment. When I got to the landing by the door I leaned over the railing and looked in the window. In the middle of floor, I saw pried-open cans of Campbell's tomato soup and a greasy frying pan on a hot plate. Bingo! I had a real scoop. But, better yet, just beyond the hot plate was a clump of bloody fur—rabbit fur—right in the middle of the wood floor, yuck.

Just to be sure, I wanted to find out if he had curry powder in his cupboard. With a quick look down the stairs, I grabbed the doorknob and just then Shinski called up the stairs, "G-Man. Hurry!" He took off running, and dived into the lilac bushes with his deputy close behind him. As Mr. Skow approached the apartment stairs, I had no choice but to climb out on to the back roof of the apartment and jump off to the ground, next to the tar barrel, safely inside Shanty Town.

That night, I wrote up the newspaper, put the date, time and a one-cent price in the upper right hand corner. I copied the paper, by hand, eight times, one for each town member and one for my parents.

Mr. Skow picked up his last check the next day. Years later my father told me, "Your newspaper story was not the only cause for Mr. Skow's dismissal." It seems Mr. Skow had insulted my mother's cooking for the last time.

Acey and I went up to the highway with two shovels. It took a couple of hours, but we ended up with a really nice new wall for the library in Shanty Town.

Of course, Dad was compelled to respond to the addition in our library. "Mighty sturdy wall, girls, but you'll have to return that billboard to the highway."

"But Dad, you said, and it was in our newspaper." Acey said, holding up a copy of The Shanty Town News.

"I know what I said, but the fact is that billboard is not our property. The best way to stop the development would have been to buy Porter's land myself."

We finished the summer of 1953 with a play about creating the ideal town for children, starring ourselves, and co-starring Beulah and Kiki. Our audience was Sesson, Mom, Dad, Grandma and Grandpa White.

We dismantled our town in the fall, when the leaves turned red and orange and the geese flew south for the winter.

Chapter 17

The Artist in the Apartment

The summer of 1954 was an impressionable time in my life, indelibly marked by wonder and beauty. My father sponsored a young Hungarian artist, who wished to escape the Communist oppression in Hungary. Twenty-five to fifty thousand Hungarian rebels—most of them students and intellectuals—had already been killed during the anti-Soviet insurrection movement. Another 250,000 Hungarians left the country as refugees.

Stephen Reteggi was twenty-one—handsome, joyful and generous. He came to live upstairs in the apartment over the garage for the summer, bringing with him a fresh new spirit and an uncommon perception.

Stephen was "getting his feet wet," investigating art schools, as he waited for his young bride, Myrna, to escape Hungary and join him in the U.S. He worked in the pasture helping Mr. B—the new hired man—fix fences, plow the fields, mow and bale the hay or whatever needed to be done. Stephen taught Sesson how to make authentic Hungarian goulash with real fresh-ground paprika. He ate all his meals with us and he wanted to repay my parents for helping him make a life in the United States a real possibility. When he wasn't working, he spent hours sketching around the yard—Shanty Town, Beulah, the apple trees, the river at sunset. Watercolors were his specialty. I was fascinated.

One evening during dinner, Mother asked Stephen if he would like to paint a portrait of the Cutter children. "I would be honored," he said. "But each one will have to pose every day," he told us, looking around the table. "I don't know how long it will take, maybe the rest of the summer."

Every day, we took turns posing for half an hour each upstairs in Stephen's apartment/studio. The apartment windows, opened over the driveway, and the sun filled the room. After the pencil sketch was completed with each Cutter child placed on the paper, Stephen began to paint. I watched as he mixed the colors on his palette. He created the characters just by looking at us and touching his brush to the paper, as if the brush was a natural extension of his eyes and his fingers.

I loved that part of the day, posing there by the open windows, holding my left arm with my right hand and wearing the brown dress I inherited from Acey with the ribbon at the top. I was so enthralled by the process of painting, that at ten years old, I thought I was in love with Stephen Reteggi.

He painted my dress precisely, showing each of the three hem lines with a slightly darker shade of brown, looking like the rings on the trunk of a tree. You could almost tell by the space between the hem lines how fast I was growing.

I asked Stephen why he used so much green paint on my face and the veins of my arms. "Why do you paint our eyes like that?"

Without interrupting his brush stroke, he answered in his gentle, blue-eyed voice, "I just paint what I see, Charlie." *Hmmm. I thought I was smiling the whole time.*

The artist painted a perfect Band-aid on Marcus's left thigh, just beneath the hem of his little-boy green cotton shorts. Marcus is dragging his one-eyed teddy bear with his left hand and he's holding on tight with his right hand. Holding on tight to Leedsie's arm.

Standing next in the back row is Acey. Her face, the look in her eyes, would just make you cry. She looks the saddest of us all. Her dress is a new one, purple with a white eyelet ruffle and no hand-me-down hem lines. At first we protested wearing dresses for this painting, but every day we put on the same clothes, climbed the apartment steps and posed.

Andrew Shinski has knobby knees. It's easy to see that he's going to be a big boy, because his head is really big, almost too big for his shoulders. He's holding a teddy bear, too. His first finger is smashing his teddy bear's button nose over flat.

Milo is next to Andrew, she's pigeon-toed, looking kind of shy and lonely. Her blue-green bunny rabbit doll has a pretty plastic face but it's broken, a jagged crack runs all along its forehead.

Oscar is painted sitting on a red hobby horse, which is obviously missing some parts on its head. She has green on her face too. Her cheeks are puffed out, like she's holding her breath. She's not really on that horse, because she was too little to sit up and pose for very long. Stephen asked me to hold her and then he just painted her like she was riding that broken down horse. Everyone has wet hair, brown shoes and white socks, except Milo who's wearing a nice pair of black Mary Janes. Stephen painted white sandals on Oscar's feet.

Overall, the watercolor was an artistic success. Mother loved it. Measuring an imposing 36" x 36", we children thought it was much too big, especially because we all looked sad, except for Leedsie who has a smile on his face, forever. My mother had the painting matted with four inches of burlap and framed with four inches of mahogany, making it even more commanding. We stood in silent horror when she proudly hung it over the fireplace.

Walking back to admire the creation, Mother exclaimed proudly, "Now I suppose all of you will want this painting after your father and I are gone." No one responded.

Other people who looked at the painting were surprised, taking in deep, calming breaths and shifting their eyes away quickly before they blurted out something thoughtless or rude. If Mother ever noticed that our faces in that painting were different from other children, she probably thought it was because we *were* different, which was precisely what she enjoyed about us.

Sometimes you have to wait a long time to understand the meaning of things. The truth is, Stephen Reteggi knew exactly what he was doing. He was a fortune teller, his palette was his crystal ball. He painted us as he saw us, with inexplicable talent and insight into our future. So to the average observer, the person who knows nothing about what's coming up in our lives, the children's bodies look pretty normal and healthy but their faces, well that's something else—far too knowing, haunted even, every one, including Oscar. The painting hangs in my living room today: no one else wanted it.

From Stephen Reteggi's obituary:

> Stephen Reteggi, a much loved and respected husband, father, painter and teacher died in New York in 1999 at age 67. In memory, one of his students wrote of his extraordinary gift for capturing the essence, all that speaks—beneath the skin.

I can never forget his magic.

Part IV

Chapter 18

Intentionally Designed

Spring of 1956: The cherry blossoms are in full bloom in the courtyard of the Ogata's Buddhist temple in Sagae City, Japan. The night before, the temple was full, the gongs were loud, the chanting long, the incense sweet. Members of the temple gathered for a special ceremony of prayer and offerings: Moshe rice balls, sushi, and seaweed cakes beautifully arranged on lacquer plates—offerings to their ancestors, placed on the family shrines behind the temple's golden altar. They were asking for a safe and harmonious journey for Ryodo, the 18-year-old son of their priest.

Papa Ogata waits on the top step of the temple for the taxi that will take Ryodo to the train to Tokyo. He will then board a ship in Yokohama where he begins a three-week journey to San Francisco, and finally a flight to Minneapolis, Minnesota.

In 1995, I wrote a children's story about a young Japanese student coming to live with an American family in 1956. A woman in my writing group suggested I change the time frame.

"It's just not a believable story," she advised. "After all, we were still occupying Japan in 1952. Relations were cold, really cold," she insisted. "Better just change the year," she said, with a patronizing wink.

If there had ever been any discussion about the success of the Japanese-American match, I never knew it and it wouldn't have mattered much anyway.

Holding up a passport photo and the personal profile of Ryodo Ogata, Mother made things crystal clear. "I'm co-director of the American Field Service program and we *are* having a Japanese student, this *particular* student," she added pointing to the photograph of her intended guest. "He is coming to live with us—period. No further discussion." She had been brewing her plan for years and it was specifically designed to include a Japanese student who possessed particular attributes.

I have a photograph, taken by my father, after Mass on Mother's Day 1955; it tells the story of our family as it was, one year before Ryodo "Mike" Ogata came to live with us.

The photo of the Cutter brood is staged in front of the fence on Park Street. It looks like a negative, because it's black and white. You can tell the occasion is Mother's Day by the clothes she's wearing, the traditional white corsage, and the fact that we're all still dressed in our church clothes. You can't see it, but Dad has already given Mom the double-layered, gold box of Whitman's Samplers candy that he gives her every Mother's Day, Easter, her birthday, and Valentine's Day.

The uninformed spectator, just driving by on that Sunday morning, would probably think, *Ahhh, there's that Cutter family. Aren't they lovely? Though a rather large family, things appear to be under control. Look at them, having their picture taken so peacefully posing together in their church clothes. Now, that's what families should look like, and then we'd have no worries about Elvis Presley and the direction this country is going.*

But, sometimes what you see driving by at 40 miles per hour, on a dusty dirt road, trying not to be obvious or rude, is not always the accurate picture.

See how Leedsie stands alone—aloof? All casual against the white rail fence.

In his baggy, beige Humphrey Bogart suit and his barn boots.

Ready to either milk Beulah, or enjoy a smoke and a stiff whiskey with Lauren Bacall in the jungle

Acey's the one trying to hang on to Oscar, who has a torn ruffle on her pinafore.

Acey feels responsible for everything that ever goes wrong—all her life.

Look how Oscar stretches and reaches for Mother's hair, anything she can touch.

But Mother's face is focused on the lens.

Andrew is the one resting his head on Mother's belly.

The new baby is under her blue satin maternity dress.

The one with giant rhinestone buttons.

Mother wears that lucky dress when she helps Dad campaign for County Attorney.

Andrew always asks for seconds, even if Mother hasn't eaten.

We thought something was wrong with him, when he hit us with hoes and croquet mallets.

But you can see, he just needed wide, thick glasses like binoculars.

Mother's not looking at him either.

I'm Charlie, the one farthest left, in the white dress trimmed in grosgrain ribbon.

I couldn't find any underpants that morning.

So, I am wearing my pajama bottoms with the legs rolled up.

That boy's haircut was thanks to Ziegler Brothers Barber Shop,

Main Street Anoka, next door to the movie theatre.

I have my arm around Milo; she has noticeable banana-bruised knees.

I dressed her for church this morning, and I know her socks don't match.

She's wearing Acey's underpants, but you can't tell.

Milo has eyes like Kim Novak, without the green eye shadow.

She's squinting hard into the sun for a better look at Mother's face.

Mother is smiling, an odd mysterious smile, looking up higher at something entirely different.

Marcus has the spot of all spots.

Yup, he's the little guy in wool shorts, hanging onto Mother's right leg.

Hanging on for dear life, right straight through that dark blue satin campaign dress.

He's five years old and, at that moment, he's happy, happy, happy.

The soft brown hair on his head is nuzzled just under the new baby.

Mother doesn't look at him but her hand rests lightly, calmingly on his right shoulder.

He probably just stopped banging back and forth, as the shutter clicked.

But all along, Mother's head has been slightly tilted to the right, looking into the camera.

She communicates something she could never say out loud to the photographer.

Her message is clear:

You see what I do every day?

Why must you be gone so much?

I wish you were here more often, I mean really here, not just Sundays.

Remember me? I love to dance and swim with you and play tennis, too.

But see how they cling and attach to my neck, my arms, my hair,

my legs and even my baby? You see? Don't you?

I can hear her pleading, right through the picture frame.
As you focused, you must have noticed,
I only have two hands.

Chapter 19

Ramsey Rams 4-H Club

It wasn't that Mother did nothing but campaign for my father and have babies. But, my father was gone a lot and she missed him. He went fishing in Canada, usually twice every summer. In the fall, he went to Wyoming or Montana to hunt for pronghorn antelope, mule deer and elk. Nickerson, near Duluth, was his favorite place for pheasant and duck hunting season.

When Leedsie was 13, he joined the Ramsey Rams 4-H Club, with his cow Beulah as his project. Mother volunteered to be the director for the annual 4-H play contest. The first play she chose was The Lottery, by Shirley Jackson. Interesting choice, considering the author's negative feelings about small towns, blind faith, tradition, and religion in general. The Ramsey Rams won the play competition that year.

The 4-H Radio Speaking Contest was, understandably, another of Mother's pet projects. She eagerly and expertly coached the Ramsey Rams prospects and guided many of them to county, even state victories. I think she was a little disappointed that none of her children excelled in the radio competition, but she was undeterred. For those who lacked skills or interest in public speaking, Mother organized ballroom and square dancing lessons. The classes were taught, by professionals, in the apartment above the garage, open to all the Ramsey Rams club members.

4-H meetings were generally held in the home of the adult leaders, way far out in the country, where families had to wind up the big-box phone on the wall, while three other neighbors listened in on the party line. The *real* country was where people made their own soap and walked through snowdrifts to go potty in their one or two-holer outhouses. Those were the signs of real farmers.

There were a few exciting times that the Ramsey Rams met on Park Street. The spring before Ryodo Ogata came to live with us, Acey and I, not yet old enough to be members, took full advantage of one those meetings.

We set up folding chairs in the dark corner by the living room bookcase, so we could quietly observe the secret world of a 4-H meeting.

Mr. Fred "Bud" Kahler, the Anoka County Extension Agent, was revered in our household, like a patron saint, wise and powerful, except he was alive. Mr. Kahler attended special 4-H meetings, particularly the ones right before the county fair. Just the mention of his name was known to end arguments on almost any subject, but especially discussions about plants, cows, pigs, sheep, goslings, mouse and rat droppings, shearing, blocking, mastitis, placenta previa, maggots, the rendering plant, and bloating.

The meeting began with the traditional 4-H pledge. Acey and I watched as the club members, mostly genuine farmers, solemnly stood and began the pledge. With their right hands on their foreheads, they spoke in unison.

I pledge my head to clearer thinking.
Then, moving their right hands over their hearts.
I pledge my heart to greater loyalty.
Hands outstretched.
My hands to greater service.
Hands at their sides, backs straight, chests out, chins forward.
My health to better living.
For my home, my club, my community, and my country.

Wow! I felt like I was in church. The Ramsey Rams sat down on our sofa, on our chairs, and on our floor to listen to Mr. Kahler. He opened the meeting with project reports for each member. He recited deadlines for project and record papers—all sacred documents. If the members missed the deadline, they would not be able to enter their 4-H projects in the county fair. And without the fair, there'd be almost no meaning in the lives of members of the Ramsey Rams 4-H Club.

It would be two years before I could join 4-H and my plan was to have a lamb as my project. In the meantime, I was content to stare at a cute guy sitting on the sofa next to Leedsie. He asked Mr. Kahler about his Holstein and something about his milk production records. The cute guy embodied the word farmer. His cheeks were rosy from the outdoor life and his forehead white from wearing a cap. He had crystal clear blue eyes, pitch black hair, and big, milk-whitened straight teeth. I kept my eye on that guy, while Mother and Sesson served up Mexiburgers and cocoa after the meeting. Later, all the official members went outside in the yard to play in the dark.

Starlight, Moonlight, Hope to See the Ghost Tonight.
I asked Leedsie about the guy. "Who is that guy with the black hair?"
"Don't bother, you're too little."
"Well, what's his name, anyway?"
"His name is Porter, forget it. I'm warning ya."
"Ahhh, like Mr. Porter." Of course he'd be a good farmer then. Porter, hmmm.
Like a train porter, carrying bags and packages for the passengers?
"What a perfect name for a farmer," I said.
"Calm down. You're acting stupid. First names are different from last names. Porter is not related to Mr. Porter and, by the way, he would never, ever be interested in a girl like you."
"Oh, yah? How do you know?"
"For two reasons," he said, as if he knew everything about farmers and boys liking girls. "Number one, you are too young; and number two, you don't have any calluses on your hands. Farmers don't like sissies," he said with authority.
"Oh! Then how could I get calluses on my hands?" Leedsie took me down to the barn and suggested that I shovel out all Beulah's manure, which I knew he hadn't done for a hundred years. The smell of ammonia was so strong, you couldn't breathe inside the barn. The floor was covered with a thick mat of cow poop caked in tangled straw and alfalfa.
Standing by the door, Leedsie said, "See if cleaning gives you calluses, and then, I might just tell Porter that you think he's cute."
After two days of prying with the pitchfork and shoveling, my hands hurt, in fact, they stung. Leedsie looked at the raw puffy pads on the palms of my hands and said, "Yah, well that's what happens. Getting a farmer like Porter to notice you might be painful. First ya hafta get blisters. That's just the way it goes. Atta girl, keep on going until the blisters turn into calluses. Might work, might not."
All along, my parents knew what was going on with me in the barn all day, but they never interfered.
I quit shoveling Beulah's poop for one reason. I remembered, I had something on Leedsie and I intended to quit making calluses and use my head. After all the 4-H pledge included more than just hands. *Head, Heart, Hand, and Health.* The ammunition I had came along by accident the year before. It was the first summer Leedsie was to show Beulah at the county fair. Three days before the fair, Leedsie came into the bedroom Acey and I

shared. He shut the door and showed me a pack of matches.

I said, "We're not supposed to have matches, ya know. I'm telling."

"Yah, well, I know, but I'm not gonna do anything with them, so ya don't hafta go be a baby and tell." Then he did do something with them. He opened the pack, tore off a match, lit it and dropped it on the floor, where it landed on some plastic doll dishes that Milo left in our room. Phooom, within seconds, black smoke filled the room, as the doll dishes clumped together and burned into an ugly, gooey ball. Leedsie stomped out the fire, but before he could pry the window up, my bedroom door flew open and Dad stood there jiggling the coins in his pocket.

"What's going on here?" He yelled. "Who is responsible for this?" Neither of us said anything.

"Both of you. Get downstairs this instant. Now!"

On his way down the hall, he said, "Whoever is responsible will not be allowed to go to the fair, period. Understood?"

We waited and listened to the coins, as he took two stairs at a time. Leedsie grabbed me. "Hey, you can't say I did it, right?" he pleaded, squeezing my arm. "Cuz I hafta take Beulah to the fair. I have my records all done and she's ready, her hooves are clean and polished, her tail is shampooed and braided. We hafta go to the fair."

I didn't want to miss the fair either. Why should I take the blame for him? He was just trying to bully me. On the other hand, if I tried to take the blame, they might think that I was less likely to have matches in the first place, and know I was lying. Then, Leedsie would have to confess.

Leedsie and I went downstairs to the living room. Mom and Dad were waiting and strangely calm for such a serious infraction. Dad's ears weren't turning purple. He wasn't jingling coins in his pocket.

Mother said, "You both know the rules. No matches. No fires. And," Mother said, raising her eyebrows, "the punishment will be severe."

Dad asked, "Now, how 'bout you tell us what was going on up there." A long uncomfortable silence followed.

"I did it," I said. "I lit a match and it dropped by mistake on Milo's plastic doll dishes. I'm sorry."

"You may be sorry now, Young Lady," my father scolded, "but you'll be sorrier still when we leave for the fair and you find yourself at home, in your room, alone."

My parents knew all along who lit that fire. Mother told me they figured, if I wanted to take the blame that was between me and Leedsie to work out.

They were right. Leedsie and Beulah won Grand Champion that year and went to the state fair. For years, I was introduced to many of Leedsie's cute friends.

Chapter 20

Gentleman Farmer

My father had always fantasized, imagining himself a gentleman farmer. The barnyard was loaded, beyond the capacity of our flimsy fences, which needed repair every year. Fifty sheep, including two rams, and Leedsie's cow, Beulah, shared space with my father's "animals *de jour*," cattle, goslings (baby geese), and chickens.

One year, before leaving for the first of his annual summer fishing trips to Canada, my father told Mother that he had ordered 30 Whiteface cattle—to be delivered while he was gone. We had no fences and Whiteface are BIG, but that was inconsequential.

I never noticed that any of my father's half-baked schemes bothered Mother. On the contrary, she seemed to take pride in that feature of his personality. She gave meaning to the terms, *relish the challenge* and *rise to the occasion*. Her life with him was radically different from the predictable, quiet, prayerful, lifestyle to which she had been accustomed.

Mother put us all to work building fences for the incoming herd. Acey and I took turns stripping the bark from the tree trunks, while Mr. B dug the post holes. Even Grandma White, wearing her housedress and white apron, appeared in the pasture to help Leedsie. Reporting early for fence-stretching duty, she diligently stayed with the job till the end of the day.

Andrew Shinski and I had pet pigs, named for the comic strip characters, Dick Tracy and his girlfriend, Model. We taught our pigs how to play tag and fed them pig cereal twice a day. We organized parades and sold tickets to Sesson and our parents on the first day of spring. We dressed Model in an antique, black velvet veiled hat from the trunk in the barn and fastened a bow tie around Dick's neck.

Marcus and Milo (M&M) were inseparable and mischievous. They attempted to capitalize on the disorganization of the barnyard. Sitting on top of the chicken coop, they watched while the two rams, Old Billy and the new young one, Butch, stomped over the broken fence for a face-off. The scraping, snorting rams backed up to opposite ends of the pasture and ran pell-mell, finally cracking smack into each other's heads. They staggered a bit, stared at each other, scraped their hooves, engaged their wooly heads for a while in close-up butting until they both dropped from fatigue. M&M tried to sell tickets to the ram fights, even offering sections of Venetian blinds with sticks as complimentary noise makers.

A disgusting addition to our menagerie was a smelly goat named Adolph, who met his demise after years of jumping the fence, chasing us, and butting and torturing Beulah. One day Acey and Milo discovered Adolf's body on the roof of the chicken coop. The evidence was there: two puncture wounds that perfectly matched the delicate shape of Beulah's horns.

No matter who the hired man was, or how many animals ran wild, our lives were simple and autonomous. The constants that gave us bearings were the river, the crop of alfalfa across the street, corn on the flat … whose growth identified the precise time of summer … the strawberry patch, Mr. Porter's cow paths, and King's Island. But even that time-honored consistency was about to be altered.

Chapter 21

Everyone's Telling on Someone

Our last baby was born June 25, 1955 and Dad named her, "Eightball." I was almost 12 and I believed that Eightball was the most intelligent and exciting of all our babies. She liked to be held and rocked in the glider and she loved to hear me sing all of Harry Belafonte's songs, especially, *Mama Look a Boo Boo.* I liked that song because I could sing out loud, *shut up your mouth,* which was otherwise not allowed. *Their mother tell them, **shut up your mouth.*** Eightball looked right in my eyes and laughed.

By this time, Sesson was working at our house Monday through Friday. Acey and I had even more responsibilities. We shared the task of cleaning up after dinner. It was a nightly race to see which one would shout out first, "Wipe, Sweep, Put Away!" The loser had to wash all the dishes. There were always diapers to be washed, which, in the past, was a dreaded chore, because we had to feed each cloth diaper, one-by-one, through two rollers that squeezed all the water out, before the diapers could be transferred to the dryer.

When Eightball was born, my parents bought the new washing machine with an automatic ringer. In the beginning, every new appliance was fun to operate and much more luxurious than its predecessor.

The modern washing tub had its own cover, a big thin metal disk with a knob handle in the center. The ringer lid was a smaller version, about the size of a dinner plate. I was taking my time transferring the diapers from the washing tub into the ringer, meticulously placing every single diaper in the proper position inside the metal tub. Acey came into the pantry and shoved me.

"Okay get out, it's my turn. I'm telling." Shoving her backward I planted my feet firmly in front of the wash tub. "No, I'm not done." Then I sang from Harry Belafonte's song, *so shut your mouth, go away, Mama look a boo-boo-dey.* Acey made her final move. At least, I *thought* it was her final move.

She pushed me out through the pantry door into the kitchen and took her place in front of the wringer. Standing in the middle of the kitchen, I gave her my parting shot. It was such a sweet little bombshell and I'd been saving it for just the right moment.

"I know you have letters under your mattress," I said, and waited for recognition of the gravity to settle into her brain. Because she didn't immediately respond, and as proof I'd seen the letters, I added, "Those letters were addressed to Dickey Rogers at the boys' reformatory up the river in Red Wing." I repeated the delicious, threatening words in sing-song fashion, "Up the river, where the bad boys go. Up the lazy river where you're gonna be." I took a breath and added in a more serious tone, "I saw, and I'm telling. A-lle-lujah."

I purposely saved a more powerful bit of ammunition for another time. In addition to the Dickey Rogers letters under her mattress, I found a stack of recipe cards with a rubber binder around them. On each card was printed a swear word followed by the meaning of that word. The cards were alphabetized, so you could quickly find any naughty word you were looking for.

Standing safely back, ten feet into the kitchen, I made a strategic decision that was my biggest mistake and one that would affect me the rest of my life. As Acey's head appeared in the doorway of the pantry, I stuck my tongue out at her and laughed. It all happened in an instant: before my smile had disappeared, I saw a metal disk, about the size of a dinner plate, with sharp edges swirling through the air, the trajectory expertly calculated for my face.

Acey stood wide-eyed, her throwing arm still outstretched, when the disk hit hard connecting with my right front tooth and cracked it in half. The same tooth I had knocked out in the playpen when I was two. The same tooth Acey told me would never, ever grow back. She was half right. The pain, the nerves waving in the breeze, knocked me to the floor. Acey cried as hard as I did. I don't remember anyone being punished for this crime— with the exception of the pain I suffered at the dentist's office.

Baby Eightball was in for a few surprises of her own. Primarily because she was the youngest, the object of affection for many; she was also the tool of revenge for others. Milo and Marcus planned a play titled, *Moses*. They decided to have a rehearsal of *Moses* one summer afternoon. Sesson was ironing sheets in the dining room, and Mother was napping upstairs with her door closed.

M&M crept quietly up the stairs to the linen closet. They removed two sheets and one bath towel. Then, quickly back downstairs to the pantry closet where Mother kept the big wicker picnic basket. Last, but not least, Milo tiptoed into the living room where Eightball was napping in her play-pen. She gently picked her up and carried her out the porch door to the driveway, where she met Marcus. They proceeded westward through the pasture, down the hill to the flat, with their costumes, their basket, and their Baby Moses.

The rehearsal was going along fine, M&M costumed with the sheets over their heads, looking like Arabian sheiks. Eightball was a happy, cooperative baby, content as she settled nicely into the picnic basket, wrapped in her swaddling cloth of a bath towel.

Moses, in her picnic basket, had just been set into the weeds between our pasture and King's Island. She would float amid the mossy rocks of the creek and eventually sail forth down the Mississippi. Just then play rehearsal was abruptly halted.

Sesson, wearing her housedress and white open-toed sandals, jumped into the mucky creek to rescue Baby Moses. Sesson then returned Moses to the "Queen," although that was not the ending M&M had in mind. Thank goodness for the eyes in the back of Sesson's head. That was one of the few times she felt compelled to, "tell on us."

Chapter 22

We Can Change the World

It was into this complex web of personalities that Ryodo "Mike" Ogata was destined.

We could never have imagined how incongruous life at The Last House on Park Street was to the peaceful, obedient Buddhist way of living that was customary for Ryodo Ogata. Nevertheless, his arrival unfolded just as my mother envisioned and orchestrated. Mom, Dad and Leedsie met Mike at Wold-Chamberlain Airport and brought him home to Anoka to live for one whole year.

Sesson managed to gather everyone on the sun porch for a formal greeting. Mike ascended the porch steps dragging his trunk and suitcases, entering the porch door between baskets of laundry: one, clothes to be folded, the other, ironing.

He dropped his bags and stood on the slate floor with his camera and light meters all dangling down. Taking in the entirety of his new family, with his hands folded in front of his face, his fingertips just brushing the end of his nose, he closed his eyes and bowed in front of us. Dressed in his ever-so-white pressed shirt, his compulsively polished black shoes and his navy blue pressed pants, he bowed again and again.

I'd never seen anyone bow to another, except Father Murphy to the body of Jesus Christ, which rested in the form of bread hosts inside the golden goblet, deep behind two sets of golden tabernacle doors, in the center of the altar, at St. Stephen's Church.

Right there on the living room floor, Mike unpacked his bags. "I bring presents from my father's temple in Sagae. For my American mother and father, I bring two books. This one, flower arranging from my mother, who is flower arranger. And another, *Living Treasures of Japan*, from my father—to sank you bery, bery much."

"For all the girls, including Sesson." He said, handing out beautifully wrapped packages of kimonos (Japanese robes) and tabi (Japanese socks, that resembled Beulah's feet).

"I bring kimonos and tabi for boys too. Chopsticks for everyone and many, many seaweed cracker and pickled prums and cherries—last whole year. Sank you bery much," he said with one last deep bow.

"Now I take picture. Everyone in pyramid, big ones on bottom, little ones on top. *Domo arigato.*"

Mike and Leedsie shared a bedroom. Leedsie had the top bunk, Mike the bottom, hundreds of seaweed crackers stashed on the top shelf in their closet. The unfamiliar smells of rice, soy and seaweed wafted down the hall, past the boys' bathroom and the girls' clothes hamper, into Acey's and my room.

Our room, where a life-size poster of Elvis Presley hung on one side of our closet wall. On the opposite wall was a 3 x 5 black and white snapshot of tire tracks that ran the length of our driveway, from the pantry door all the way to Park Street. Every night before she went to bed, Acey kissed that picture of tire tracks. I saw her. That photo was my collateral, my bargaining chip for anything I could ever want, including a nice little sip of cold water in the middle of an unbearably humid summer night.

The tracks were made by the Knodt's Grocery Store delivery van, which Tom Garvey drove, when he brought our groceries to the pantry door twice a week. It was never any trouble for Acey to pull the hairpins out of her spit-curls and rush downstairs, with a smile on her face, to help unload our order. Aside from Dickey Rogers and Johnny Mathis, Tom Garvey was Acey's first obviously unrealistic crush.

For most of the summer, Dad anchored his Seabee on the river. One silver wing of the plane rested just under a gently drooping elm branch.

Early in the summer, my father took Mike and Leedsie to Canada where they fished for 25-pound Northern Pike. Lifting off the river, making a low-altitude circle over the house, dipping the wings back and forth, they said, goodbye.

Mike Ogata was interested in learning American slang, so during that precious week in the Canadian wilderness, Mike carried his notebook everywhere recording his experiences and all the slang he heard. He learned about campfires that permeate your clothes with the sweet and lasting scent of cedar. He learned how to fly an airplane and repair it too. He ate fricasseed butterfly wings (oatmeal) and monkey beds (dried apricots) and porridge closets (mushrooms). He learned that the fish you catch, you clean. In the evenings they bathed in the frigid Canadian River water, and communicated with the natives through sign language and drawings in the dirt. When they returned from Canada, Mike was exhilarated.

During their homecoming dinner of grilled Northern with butter and lemon, Mike told us of his great adventure. "That trip with Dad make me so exciting," he said, with tears in his eyes. "Dad bery, bery kind, teach me many things. I remember all detail all my life."

Shanty Town was still part of our lives when Mike arrived, but Leedsie, at age 15, was becoming too sophisticated to participate in our town's business. One less man in Shanty Town. Mike humored us, though, and soon he reluctantly traded in his white shirt and pressed pants for overalls. He was the Shanty Town photographer and he attended Acey's school, with hopes of learning more slang.

Mike walked the cow paths with us, first to the river to meet Willow Island, then the creek and finally to the ferns and ancient looking trees of King's Island. We wanted him to know how important our landmarks were, in case he needed them in an emergency—to help him relax, or find his way home.

Mike adopted the position of 2nd baseman on our softball team under the cedar and elm trees in our front yard. He joined in swimming lessons at 5 o'clock every summer evening. On Sunday mornings, he knelt with us on the hard oak benches at St. Stephen's Catholic Church. Bowing his head, he prayed for the Russians. At the end of Mass, Mike joined in the affirmation—the mantra—*we can change the world, we can change the world, we can change the world.*

Chapter 23

The Greatest Invention Ever

The spring of Mike's arrival, Mom and Dad had conspired on a new adventure. Plowing under all the remnants of strawberries and corn, they planted the entire flat to cucumbers, which with any luck would yield thousands of pickles. With very little knowledge of the work involved, my parents negotiated a contract with Gedney Pickles to grow 30 acres of cucumbers. By the end of that summer, the fruit was maturing nicely and on schedule.

With things comparatively under control on his "gentleman's farm," my father could take his traditional two-week fishing trip with his flying pals to Canada—his second trip of the summer. Two nights before he left, my parents invited their friends over for tennis, swimming, and a picnic at the big rock fireplace down by the pool. The children had to stay upstairs. Mother delivered her usual orders, "Big kids take care of little kids and no coming downstairs for crackers, pickled herring or anything else."

Acey and I spent most of the evening looking out our bedroom window, where we could see and hear some of the party action.

My father and his buddies gathered around the cedar tree, just below our window. "Yes, sir! A pickle picker," Sy, our swimming coach, shouted, slapping Dad on the back. "I'll say, that is the greatest invention ever." The men laughed and guffawed down on the front yard.

"What are they talking about?" I asked Acey

"Just shut up and listen."

"Not supposed to say shut up."

Dad stood proudly on the pitcher's mound in the center of the softball field. His buddies gathered around kidding him, among other things, about the ragged looking lawn. He never apologized for having a torn up yard. Instead he repeated his classic response, "You can either have a beautiful lawn or a house full of kids. I prefer the kids."

Chalky, a long-time friend of Dad's, smoked a cigar, and wrapped his arm around my dad, almost spilling his drink. "You sure pulled this one off in fine style, LD. Oh boy, did ya."

Eugene Bird chimed in. "Congratulations Darrah, you always said you wanted to be an inventor and this time you've beat 'em all."

Acey leaned forward with her nose pressed against the screen. "So, Dad invented something. Sy said so, and Eugene said so." That was all the proof she needed.

"Yah, so what did he invent?" I sure didn't know. My idea of a good invention was the Valentine's gifts he made for all the secretaries at the office. The hand-carved wooden hearts with a hole drilled in the center for a glass tube to hold one single red rose. He cut the hearts out with his saw in the basement. Then he sanded and painted them red. He engraved each woman's name on the bottom of the wooden heart. On Valentine's morning he placed one red rose in each glass holder and went to work. To me, that was an invention.

But, I said to Acey, "Let's ask Leedsie and Mike; they probably know." We dragged Mike into our room and told him to sit by the window.

"Do you know what Dad invented?" Acey demanded, with her hands on her hips.

Mike looked confused. Starting over, using her best teacher approach, she pointed down in the yard. "An invention, it's what all those people are talking about down there. Sy said something about a pickle picker. Do you know about any invention?"

"I don't know about invention," Mike said looking out the window at the men. "But I watch Dad take washing machine apart in the basement."

"No Mike, that's not an invention," Acey said impatiently. She was usually the expert on everything. I believed everything she told me, all my life, including the time the sky over the river turned deep orange and she said, "Oh boy, look out! When the sky turns orange that means the Russians are coming."

Acey continued explaining English to Mike, nodding her head for emphasis.

"An invention has to be something no one has ever done before ... or even thought of, something unique and interesting ... that ordinary people need. It can be exciting and wonderful, Mike, or it can be dreadful and dangerous. That's an invention, Mike. Okay?"

Two days after the men congratulated him out on our softball field, my dad prepared his dried fruits and oatmeal and packed his red wool plaid jacket and hip-waders for another fishing trip. Before he left, he gathered all of us in the living room. Every time we were all together Mike wanted to make a pyramid.

"Leedsie, Acey, Charlie, and I on bottom. Andy, Milo second row, Marcus, Oscar next row and someone, maybe Mom please hold Eightball on top. Dad, please take picture. *Domo arigato.*" After snapping the pic-ture, Dad reminded us, "Tomorrow, I'm going to Canada for two weeks." We knew he was going. It seemed to me that he was gone most of every summer.

Milo asked, "Will you fly over the house and wave when you go, Dad ... dip your wings?"

"Yes, but there's something much more important for you to know. Maybe you heard, I have a new invention, a pickle picker." The pyramid collapsed on the living room rug. I thought for sure he was going to show it to us. Acey jabbed me in the ribs, and we were silent while the little kids scrambled to attention and Mike shouted, "Dad, I know what invention is. Is something very exciting, ney?"

"That's one way to look at it, yes ... exciting, that's for sure, Mike."

Dad cautioned us, "Your mother is in charge. She's knows where the invention is. Don't even try to find it. When the time is just right, she'll show you, but you must wait, be patient and follow her instructions pre-cisely. Do you understand?" Everybody mumbled disappointingly yes, yah, okay, well where is it anyway? Even Leedsie, who was 15, didn't know where the invention was hidden.

At 6 a.m. the next morning, my father began his ritual of saying good-bye before a fishing trip. Beginning in our room, he tapped Acey's shoul-der, tipped her head back and kissed her forehead. "Take good care of your mother." Then, just across the room he kissed my forehead with the same instruction, leaving behind the familiar sweet scent of his last Canadian campfire. Across the hall to Leedsie and Mike's room, then down the long hallway to the boys' room, the girls' room and the nursery.

By 7 a.m., we heard the low drone of the Seabee flying over the house. We ran to the pool and watched as Dad dipped the wings back and forth three times and then gained altitude and flew north over the river.

Leedsie and Mike immediately took off on their own quest. They looked in the shop for something small like a motor with an improvised do-dad or gizmo attached to it. They looked for something really big in the garage and the back of the shed under the tractor and the hay wagon, even in the wood piles. They looked down by the flat in the mud near the irrigator pipes and behind the tar barrels by the farm road. Every day they looked someplace new, in the barns and corn bin and places that were dark and dusty with spider eggs and webs and mice running up the walls.

For that whole week in August, Shanty Town closed down. We made signs for our shop doors, "Gone Hunting." Acey and I listened at the kitchen, dining room, and library doorways hoping to hear mother confiding something to Sesson about the invention, or maybe talking to one of her friends on the phone and spilling the beans by mistake. But Mother was exceptionally careful.

On August 15th, an otherwise ordinary Minnesota summer morning, Leedsie came back from the alfalfa field after milking Beulah. Mike followed behind him, carrying his notebook and camera recording anything and everything anyone said, looking for examples of English slang. Mother carried Eightball on her hip as she herded the little kids outside.

"Today is the day!" she declared from the pantry steps. "The time has come to unveil your father's greatest invention. Big kids take the little kids down through the pasture, last one through, close the gate. Then, I want you to go down the hill to the farm road, beyond the pinecone woods, where the big elm tree is dying, beside the cow path. I will take Eightball with me and the rest of you, climb up on the dead limb and wait. Do not come looking for me, just listen carefully, be patient and wait."

Mike took pictures of us all lined up on the dead tree limb while we waited, swatting mosquitoes, wiping little kids' noses and trying to keep everyone on the limb without making any noise or falling off. "Talk about being out on a limb," Leedsie said.

"What does that mean, *out on a limb*?" Mike asked.

"It means, we're all sitting here on a rotting tree limb, waiting for something to happen, that may never happen. In the meantime, the limb could crack off, from the weight of us, and dump us on the ground."

After a while, Leedsie was impatient. He started walking down the cow path toward the creek. Acey called out, "C'mon Leedsie, Mom said. You know it might not happen if we don't do what she told us." Leedsie grumbled, picked up a dried cow pie, threw it up in the air and watched it land and disintegrate in yellow dust on the hard, dry ground then he came back to his place on the limb.

Andrew Shinski said, "Shhhhh, I think I hear something coming up in the air." Everyone looked up at the sky. "No, wait!" he said. Then he lay down in the dirt with one ear to the ground, just like a real native. "It's coming from up the hill, way down Park Street." We were so quiet we could hear Mike's camera clicking and advancing for the next shot. We could hear the sound of pine needles dropping in the woods behind us.

Pretty soon the noise got louder; and then, we could see it all at once. Coming over the crest of the farm road in a cloud of grey dust was Mom, driving the Ford tractor, with Eightball bouncing up and down on her lap. She was pulling the hay wagon.

Leedsie was disgusted. "That's not it. That's nothing. Where's the invention?"

"Maybe that's just a part of it, guys," I said, hoping for something more.

Mom smiled proudly, as she drove the tractor completely down the hill, stepped hard on the clutch, shifted and hit the brake right beside the tree limb, where we sat. It was only then that I saw the pile of old peach crates in the center of the hay wagon.

Mother stood up from the tractor seat holding Eightball. "Okay now I want four of you to lie down on your tummies on the left side of the wagon, and the other four, including you, Mike, on the right side. As I drive through the rows of cucumbers, you all pick as fast as you can, and put the cucumbers in the boxes in the middle of the wagon. And no grumbling." She must have laughed all the way through the cucumber field.

By the time we finished picking all the cucumbers, Mother was tired. She had kept the spirit alive while he was gone, but after the initial euphoria of unveiling the invention, she felt weary of the sole responsibility of managing the gentleman's farm. Undeniable fact was: He was late, again. Could it be the last straw?

Finally the telegram arrived, informing us that Dad would be home in two days. Mother revived, as usual, hung up the phone, and sighed, "Just in the nick of time, while I still have a sense of humor." Mike recorded in his notebook, *just in the nick of time.*

This year, the year of Mike Ogata, Mother did something unexpected. Before leaving to meet my father at Pierce's landing strip, she sprinkled her hair with ZBT baby powder until it was completely white—to remind him that he had been gone far too long.

By the time they returned home, half the baby powder had fallen on her shoulders, but Dad was obviously amused by Mother's message. "I know her like a book," he said giving her a hug. "But I must admit, in a nutshell, that was really out of left field." Mike Ogata couldn't write fast enough.

Chapter 24

Fitting In

This is the year I began working for my father at the Abstract office. My job title was "gofer." Technically, the job shouldn't have been mine. Leedsie turned it down, in favor of milking Beulah. Acey wanted to work at Bimbo's drive-in across the alfalfa field; that kind of work was frowned upon in our house, but Acey was holding out for something more exciting than working at the office. "You take that office job, Charlie. I don't want it. I'm going to be a carhop at Bimbo's. I can make enough money to buy lipstick and records, too. Just you wait. Pretty soon you'll see me walking across that alfalfa field to my job."

"They're not gonna let you work there. Besides, you have to be 16."

"Oh, yes they are, and I do not have to be 16."

Every day after school, I walked the three blocks, from St. Stephen's School to the Abstract office, located behind my dad's law office at 316 East Main. I filed documents, fetched donuts for the typists. I made coffee in the basement break room, and I delivered documents across the street at the courthouse to the Auditor, Treasurer, and the Register of Deeds. All of this meant I would not have to take care of little kids at home, or help with dinner, or set the table; Acey would.

I looked forward to riding home with my dad. Maybe I would discover the reason he sometimes sat for so long in the car, staring out at the river. But for a long time, there was almost no conversation on our rides home. After the peace and quiet of the car, we'd walk into what sounded like a birthday party for 100 four-year olds. The table was set—by Acey—for 11; dinner was ready and Dad and I took our places to eat.

Mike never complained about our food. He spent lots of time with Sesson, watching her prepare and fry chicken and other specialties. On those days when Sesson sensed that Mike might be a little homesick, she'd invite him into the kitchen.

"C'mon now, you sit down and I'll have a nice little B.L.T. ready for you a two shakes of a lamb's tail. Mike wrote in his notebook, *two shakes of a lamb's tail.*

Mother served pork roasts and lamb chops, hot dogs, Mexiburgers and mashed potatoes with gravy; Mike thanked her for every new experience. *Domo arigato.*

After the mighty Tornado high school football games, Mike invited the whole team and all the cheerleaders over to roll up our rugs and dance the lindy, the waltz and the jitter-bug on our living room floor. Acey and I sat at the end of the living room on the rolled up carpet watching the older kids dance. I wondered if I'd ever get old enough to wear penny loafers and fluffy crinoline slips that make your skirt look huge like Cinderella.

The Platters sang out from the hi-fi at end of our living room, *Oh Yes I'm the great pretender,* as the homecoming queen danced in her stocking-feet with the captain of the football team. "For sure they're gonna get married," Acey whispered in my ear. The chandeliers shook as The Crew Cuts sang, *Sh'Boom, sh'Boom* and all the dancers stomped on the floor. One by one, the girls danced with Mike Ogata, the honorary mascot of the Anoka Tornadoes.

Christmas time introduced many strange traditions to Mike, including midnight mass, Santa Claus leaving presents under our tree, angels with our names painted on them, stockings hanging from the mantle, decorating the house with more angels, and snow sprayed on windows and mirrors, candles, and lights. That year, Mike's name was added to our Christmas card.

He joined the celebration with the Ramsey Rams 4-H Club as we sang Christmas carols on the back of our hay wagon, piled with fresh fragrant straw. Dad drove the tractor, pulling us through the snow all the way down the farm road to the creek and back.

New Year's Day on the frozen river along the banks of Willow Island, Dad, Mike and Leedsie shoveled snow to create a huge skating rink. They gathered fallen branches and built a bonfire to roast hot dogs and marshmallows. For Dad, the ritual of preparing the skating rink on New Year's Day was a labor of love. He'd been skating on the river for most of his life. He'd been a member of the speed skating team at the University. Now, he shared that part of his history with his brood and with Mike Ogata.

Skating on the river was worry-free, because no one would laugh at you if you fell down trying to do something risky like a fast, fancy turn. Acey had taken on the role of skating coach for Oscar. Dressed in her red velvet coat, and white furry hat with matching mittens, Oscar was inspiring, and for a four-year-old, she was a pretty good skater. "You keep this up, Oscar, and you'll knock their socks off," Acey cheered skating along beside her. Mike took a picture of Oscar skating backward and wrote in his notebook, *knock their socks off.*

Acey taught Oscar how to turn with her arms outstretched. Oscar was a natural-born athlete; she could skate backward, forward, even sideways, and stop on a dime—all at Acey's command.

Acey's big-picture plan was to get Oscar on The Ed Sullivan Show.

Chapter 25

Arbor Day

One early bone-chilling morning in April began with the sound of the tractor coming up the driveway and stopping at the porch door. "Get your warm clothes on and get out here, now!" My father ordered us into the yard, "Everybody! Including Mike." I knew without looking at the calendar what this chilly damp day meant: Arbor Day, and long, cold hours of work in the trenches.

The very first Arbor Day was April 10, 1872; it was the brainchild of Julius Sterling Morton, President Grover Cleveland's Secretary of Agriculture. Morton encouraged people to plant trees for cleaner air, improved properties and a healthier planet over-all. In 1970, President Nixon proclaimed the last Friday in April as National Arbor Day.

Dad was an environmental soldier. He believed as Franklin D. Roosevelt said, *Forests are the lungs of our land, purifying the air and giving fresh strength to our people.*

Leedsie and Mike helped Dad attach the disc to the back of the tractor. Then they loaded 10-gallon buckets, some filled with water and others with hundreds of pine seedlings. While we waited in the cold, they anchored the buckets on wood platforms that Dad had rigged up on either side of the disc.

My father drove the tractor out beyond the swimming pool, through the pasture to the other end of the burdock field almost to Mr. Porter's milking shed. We all dragged unpleasantly behind, cold, tired, and complaining.

"Why do we have to do this every single year?" Acey whined.

I agreed, "Yeah. Last year it was Bunker Prairie, the year before that, the other sandbur patch; and I'm cold and I hate this job." Acey and I couldn't even wear mittens because we had to pick up those little trees.

However unpleasant at the time, Bunker Prairie was our biggest accomplishment. It was a 2,000-acre plot in Coon Rapids, purchased by my father for the price of delinquent taxes. When we started planting pine seedlings on that land, it was overgrown with sandburs and burdock and scrappy shrubs. Today, Bunker Hills is rated in the top 25 of U.S. 27-hole golf courses, famous for its lush tree-lined fairways and trails.

On this Arbor Day, the tradition began as usual at the edge of another empty forlorn field. In a way, tree planting on Arbor Day was another of my father's ingenious *inventions*. We had to move fast, not missing a beat, almost with machine precision.

Lowering the disc, my father drove slowly forward creating a shallow trench. Leedsie and Mike followed the trench on one side; Acey and I on the other. We lifted baby pines from the buckets of freezing water, carefully untangling their roots, then dropping them root first into the trench. Then, we poured water over the roots, and the middle kids followed behind us pushing the trench closed. They were followed by the little kids stomping the dirt tight around the trees, row after row, until we had planted another thousand trees. And for all of that experience, we had Julius Sterling Morton to thank.

Mother always prepared a special dinner to celebrate our accomplishment—the food made all the cold, wet discomfort disappear. My father beamed, at the end of the dining room table, because he loved Arbor Day.

Besides thousands of new trees planted, spring brought new baby lambs to our pasture. If one of the ewes had twins or triplets, she would be unable to feed all of them. We frequently took baby lambs into the basement to feed them until they were strong enough to fend for themselves.

Toward the end of Mike Ogata's stay, a *real* newspaper reporter from The Minneapolis Star Tribune interviewed Mike and ran a photo of him and Leedsie feeding a bottle to a baby lamb. In the article Mike was quoted, "I like very much doing chores with my American brother, but I am a bit disturbed that in overalls I don't always look as neat as I like."

Mother told the reporter that Mike was an excellent student and had a positive influence on Leedsie's schoolwork.

"Leeds has been inclined to have a somewhat casual attitude toward study," she said. "But since Mike's arrival, he's doing much better in school, learning karate, judo, and even some Japanese words."

Mike had been exposed to more than a new wardrobe that year. During the month of May, the son of the Buddhist priest, prayed with us every night, kneeling on the cold slate floor in the sun porch, while we recited the rosary to honor the Blessed Virgin Mary.

During Lent, Mike observed our rituals and rules of fasting—no meat on Fridays, no food after midnight, fasting until after Mass the next morning. Palm Sunday, the day that Jesus arrived in Jerusalem on a donkey and walked over a path of palm fronds, Mike went to church with us. He attended the longest, most arduous Mass of the year, on Holy Thursday.

And on Good Friday, the day Jesus carried his cross and died for the sins of man, Mike studiously followed along in a prayer book, as the priest prayed at each station of the Holy Cross. Finally on Easter Sunday, Ryodo Ogata celebrated the joy of the risen Christ at High Mass. He enthusiastically helped hide Easter eggs in the yard in nests of fresh straw, under the pine trees, and in the knot holes and crotches of the trees.

Chapter 26

Sayonara

Mike Ogata taught us a few Japanese words. He pointed out that changing even one letter in a word could cause, embarrassment, shame, even dishonor. "Be very, very careful, how you speak another's language. For example, '*Butta*' means big fat pig, but Buddha is our spiritual teacher. Be careful. And, do not use '*Sayonara*' lightly, as most Americans do. The word is reserved *only* for final goodbye."

He was not brought up to cry and, so that year he never did. Instead, in emotional situations, I noticed, he would press his lips tight together and bite his upper lip, which is exactly what he did that last night in June, the night before he left to return to his home in Japan.

Mother had prepared Mike's favorite dinner: standing rib roast rubbed with coarse salt and cracked pepper mixed with chunky chopped garlic, mashed potatoes, tender green beans, salad vinaigrette, and Beulah's milk in the tall red glasses.

"There's one more surprise," Mother announced after dinner. "After that, we'll have Mike's favorite dessert, strawberry shortcake with ice cream." Mike stood gleaming in the doorway between the kitchen and the dining room, grinning so completely that I could hardly see his eyes, as he presented a still sizzling, cast iron skillet.

"I made from Japanese special recipe," he said. "Little kids help me catch grasshoppers in sandbur field, right out there, where we plant trees on Arbor Day. Eat these grasshoppers. Good for your gut," he said, rubbing his tummy with one hand. "Thank you, thank you very much. *Domo arigato.*"

Mike Ogata lived the words of Thich Nhat Hanh: *If you touch one thing with great awareness, you touch everything.*

On his final night at The Last House on Park Street, he bowed deeply and biting his lip, he held the pan of grasshoppers to the side and said, "*Sayonara* my American family." He must have thought that dinner to be the last we would ever have together. It wouldn't take long to realize the power of his presence. Mike Ogata touched our lives with great intention and awareness.

Chapter 27

Transformations

In the year Mike lived with us he never talked about the war or its effects on the lives of the Japanese people. But, something about the toll of that war dissolved, as the remnants of Mike Ogata's visit lingered in our walls.

If I noticed something unusual about my father's behavior, when I was only eight years old, then Mother must have been aware of it too. But, my father changed after the year of Mike Ogata. Mother must have imagined the healing power of simply looking into the face of compassion: a joy-filled, open-minded Japanese Buddhist boy. She must have anticipated the curative power of living with that—every day, for one whole year—teaching the virtue of forgiveness by his presence alone.

My mother's task was to push the envelope, discover and employ all that could be known, all that could be experienced, shine a light in the darkness and exploit the resulting brilliance *so that no man's efforts are wasted.* That she did.

After the experience of Mike, my father didn't seem so sad, so isolated and stuck in that unreachable place. Laughing as he played with Eightball on the floor in the living room, crouching down to hide inside a fort made of giant red cardboard building blocks, he seemed to have discovered some peace, some understanding, maybe even forgiveness—for himself and others.

He patiently taught the little kids how to make moving vehicles out of empty thread spools propelled by rubber binders; he helped us pick gooseberries, instead of ordering it done; he took us flying more often to visit long-ignored, aging relatives, traveling back to places he had enjoyed as a child.

Gradually our rides home from work evolved, too. My father asked questions about my school and my friends. He bought clothes for Acey and me, quilted skirts with attached crinolines … a surprise at the ends of our beds one Valentine's Day morning.

There were times when he would take longer to come into the house at night, but those times grew fewer and fewer over the next few years.

The usual domestic cycle at The Last House on Park Street continued: Leedsie got his braces off; I got my braces on. Acey was midway through her term with wires on her teeth and she landed a job at Bimbo's. She had to compromise, though. She was not old enough to be a carhop, so she took an inside job washing dishes, in hopes of the more glamorous and lucrative future position as carhop. Acey does not give up, and she's a hard worker. She walked home, in the dark, across the stubble in the alfalfa field, scratching her legs all bloody.

"Is it worth it?" I asked her one night, while she was trying to sleep. "Do you wish you were working at the office, now?" I would have given her that job, just to save her legs. It was rightfully her job, if she wanted it.

"It will be worth it, and no I don't want that office job. Go to sleep."

"But you're cutting your legs to pieces, and it's gonna take another two years to get what you want."

"I know what I'm doing. Gotta be painful, if ya wanna get anywhere. It's all in the timing. Now, shut up."

"Not supposed to say shut up. I'm telling."

While Acey waits to be a carhop, she's training Oscar to do Mae West impersonations. Oscar has an unusually deep voice for a little kid. Acey curls her hair with strips of rags, dresses her up and sends her downstairs to perform in front of Mom and Dad's dinner guests. "Why doncha come up and see me some time, Big Boy?"

We were all required to take piano lessons from Mrs. Annon, who lived on Park Street, in the house where my father was born. Because of that history, her home was comfortable, but I did not excel at piano. Leedsie did, and he was good, especially at boogie-woogie. Acey tolerated the lessons and all the younger kids learned piano, and at least one other instrument.

Fortunately for me, after eight years of struggle, Mrs. Annon gave up. "I will suggest to your parents that they needn't waste their money on your piano lessons any longer." There was no discussion, my parents were not disappointed. They were not surprised. I was simply allowed to pursue other interests. And soon those interests emerged.

One summer night, company was arriving, and Mother was still upstairs dressing. My father asked me to make cocktail sauce for the shrimp appetizer. Even though I simply followed his directions—using plenty of fresh lemon juice and a drop of Tabasco—he told me that I made the very best shrimp cocktail sauce he'd ever tasted.

My most powerful culinary encouragement happened late on a snowy afternoon, New Year's Day the year I was 12 years old. I sat warming my feet by the fire in the living room. Across the room on the sofa, my father rested, reading his favorite book, *My Day in Court,* by Louis Nizer.

After our traditional New Year's Day dinner of standing rib roast followed by our annual family skating event and bonfire on the Mississippi River, everyone was exhausted.

While Mother and all the little kids napped, I began to feel gnawingly hungry. It seemed like hours since we'd eaten.

The memory of the rare roast beef with the crispy edges all rubbed with salt, cracked pepper and chunky garlic made me ravenous. The lingering aroma of roasting beef still hung in the air and drew my mind to the kitchen and the refrigerator, where I knew there were leftovers.

I watched the embers in the fireplace and imagined what I could do with that meat and a couple slices of white bread that Grandma made early that morning

I looked across the room at my father. "Hey, Dad? How would you like a sandwich?" I asked, hoping he'd say, yes.

Engrossed in his book, he mumbled absently, "You bet. That sounds fine."

Up to that moment, I'd only opened the refrigerator to remove a bottle of milk or get something out for my mother; I'd never looked deep inside and I'd never so much as touched a really sharp knife.

My first adventure was to discover exactly what was in the refrigerator.

Besides the roast, I chose a tomato, a big white onion, two leaves of lettuce, fresh parsley and a jar of mayonnaise.

To begin the sandwich, I cut two slices of Grandma's bread, trying to keep the serrated knife straight and the bread even and thin, but not flimsy. On to the beef. I took a deep breath, inhaling the scent of the meat, which I cut in one round thin slice, so clean and straight, no one would even guess that I had tampered with the leftovers.

Feeling more confident with the knife, I sliced four thin rounds of tomato, peeled the onion and carefully planed two paper-thin onion wafers. I held one up to the kitchen light and could see right through it.

I spread one slice of bread with a bare coating of butter and a thin sheet of mayonnaise on the other slice—all the way to the edges. I placed a ruffled lettuce leaf, just so, over the mayonnaise and sprinkled the leaves of parsley over the lettuce, which was the bed for the tomatoes. That way, I figured, the bread wouldn't get soggy. After trimming the thin rim of fat from the roast beef, I folded it carefully over the tomatoes. Then I added just a dash of salt and a grind of pepper over the meat and arranged the onion slices on top of the meat.

With the buttered side of the bread to the onions—because butter and onions go well together—I sealed my creation. Holding the sandwich firmly, without squashing the bread down, I gave the sandwich an authoritative diagonal cut—fancy, restaurant style. I stood back to admire. The ruffle of lettuce showed just slightly around the outside edge of the sandwich with a simple elegance that made me feel proud.

At this point, I was beyond excited and feeling totally in control of everything. I found a salad-size Christmas plate in the dining room and arranged the sandwich with the diagonal cut perfectly joined. From the top shelf in the pantry, I removed a wicker tray, usually reserved for summer parties. I placed a white linen and lace napkin on the tray and added a red Christmas goblet filled with Beulah's milk. The sandwich plate rested in the middle of the tray, which I carried with both hands underneath, like a restaurant waiter, as I made my entrance to the living room sofa.

My father set his book down, sat up and surveyed the tray.

"Hmmm," was the only sound I heard, as I backed up to the fireplace to wait. He said nothing, he only stopped to wipe a bit of mayonnaise from the corner of his mouth then bit into the second half of his sandwich.

When he finished, he picked up a crumb from the plate and licked it off his finger.

He was taking forever. What would be the verdict? Finally he wiped his hands, folded the napkin and placed it back on the tray.

Then, as if he had no concept of the power of his next words, he looked across the room right into my eyes and said, "That, young lady, was not *just* a sandwich. *That* was an experience." I had forgotten that I'd been starving earlier and at that moment I felt completely full. I did not need a sandwich after all.

My father's new level of involvement included reading the Sunday funnies out loud to any of us who crowded in close to him on the sofa. He *let* us crowd in close to him. He quoted limericks over and over again. *Th ~~e once was a man named Finnegan. Now my story's begun. He took off h hat and his hair blew away. Now my story is done.* And, when I went to ve him a goodnight kiss, he no longer scrunched up his face, turning or a scruffy cheek—as he had done for years.

When we approached adolescence, our parents came up ' .h indefensible rules; but they were in charge of enforcement; so we had pay attention.

Mom told Acey and me, "Until you get your braces of' ou may not wear lipstick or date boys." That rule wouldn't apply to me f a long, long time. For one thing I was only 13. And another thing, whe Dr. Devries put the braces on, he told me I would have to wear them for least two years.

The other rule was: no jewelry or clothing from ys; only stuffed animals and records are acceptable gifts.

It was true—and my dad knew it—that last year I had developed a huge crush on Teach, one of Mike Ogata's Japanese friends; but the chances of Teach ever paying attention to me were less than zero. Besides, he had gone back to Japan with Mike. I did, however, write letters to Teach and he wrote back.

All our mail, addressed to The Last House on Park Street, came to the Post Office, next door to Dad's office, and he picked up the mail every day. Dad was aware, but, thankfully, he never asked about the letters from Japan.

One afternoon, I was just kicking off on the girls' swing in the yard. Dad came around the side of the house, carrying a small package. Handing it to me, he said, "Go ahead, open it up, but if it's jewelry it will have to be returned."

I looked at the brown paper wrapping, with the neatly, tightly folded corners. So careful, so Japanese. Of course it was from Japan, all the stamps made that clear.

Dad stood, waiting in front of me—inside my circle of dirt under the swing. The size of the box was obvious too, not long enough for a Japanese fan, or chopsticks, not deep enough for a Kokeshi doll. I turned the box over and over, trying to stall. *Why didn't Dad just go in the house and leave me alone?* He did not budge from that circle.

I opened the box. The contents sparkled in the sunlight. It was a delicately etched silver locket with a door of jade framed in silver, hanging from a silver chain. Inside the locket was a teeny photo of Teach. I was only 13, but it was the most beautiful thing I'd ever seen. My heart raced, I wanted to swing really high, over the tops of the oak trees.

"I'll leave this up to you," my father said, slowly, "but the rule is: no jewelry from boys." Even though I knew it was coming, I cried.

"And, young lady," he said, as he turned to go back to the house, "feel free to do the packaging and deliver it to the Post Office yourself."

He didn't say when I should repackage and deliver it to the Post Office, did he?

Leedsie was almost 16 when our parents devised an outrageous rule. It seemed to fall on us, out of mid-air. Dad said, "If you want to get your driver's license, you will first have to get your pilot's license." *What?*

On October 4, 1957, the Russians launched Sputnik I, the first artificial satellite to orbit the earth. They launched a second satellite, Sputnik II, on November 3, 1957—the day before Leedsie's 16th birthday. My father was exhilarated by the dawn of the Space Age and he intended his children to share his enthusiasm.

"Why do we hafta do *that?*" I groaned, imagining myself being even more obvious as an oddball. This family was spinning out of control. My parents seemed to be inventing rules to suit the occasion and sustain their best interests.

"You have to do that," Dad said, "because learning to fly an airplane will make you a more conscientious, responsible and careful driver … and, you won't take things for granted. In addition, flying an airplane helps you learn how to react in emergencies."

By July of 1960, it had been three years since Mike Ogata returned to Japan, I was almost 16 and had just been released from three years of braces, which meant according to my parents' rules, I could wear lipstick and go out with boys. It just so happened that summer that I could also wear a bikini and not appear too silly.

I still worked at the office every weekday 9 a.m. till 5 p.m. and on Saturdays until noon. I had been promoted, adding proofreading to my duties. I enjoyed being with the women at the Abstract Company. By this time, I knew all their favorite sweet rolls. Evelyn always ordered two cinnamon-sugared donuts; Dorie, a lemon Bismark with glaze; Francis, a regular glazed donut. Small details of the office amused me, like when Dorie would open that little bread board on her desk and put her feet up for a rest. She could talk on the phone, eat her sweet roll, smoke a cigarette, drink coffee, and type, all at once. Fascinating to witness.

The Abstract women typed furiously and sometimes the clatter of typewriters sounded like heavy hail on a tin roof. When they took a break, the typing instantly ceased. They told stories about their kids, their husbands, and their parents. Those women had a long history with the Abstract Company. Three of them had worked for my grandfather. Evelyn and Arlene were sisters; their mother was my dad's babysitter when he was little. They gave me their mother's recipe for pecan pie. "It's your dad's favorite," Arlene told me.

I still have that recipe.

When my Dad came back from court, through the back door of the office, Dorie dropped her feet to the floor, closed the bread board, and sat straight up at her desk. The other women stopped talking, stopped proofreading, stopped typing.

"Good morning, Sir," they said in unison.

Nodding in their direction, my dad would tip his fedora. "Mornin', Ladies," he'd say with a smile, as he passed swiftly through the room, heading to his own office down the hall. I loved those moments, in that office.

It was during our rides home that I recall more conversation with my father than ever before. One day I told him I wanted to be an Interior Decorator. He drove all the way through downtown, and over the Rum River Bridge, before he responded.

Finally, he said, "I can think of nothing more sensible and secure than the position as County Surveyor. What do you think of that, child?"

Another time, as we talked about his next, and third, trip to the Arctic

Circle, I asked, "Well, if that place is so beautiful and peaceful, why don't you just buy some land up there, then we can all go for the whole summer?"

Without a moment's thought—or maybe it was after *years of thought*—he replied, "It's not a place that can be bought or owned. The essence of the Arctic would be irreparably altered, even destroyed, if people started buying property up there."

After work on Saturdays, the afternoons were mine, more or less. Except that this summer I *had* to take flying lessons, if I wanted to get my driver's license in the fall when I turned 16. Leedsie already had his private license and two days a week he took me out to Pierce's airstrip. He waited in the car, while I finished my hour of flying with Mr. Christiansen in our yellow Piper J-3.

I didn't want anyone outside our family to know that I was taking flying lessons. It was just another strange thing about our family, something no one else my age had to do.

Certain farm chores I did enjoy, more than inside chores like cleaning, ironing, making beds or dusting. One steamy, hot Saturday in July, I put my bikini on and made my debut to none other than the manure spreader. Happily shoveling manure into the spreader, I then hitched the spreader to the tractor, put it in high gear and sailed down the driveway across Park Street to the alfalfa field with the summer breeze on my face.

Singing at the top of my lungs, Wake Up Little Susie, by the Everly Brothers. Bouncing up and down on the tractor seat, I felt like the free-est, most powerful human being alive and loving the sun and the manure flying 20 feet in the air behind me. Then I sang like Patsy Cline herself.

I was born the next of kin, to the wayward wind.

I made a turn at the south end of the field singing to the skies above, when I spotted a line of boys leaning against the fence, gawking. Their cars were parked along the edge of the ditch on the dirt road. As I pulled the tractor and the manure spreader up to the fence, I realized I didn't really know any of those boys. But I did know they were all friends, odd-ball guys, social outsiders, but interesting characters. They were not the cliquish, annoying jocks who strutted around the halls at school bragging about how many girls they did "it" with. They weren't part of the nasty group of guys who bullied me because I was skinny.

"If ya stand sideways and stick your tongue out, you'd look like a zipper."

Billy was the first to politely ask me out. That very evening I prepared for the first date of my life. My father paced the floor, nervously jingling the change in his pocket, waiting to meet poor Billy.

"All right, young man," he ordered, gruffly. "Have her back here by ten, or there'll be no further dates. Walk her to the car, open the door for her, and walk her back up the steps when you return *promptly* at 10 p.m. And, do not, *ever* beep the horn at her. Understood?"

Whoa, gad! What was the matter with my father?

In the next two weeks, I went out with the other four boys, one at a time, one date each—all resulting in good and lasting friendships.

Coming home from work one night, I reminded Dad about my birthday. I knew he was leaving in August for another fishing trip.

"Dad?" I said. "You remember this year is my 16th birthday? You know what they say? Sweet 16 and never been kissed."

He laughed and said, "Oh yah? By whom have you *not* been kissed?" So that was his problem.

"Very funny. I haven't kissed that many boys, really. You will be back from your trip for my birthday, won't you?"

"You betcha," he said. "I wouldn't miss it for anything."

But gradually over the summer, my father's attitude shifted. He barely tolerated the boys' presence, when they came over to swim or play tennis or wash their cars in our driveway.

"Respectable young men should make appointments with young ladies, not show up willy-nilly, whenever the spirit moves them." Maybe having him gone for a couple of weeks wouldn't be so bad, after all.

There was one guy in that group I hadn't dated. Ned Hayden was the most interesting to me, although I'd only seen him in the halls at school. I'd never met him. Ned was their ringleader, the one they respected the most. I asked each of them about him, dropping hints, nudging an introduction, and the more I heard, the more I wanted to go out with Ned.

At last he got the message and called for a date. Ned Hayden was the one, the perfect combination—tall, really funny, generous, and polite. He liked plays, was even in one at school, so of course, Mother would approve, but best of all he had a big nose just like my dad's. Dad would approve, if nothing else, of Ned's nose. Oh yes, I knew it! He and Ned would get along fine.

With the confidence of my parents' assumed approval, we went out every single night for two weeks in Ned's two-toned blue Ford that he paid for himself. That was admirable for a 16-year-old. I'd remember to mention that to Dad, if I had to. He'd be impressed, I imagined. Sometimes on our dates, we took Billy or one of the other guys with us, because Ned knew when those guys needed attention, and he was loyal to his buddies. Surely, my father would respect the virtue of loyalty.

Ned and I played miniature golf or went to one of the local drive-in movies. Later in the summer, we went to the county fair. Ned spent 10 dollars and finally knocked over all the milk bottles to win a very small teddy bear with teeny bells in his ears. Perseverance too; how impressive would that be to my father? I felt like Sandra Dee in "A Summer Place" with my very own handsome Troy Donahue.

By mid-August, Ned and I had secretly exchanged friendship rings, and we had our own song, Walk Don't Run, which wasn't really a song with lyrics, but the music was lively and danceable and the title completely fitting. I couldn't believe my luck. I would return, as a junior, to high school in the fall, with the coolest boyfriend in the world, who would walk me to all my classes. On Friday nights, we would show up together at the Rec Hall, dance to Walk Don't Run, and Ned would bring me home after football and basketball games. We'd go to the Homecoming dance together just like other kids. Life was getting more and more wonderful.

My father had simmering problems with Ned and his constant presence. One afternoon we were lying on beach towels down at the pool, with a purpose though, watching the little kids swim and also admiring our friendship rings. I could hear the change in my father's pockets clanging, as he walked down the porch steps from the house, which meant he was on a mission *and* he was in a hurry. Without looking, I could tell how fast he was walking by the sound of the coins and it was getting more and more shrill.

I slipped my friendship ring off and pushed it under the towel. He walked up, casting a shadow over our beach towels, and with his hands still in his pockets, jingling the coins, he growled, "Well, young man, if you're going to hang around here, you might as well be useful as well as ornamental." *Hang around! Useful as well as ornamental?* I was furious and embarrassed for Ned. Why couldn't my father be civil to any of the boys that summer, especially the one I really liked? My Dad was wearing me down.

He said, "Up and at 'em, young man, I'll show you how to work the circulator pump for the pool." Off they went to the dark, damp, smelly pump house. Dad was on a mission to make Ned look stupid and subservient, like someone I'd never want to see again. Dad knew his name but he acted like Ned wasn't important enough to be called by his name.

But Ned persevered. He was in our yard the next afternoon, under the cedar tree, where my father was preparing his yellow rubber raft and the tent for his annual trip to the Arctic. Ned was pressed into service again, happily, quietly assisting my father setting up the tent, cleaning it, and folding it up again. I held my breath and prayed that my father would not humiliate him again.

August 16th at 5 a.m., I woke up to the sound of my father stomping around in the attic above my bedroom. I could just see him up there, shoving boxes of old books and magazines around, gathering his fishing pole, lures and nets, and his red and black checkered wool jacket.

As he did before every fishing trip, he tiptoed quietly into our bedroom first. I watched across the room as he pulled the sheet back from Acey's face and bent down to kiss her forehead.

"Take care of your mother," he whispered. "Bye, Dad," she mumbled sleepily. The slightly stale pine smoke from his wool jacket preceded him, as he approached my bedside. I pretended to be asleep and kept the sheet tight over my head. That'd teach him to be rude to my boyfriend. Tapping the top of my head he said, "I'll be back for that Sweet Sixteen. Meantime, be good, and take care of your mother." From under my sheet, I heard his goodbyes next in Leedsie's room, then down the hall in Andrew and Marcus' room, next door to Milo and Oscar. He completed the circle with Eightball in the nursery across the hall from our bedroom.

Ned and I continued to go out almost every night. My mother, now the sole authority, was growing anxious and annoyingly obvious in her attempts to chaperone by proxy, or better yet, curtail our dates. Frequently she would send one or two little kids along and insist on earlier and earlier curfew times. "Be home by nine; the children have to get to bed."

Of course, Mother was well aware of the possibilities in the back seat of a car, at the drive-in movie, with a boy she knew I liked. She was probably right, too. It was only a matter of time and opportunity, both of which she intended to control. Why is it that we cannot comprehend the fact that our parents were teenagers, and not so long ago?

One night, after my father had been gone for a week, Ned brought me home at the scheduled time. Following the rules, he opened the car door for me, walked me up the porch steps and very quietly asked, "What time tomorrow night?" Before I could speak, a voice from above interjected, "No, she *won't* be going out tomorrow night." Ned and I looked up to see Mother, sitting in the window of the upstairs nursery with her knees comfortably pulled up under her nightgown, looking as if she was just waiting for something interesting to happen along that night, way out there in the country. Well, that moment was mortifying, but paled in the wake of what was to come, and Mother was regrettably right.

Chapter 28

Baker Lake, Northwest Territories

A quote from my father's journal in 1939: *Now from the top of the rock north of the lonely roadway was a wilderness of stone, brush and small trees. Forbidding to one who did not know it.*

With his friend and co-pilot, Dave, and another pilot, Bob Taft, my father was about to undertake the adventure of a lifetime. That August 16th of 1960, they climbed aboard their Seabees on the grass strip at Pierce's air strip and headed for the incomparable land of excitement and challenge: the Arctic Circle, a region they had visited and fished twice before.

Because the northland is mostly uninhabited, except for a few Native Eskimo, the terrain and the elements present a cruel struggle between nature and survival. Few white men had ventured into this Arctic region before 1960.

My father became increasingly attracted to the area, which was entirely different from his everyday life. In the Arctic, there were no boundaries, no fences, a scarcity of tall trees; wild herds freely roamed the peaceful landscape for miles and miles. The three men must have felt the exuberance of genuine explorers crossing the border and landing at customs in International Falls. Imagine flying into Winnipeg for lunch, then spending a peaceful night at Lynn Lake. The next day, they gassed up their Seabees and took off for Yellowknife and the Great Slave Lake, making good progress toward their goal.

But engine problems and delays added 10 days more to their intended schedule. They finally set up camp on a fairly large island in the Back River. I'd heard about Chantrey Inlet and the Back River north of the Arctic Circle and I also knew the water there is cold, 34 degrees, and the fish are big, 45-50 pounds.

Dressed in the requisite cold-weather gear, hip-high rubber waders held up with 2-inch wide suspenders, canvass pants, wool and quilted jackets, the fishermen were prepared for the elements of the Back River. They anticipated serious fishing near a remote settlement, on the other side of the river, where the Eskimo from King William Island came to catch the huge trout.

September 5, 1960: 7 a.m., the first day of my junior year in high school, was too hot to even turn over in bed. I couldn't bear the thought of going back to school. Why, oh why couldn't I just stay home and wait for Ned to come over for a long, cool swim and more amazing admiration of our friendship rings.

The morning was still. I could hear Acey breathing across the room and the coffee pot percolating downstairs in the kitchen. Mother would be starting breakfast pretty soon. The leaves on the oak trees outside our bedroom windows did not flutter even the slightest bit. Nothing moved in that humidity. So I lay there under my sheet, listening to the quiet, counting the beats of my heart, waiting for Acey, the responsible one, to make the first move.

The phone rang downstairs on the kitchen wall, where I imagined Mother was sitting near the stove at her end of the table, reading, either a book on child psychology or The New Yorker magazine. She'd enjoy a peaceful moment and a cup of coffee before the circus of school days would begin for another year. Today was going to be a big day, too, because Eightball was starting kindergarten. The last of the Cutter kids off to school.

Pretty soon, Mother would come upstairs and begin waking the children. I hadn't heard Sesson's car come up the driveway, so I knew I wouldn't be late for school, yet.

Mother answered the phone and I waited for her to say something, but she never did. She hung the phone back on the wall and everything was more still than before. I closed my eyes for a second, feeling the weight of my sheet, and Mother seemed to materialize at the end of my bed. Dressed in her baby-blue chenille robe, she carried an open issue of The New Yorker.

Looking like The Blessed Virgin Mary, descending on a cloud at Fatima, not touching the floor, she floated in a small space at the end of my bed. Acey and I sat up quietly, holding our sheets.

Mother's journey to deliver the message began at the top of the stairs in our room, where the air was locked in place. Staring straight ahead at a spot somewhere over the massive headboard of my bed and barely moving her lips, she whispered, "Your… father… is not all right." I had to read her lips, and was sure I got it wrong, until she began floating out our door. Was he hurt? Or sick? Is that what she said? Is that what she meant?

"What did she say?" I asked Acey.

"You heard her," she snapped, dropping hard onto her bed and pulling the sheet over her head.

Mother moved across the hall to Leedsie's room, repeating the same numbed monotone message in every bedroom, as if she were a passive stranger on a slow conveyer belt.

One sound at a time, the squeals and cries rose up from the bedrooms, into the hallway until the entire upstairs sounded like a ship of shrieking, terrified passengers going down with no life belts, no hope of survival. "Your father is not all right." "Your father is not all right." "Your father is not all right." That was it, and I think that's what she wanted to believe for a long time: that his death was not real; it was just another one of his late arrivals.

Staggering out of his bedroom into the hallway, Leedsie crumbled against the wall outside our door, screaming, "No… no, no, no, no." Then he lay sobbing and shaking, pounding his fist on the floor. The little kids scrambled out of their rooms, screaming and crying into our room and onto our beds. Mother had floated away … alone.

The call had been from Father Murphy at St. Stephen's Rectory. He phoned to read a telegram he'd received from a mission priest at Baker Lake, Northwest Territories:

Cutter drowned stop Rest okay stop.

Part V

Chapter 29

The Aftermath

Not counting their four years of wartime "camping," my parents had lived together a mere 16 years. They had eight children, aged five to 19, and he was gone. The news of my father's death spread rapidly through town. I could not go to school. I stayed in my room, on my bed, remembering his last night and the sheet I'd stretched tight over my head. I listened to the sky and waited for the sound. He promised to be here for my 16th birthday on August 31st. He was just late.

The local radio station announced a few random details every hour: My father's age, number of children, service to the community, and number of years in the Navy Reserve. What little I knew about my father's death, I learned from the radio. His yellow rubber raft overturned during a sudden Arctic storm and he and Dave Hymanson were thrown into freezing water to swim for their lives.

Every day for the next ten days KANO radio reported, "The body of Darrah Cutter has still not arrived home."

The Children's Funeral

As our house filled with stunned, confused friends and relatives, Leedsie began an unintentional but necessary exile. He led us through the tunnels of bereaved and hysterical people—shaking and crying, anchoring themselves to the dishwasher, the kitchen table and the door jams, wiping their noses on fluttering handkerchiefs.

They kept asking, "What can I do for you, Mary Helen? What will we all do now? Oh my God what *will* we do?"

Grandma White prayed in the living room by the fireplace with her eyes closed behind her glasses, her lips moving and her fingers rubbing each bead of her Rosary, shaping her intentions as she passed the beads forward to the Glory Be that ended each decade.

> *Hail Mary full of grace, The Lord is with Thee, Blessed are Thou among women and blessed is the Fruit of Thy womb, Jesus. Holy Mary Mother of God pray for us sinners now and at the hour of our death, Amen.*

In between Hail Marys, Grandma barely mumbled out loud the beginning of each of the five sorrowful mysteries, as if she wanted to make something very clear to Whomever was listening to her prayers: *The first sorrowful mystery, the agony in the garden; The second sorrowful mystery, the scourging at the pillar; the third sorrowful mystery, the crowning of thorns; The fourth sorrowful mystery, the carrying of the cross; the fifth sorrowful mystery, the death.*

Keeping the rhythm of her prayers, Grandpa White rocked slowly beside her with his long pale fingers knitted together, his head of pure white hair bowed and his weary eyes closed. They were profoundly, devoutly Catholic, and they truly loved my father.

Leedsie was the grand marshal of our pitiful parade, as we ambled down the main hallway, beneath the photographs on the wall—three poses of our father in his Navy uniform and his county attorney campaign photo. Just before the kitchen door, I glanced up at a picture of my father at three years old, taken outside by the porch. Wearing a white linen suit with a wide collar, long black stockings and white high-top shoes, he's petting his dog. With a chubby little hand, he's holding a galvanized bucket with a red Texaco star painted in the middle. I think I never noticed what a beautiful baby he was. Had I ever noticed that he was a child once?

Leedsie walked in a daze through the kitchen, onto the cool slate floor of the sun porch and down the steps, outside into the sunshine.

He didn't know it, but we were all there behind him, with Eightball dragging her silky-edged "blankey" at the end of our line. We just automatically followed him because he was the eldest boy, the leader. He'd gathered each of us in the same way we made snowballs, starting with a substantial tightly packed core and adding layers, by moving forward through similar material, growing larger because of a natural need to be connected to something.

Drifting out in the yard to the Cutter family softball field, our line began to splinter, like creeks to the river and rivers to the sea. We each chose a tree as our counselor. Leedsie turned left at home base and trailed off straight east, past the girls' swing tree, over the driveway, across the tennis court, just like he knew exactly where he was going. He pulled himself up and sat on the swing hanging from the boys' tree, a very old elm.

Acey followed him for a while with her head down and by her heart, stopped at the huge oak tree where the girls' swing hung from the lowest branch. She sat on the board initialed by all five girls. She didn't move or even kick at the worn spot of dirt under the swing. She sat with her head dropped down like she was unconscious, too tired even to take care of the little kids. It was the saddest thing for me, watching Acey and wondering where she would land in our yard of trees. Sad for me to notice that she could not, for these moments or hours, be responsible for the little kids, even though they depended on her. But they must have sensed her need to be alone without responsibility, because they all wandered aimlessly away from her, finally gathering in that small grove of pine trees at the end of the driveway, where Mother always hid their Easter eggs.

When I finally realized where I was sitting, I was grateful. It was the spot where my father had packed his dried fruits, dehydrated cereal, and soups. The spot where he asked Ned to help assemble his tent. I'd stopped at the spot where he inflated his yellow rubber raft, washed it with the hose, deflated it and packed it tightly to fit in the back of the Seabee, the night before he left. The tree was comforting too, because from my spot under the cedar tree, I could see all the rest of the children.

It was Leedsie I worried about the most; he seemed to take it so differently. He sat the farthest away. As we departed the house, the people kept repeating, "Oh and those poor boys. They've lost their father." When he cried on the floor of the hallway, I was afraid he might never get his body up; he might never go back to college; he'd never dress up in his coonskin coat and hat to go to Gopher football games with his friends. Luckily, Leedsie had a girlfriend, Corrine. I knew if he started thinking about her, he'd eventually get up off the floor.

Leedsie was a nerd. He never had a real girlfriend before Corrine, and she was just perfect for him—the bookish type. They were both AFS students. Leedsie had spent a summer in Milan, Italy, living with a host family. And Corrine went to Germany for a year. It was his first year at the University when he met Corrine at an AFS reunion party, and they'd been dating ever since.

As he sat so still in the boys' swing, I thought about Corrine helping him.

They wanted to get married some day, someday soon. But, he would have to finish college first. She told him she'd like to raise sheep with him. She was a good sport, an authentic person. I could imagine Corrine pulling the roll of barbed wire across the top of the fences Leedsie would build. They'd be strong, solid fences those two would build. If it's true that there's one person for everyone, then Leedsie was lucky to have found his one person already. But, for now, nothing in the world but living through it would ease his suffering.

I sat in a nest of needles under the cedar tree my father planted when he was nine. Scrunching down into the needles sent up a sweet fragrance of cedar; the sharpness on my legs reminded me to suffer for the poor souls in purgatory.

That tree was our first base. It had a big crotch about five feet off the ground where we hid things like Easter eggs and stuff we'd taken from each other. Inside that tree was a forbidden book I had taken from under Acey's mattress. I stood up and dropped my friendship ring deep into the crotch of the tree and heard it bounce off the hard cover of *Peyton Place.*

We stuck stubbornly and silently to our trees through the day until the sun just began to dip behind Willow Island. We had ignored all the adults who paraded up our driveway with trays of cookies, baskets of dinner rolls and roasting pans overflowing with ham and turkey.

Throughout the day, people came, carrying hot pots of beans and tuna casseroles, apple, cherry, and peach pies.

My father's office workers, the proud legacy of his father, appeared inside the shadow of my tree. Their open-toed sandals crunched the brown cedar needles close to my nest, but I didn't look up. I only stared at their feet, their toes popping out the small holes in the front of their sandals, some with nylon stockings, others with red nail polish, and two women whose big toes curled out and around the open-toe of their shoes.

I knew their toes pretty well because of my job at the office. I noticed their feet under their desks when they were typing, tapping their toes to the music on the radio at Dorie's desk. I paid attention to those women.

But now, I wanted the women to go away, to leave me alone under my tree, but they cried.

Through their tears they whispered, "Oh dear, you've lost your father. Oh you poor, poor thing. What will we all do now?" Their white cloth hankies trembled under their noses. "Oh my, we loved him too, you know." I knew they loved him. *They* wanted *me* to help them. I heard a calm voice, I think it was Arlene, the one who liked cinnamon sugared donuts.

"At least, Charlie," she offered in a gentle tone, "he was doing something he loved."

If my father was simply lost, I'd find him someday, but what really confused me was the part about doing what he loved. Nobody loves to drown in freezing, black, stormy water, thousands of miles away from his children, his wife, his trees and his place on the river. I looked up the noses of the voices and wondered about words for the sake of words. Sister Sabina told our seventh grade class that for every unnecessary word you speak, you will spend another day in purgatory.

After the women left my tree and the last visitors quietly spilled out of the porch and pantry doors, shuffled over the gravel driveway to their cars and drove slowly down Park Street, I stood up from my pile of cedar needles. I walked down Park Street toward town, past the house where Grandma and Grandpa Cutter had lived, two doors down from Mrs. Annon's house, where we took piano lessons. We took turns waiting upstairs in the bedroom, overlooking Park Street, sitting on our teacher's lavender satin bedspread in the very bedroom where our father was born, 45 years ago.

I walked past Hoglund's flower shop, the halfway point on my way home from school. Hazel Hoglund always let the Cutter kids come in to warm up in the winter, to smell the fresh, warm dirt and the flowers in the greenhouse. Hazel let us use her bathroom.

Walking across the Rum River Bridge, I looked for the men, who usually sat there, *the bums*. They shared drinks from brown paper bags, as they visited together on the concrete benches. They knew me and I was comfortable sitting with them, watching the rushing water catch long branches, carrying them over the dam and under the bridge. There were no men on the benches that evening.

I marched past the Post Office, the Courthouse and my father's office straight ahead to the Anoka High School football field, where Ned was out on the track jumping hurdles in the late summer evening. Poor Ned. I'd ignored his calls, hoping I'd never have to tell him my father died, and that I could never go out with a person who was happy to sit around in the sun looking at friendship rings—rings that were against the rules. I couldn't possibly go out with a boy who didn't know how to run the circulator pump, or wash my father's yellow rubber raft without instruction, a person my father didn't approve of, for whatever reason.

I found Ned's car in the parking lot, opened the door and removed the friendship ring from his keychain. Then I turned around and walked the three miles back home. Of course, my father was right. Ned was purely ornamental.

Father Murphy came to our house to talk to Mother about the funeral. I'd had my doubts about Father Murphy since I was in fourth grade. He'd come to visit our class to talk about confessing more *important* sins in the confessional.

He scolded us, "I'm tired of hearing the same old sins, week after week. Think about your sins and take your time. And if you need help," he told us, "look at the pamphlets in the vestibule to get some ideas." Then he walked down the aisles patting all the kids on their heads muttering, like he always did, "God bless you, Jesus Mary and Joseph, Peace be with you." Little short prayers called ejaculations. But when he got to me, he lowered his mumble, and quickly spit out, "You, your mother and your brothers and sisters will go to heaven, but not your father because he is *not* Catholic." He said it so quickly, like a stutter, that it took me several minutes to comprehend his words.

Now, a week after my father died, Mother showed Father Murphy into the library and closed the sliding door, a door that was hardly ever closed. I didn't even know it worked.

Sitting on the bottom stair in the hallway, I listened as Father Murphy told Mother that my father could not be buried in the Catholic cemetery.

"But he was always so generous in his donations, Father," Mother reasoned.

Father mumbled, "It isn't a question of money. He is not a Catholic and that's the way it has to be. Rules are rules and they're not made to be broken."

He is not a Catholic and that's the way it has to be. Rules are rules.

Mother came out of the library looking limp, hungry, and hopeless. At the bottom of the hallway stairs, she said goodbye to Father Murphy, not escorting him to the porch door. Father Murphy, all stiff-necked in his black suit and choking rigid collar, his light, white hair that I could see right through to his pink scalp, walked hard like a ramrod down our hallway, through our kitchen, past Sesson, and out our porch door and got himself into his plain black car.

I could tell Father Murphy had insulted my mother and my father. It's hard to believe today but I thought I could console her.

"Everything is all right," I told her. "Dad will go to heaven even without Father Murphy's help." Mother actually asked me what I meant. With all her grief, all her sorrowful mysteries; with all that, she sat on the bottom step in the hallway and asked me what I meant.

"Do you remember when Mr. Clark died, when I was in fourth grade choir?" I asked.

She nodded wearily. "And," I went on, "Remember, his funeral was at St. Stephens?"

"And your father was a pallbearer, yes I remember," Mother nodded.

"I was singing alto up in the choir loft, for Mr. Clark's Requiem Mass. When Father Murphy led the funeral procession from the vestibule in the back of the church, I waited in the loft until I could see the top of his white head and his incense burner swinging wide between the aisles. Then," I said, "I knew Dad would be close behind carrying Mr. Clark's coffin."

"All in the time it took to sing the word *eterna,* I stepped off the bleachers and ran quickly to the holy water font at the railing before Sister Arthur could stop me. I sprayed a shower of redeeming grace down on Dad's head, as he passed under the choir loft, while I said, 'I baptize you in the name of the Father, the Son and the Holy Ghost'."

Mother reached over and patted my leg. I was sure I had relieved some, if not all, of her suffering. She gave me a hug and said, "Thank you."

September 14: With a distant 10-mile stare, Mother thanked the few invited friends and family members at my father's private closed-casket service held at the funeral home on Jackson Street, in the same room where we held a private wake the night before. My father's sisters, Fritzi and Mary, were there. Sesson sat with the little kids and Leedsie, Acey, Andrew and I sat in a row by ourselves. There was one remarkable incident the night of my father's funeral.

From deep behind the thick walls covered with crimson-flocked wallpaper and heavily draped windows of the funeral home, there was a knocking on the door and someone yelling in the street. Mother asked me to go and see who was out there.

I walked down the narrow hallway under crystal chandeliers, unlocked the door and opened it just a crack. Someone on the other side forced the door wide open. There stood three little old ladies I'd never seen before, dressed in nice suits and black hats with veils.

"Why is this door locked?" One lady asked, angrily. Another demanded, "Why can't we come in?" I explained that it was a private service.

"We have to see him!" They were insistent and shouting at me, their tone suggested they were entitled to say goodbye to my father.

I told them the casket was closed, so they couldn't see him anyway. It was strange, but they said they had a right to see him. "It's just not fair to have a closed casket."

"I'm sorry," I said, closing the door. Afterwards, I thought about those anonymous women. They must have felt my father was a part of their lives. Maybe they had known his parents, maybe he had represented them in court, or found a job for them when they needed money. Maybe he had worked pro bono for their families at one time. I agreed with those women. I wanted to see him, too.

After the funeral, the hearse led the procession through Anoka, down Park Street to Forest Hills Protestant cemetery where Mother had purchased 10 burial plots together on the side of the hill, 23 steps from Grandpa and Grandma Cutter's graves.

My father's grave is under one lone pine tree.

Several days after the funeral, the fishermen, Mr. Taft and Mr. Hymanson, came to see Mother. Sesson hustled all the kids, except for me, into the kitchen. She opened the porch door to show the two men into the living room. Still wearing their heavy wool pants and quilted jackets, the men looked weary, unshaven, and worn out, as if they had just landed at Pierce's airstrip and come immediately to our house. They must have been apprehensive about this moment in their journey. Even at 16, I would have been scared.

I watched from the glider rocker at the far end of the living room; from there I could smell my father's campfire on their clothes.

Mother waited on the sofa with her hands gently folded in her lap; she didn't even stand when the men walked in. Sitting awkwardly in chairs opposite the sofa, they told Mother they were sorry. There were long silences, gaping holes, where it seemed no one had the energy to utter another word. I stayed in the room because I wanted to know if my father was really dead, or if he told his friends that he promised to be home for my birthday. It seems frivolous and self-centered now, but I wanted to know if he was capable of breaking a promise.

Mother surprised me. She didn't ask one single question. In fact, she hardly said anything at all to the fishermen, the friends who knew him so well.

What child doesn't believe she is totally responsible for her parents' sadness or happiness, for their disappearance, or even their death? I wanted to know if he talked about us on his fishing trips. Did his friends know our names? Did my father try … to live? The fishermen were in our house for less than 15 minutes, and the opportunity to talk to them never arose again.

But, there was still hope that my father was alive because Mother never saw his body. She never said he was dead, ever. What she did say was, "Your father is not all right."

Maybe she didn't ask the fishermen questions because the truth might be undeniable. Someone, maybe Sesson, told me the body was badly decomposed and it was recommended that my mother not see it. That was the first time I imagined the impossible: my father separate from his body. At that moment, when Sesson referred to my father's body as *it*, I felt as if the Holy Ghost flew from His position in the center of the Trinity, and departing my soul, waved a white wing tip at The Father and The Son, on his way out.

Nevertheless, the glimmer of hope remained in my mind: If there was no body, maybe he wasn't dead.

After the fishermen left, I walked through the pasture on the cow paths and across the flat, prickly with the edges of tall corn stalks, to the spot on the river where he anchored his plane. I sat on the bank, facing Willow Island, under the bowed branch of an elm tree and stuck my feet deep into the muddy water, stuck them down hard, till the mud sucked them in like quick sand, and I couldn't move if I wanted to. Pretty soon I'd hear that familiar sound of his Seabee, something like a lawn mower driving through a bath tub full of water. If he was returning just a little bit late, I was going to be there to hear him coming home.

The Anoka County Union reporters pestered Mother for an interview. She refused. KANO Radio station tried to get through to her, but they also failed. They didn't know about Sesson's loyalty and her fierce protection of Mother.

Letters arrived from every one of Lt. Commander Cutter's surviving crew members telling Mother how much they respected her husband. "He was a good skipper, disciplined and conditioned." The letters made her sad for hours and days. She'd sit in the rocking chair, looking out the window, with her hands folded like weights over the letters in her lap.

It was during this time that Mother told me of a strange thing she saw the day my father died. She said, "I knew something was wrong as early as the morning of August 30, the day before your birthday."

"I woke up to the sound of tapping on the bedroom window," she said. "I got up to look and there it was, a male cardinal frantically tapping on the window with his beak, fluttering like a humming bird. I knocked on the window to make it go away, but the bird kept beating on the window, like it was caught against it. So, I went downstairs to get away from the bird, but he was tapping on the kitchen window above the sink." She told me the bird had come back one more time since August 30 and so, she knew. "Something had happened to your father."

Mr. Christiansen, my flying instructor, called. He wanted to know if I still wanted to fly. Half-heartedly, I did. I wanted to fly.

Sweet Sixteen
Friends car-hopping at the A&W, trampoline jumping,
Squirting ketchup on cars
Making out at drive-in movies
Swimming in the new city pool
While I was making the pre-flight check
On the Piper J-3 at the grass runway south of town
Mr. Christiansen took me up 2000 feet
Put it into a spin and ordered,
"It's your airplane. You recover!"
I pushed the stick forward, worked the rudders,
And leaned fearlessly into the dive
Then he said, "Now you're on your own. Solo!"
I did it all by myself
Even today I wish my father had been there
To see my recovery
To see me solo

Nearly a quarter of a century later, in preparation for my 40th birthday celebration, I wanted to go to the Arctic, to feel the ground and breathe the air, in the place my father last lived or maybe was still living. By 1984, his fishing companions had all died, eliminating the possibility of finding the exact location of their camp in 1960. I asked my siblings if anyone could pinpoint the location where our father spent his last days. My youngest brother, Marcus, sent me an amazing news story I hadn't known existed, perhaps because Mother didn't want me to know the many details describing the moments of my father's death.

On September 23, 1960, <u>The Anoka County Union</u> reported the story of Darrah Cutter's last fishing trip. The 2,952-word account included the geographical description of the Arctic region, several mechanical problems with the aircraft, people the fishermen met along the way and statements made by Mr. Hymanson, my father's fishing buddy and co-pilot on his last trip.

The most exhilarating information I learned from the article was that there was a child on that last fishing trip, the 13-year-old son of Bob Taft. He would be 37 years old. That boy might be able to answer questions, ones that Mother neglected to ask that September day 24 years ago. As I read the story, I felt a heart-pounding hopefulness that Bill Taft was alive and might remember the trip—if I could find him.

In the newspaper account, Dave Hymanson described the northland: "The Canadian Northwest territory is a vast area that staggers the imagination, a wonderful country full of exploration that can excite men."

The story continued, "While flying into Great Slave Lake, Bob Taft had trouble with his oil cooler and so the men stayed with a trapper named Gus. He'd been trapping for 33 years and happily living in the wilderness with a Native woman. Darrah and Gus hit it off and arranged to meet up again during my father's return visit the following winter." Hmmm. I didn't know there was a return trip planned for the following winter. That would have been an unusual time for my father to return to the North Country.

Another related reference made by Dave: "To be with Darrah on a camping or hunting trip was to know him. He loved the north woods, understood the people, their food and ways. When he lived there he lived like the trapper."

The article satisfied some of my nagging doubts but it also created new questions in my mind. For instance, Dave recalled a curious event which occurred early in their adventure, interesting because my father had written a similar scenario in his journal in 1939, one year before he and my mother were married.

Cynic on modern attitude toward romance: Plot to involve male who has outstanding capabilities in several fields but who goes only so far in each and stops either of his own volition or by failure induced by lack of interest. His shortcoming will be a lack of social adaptability. Character number 2, the girlfriend, made it look like a conventional perfect mating romance, but he comes to his senses and prances off into the woods—Canadian preferably—to trap or prospect, if an excuse be needed. Might bring in another love affair early, and get in a dig through fickleness.

The detailed events leading up to my father's death were riveting because each engine problem, every cloud passing, and fogged-in morning represented critical moments in a series of missteps and bad timing, all culminating in sudden disaster.

In this unfamiliar territory, where every second telegraphed new challenges, the fishermen spent precious moments engaging in child-like tourist pleasures. For example, on a hill on the island where they camped was a rock image of a man created by the Eskimos. An amazing larger-than-life sculpture, simply and expertly constructed, balancing tips and edges of massive, incongruous jagged rocks to form an icon: Man of stone.

On that Monday morning, before they left to cross the river for the big fish, the four men took the time to walk to the sculpture, and then took turns taking each other's pictures posing beside the stone man. Meanwhile just around the corner of the island a dangerous, black storm is brewing.

They all took off for the other side of the river, Dave and my father in one boat and Taft and his son in another. Dave noticed that one of the rods on my father's rubber raft needed stabilizing. They stopped, mid-river for 20 critical moments, to secure the rod in the freezing water, while Taft continued safely on to the other side of the river. After repairing the boat, my father and Dave returned to the stone man island, where they each ate a candy bar and Dave smoked a cigarette. After which, they resumed the trip across the river to the Eskimo encampment for fishing.

I had never known my father to eat candy. He took great pride in having absolutely no cavities and we were not allowed candy, pop or gum—ever.

The pieces, the details I hang on to are, in part, what I wanted to hear decades earlier from the returning fishermen when they came to see Mother.

The article outlined precisely the moments leading up the tragedy:

> It wasn't until they were already in the middle of the river that they saw the weather had dangerously shifted. The sky was dark with low angry clouds forming. Arctic storms in August descend rapidly and with vengeance including five-foot icy waves and tornado-like squalls.
>
> Suddenly, one of those wind squalls hit Dave square in the shoulder and instantly swamped the raft. As he tried frantically to restart the motor with no success, my father attempted to lock the motor oar and another wave hit and took the oar with it. The river was relentless and alive with wind and wave. The raft was sinking in the storm and the two men were forced to swim. They struggled in the frigid water, disoriented and fighting to stay alive and stay together, focusing on the nearest land, that small rock island.
>
> Fortunately, the Eskimos on the opposite shore had seen the two go into the water and quickly summoned Bob Taft, who placed himself low in his boat and took off into the teeth of the squall to try to rescue his companions.

It had been 20 minutes since their boat sank, the howling wind receded a bit and Taft could make out one of the swimmers between the alleys of waves about 100 feet from the rock island. Taft, blinded by the waves reached into the water and grabbed the man's wrist, hauling him into the boat.

"Where's Darrah?" He yelled above the crashing waves. "When did you last see him?"

"I don't know," Dave said, barely responsive. "We were going to stick together."

Bob Taft spent the next 25 minutes in the storm looking for Darrah. He then returned to the other side of the river, picked up his son and spent the next two and a half hours crisscrossing the river searching in a grid pattern. All he found was their gas can floating on the waves. They returned to the island mute, heartsick and almost paralyzed with fear.

A few hours later, they spotted my father's life jacket in the water near the spot where the raft went down. According to the news story, "Bob got Darrah back to the island. The three of them put him in his sleeping bag and covered him with an air mattress."

Tuesday and it started to rain. Bob went back to Darrah and covered him with a boat. It rained until about 2:30 p.m. To make matters worse, the wind had beached their planes. Now they had another problem. How to get Darrah back. Neither felt comfortable flying with the body of their friend sitting alongside them. They made a decision and told the Eskimos in pictures and sign language what they were going to do ... take off for help and return soon for the body.

I can see the anguish of those rough hewn men on a stone island caring tenderly, covering my father's body in the rain and asking the Eskimos to watch over him. I hoped somebody thanked the Eskimos.

The fishermen must have felt cursed somehow, when they took off in both planes but soon ran into heavy fog and had to return. Another sleepless night followed, and another day of fog; then hours of low flying finally reaching an outpost where they could at last send a telegram to Anoka.

This passage in the story linked the fishermen in Baker Lake to our family back on Park Street. It was the only reference to us, remote but nevertheless comforting.

"At Baker Lake there is a town consisting of a Hudson Bay store, Catholic and Protestant missions and a DOT. Here they informed the Northwest Mounted Police of Cutter's death, then sent a telegram to Anoka. They never did get a confirmation of receipt of the telegram during the entire eight days they spent there, although they inquired each day." (If Mother had confirmed receipt of the telegram, she would have to confirm the information in it.)

After they sent the telegram, the fishermen spent the eight days (waiting for the Mounties to arrive) from Wednesday to Wednesday—in three extra upstairs rooms at the Catholic mission with Father Choque, 39, a Belgian who has been in the north county for about 15 years.

On Thursday night, the Mounties arrived and with Bob took off in an eight-place large single-engine rescue plane called the "Otter," to try and bring back Darrah's body.

They were within 80 miles of Chantrey Inlet, the location of my father's body, when they ran into wind and had to come back. The wind was so strong it damaged the Otter and at Baker Lake blew the two Seabees eight feet on shore.

"The wind started howling again that night, and continued to do so for three days, again beaching the aircraft. They finally pulled the planes further on the beach to prevent more damage."

There was no response to the telegram? For eight days? How strange. Mother was obsessed about getting our thank-you notes out on Christmas day, before we played or ate or went ice skating. Of course, thanking someone for sending *that* telegram is quite a different circumstance.

Maybe it's not unusual to notice the weather pattern after a loved one dies, but as I read the newspaper article, I couldn't help remembering the moments and the days after Mother died at 4 a.m. on September 10, 1982. The wind blew violently forcing the rain at hard angles, creating waves on our windows and flooding the yard. At 6 a.m. lightning struck our well. We were without water for 48 hours and the rain continued unrelenting, for a total of nine days.

A similar pattern persisted at Baker Lake where the fishermen were desperately trying to return my father's body and were thwarted by fog, wind, and rain.

"They repaired the Otter (Mounty's sea plane) Friday, went up and fog forced them back again. They made it to the Back River Saturday and returned with Darrah's body at 2 p.m. The Mounties flew Darrah to Churchill. His body was later shipped to Anoka."

Thanks to the news story, important questions are answered, doubts resolved that had gnawed at me since that September afternoon in 1960, as I waited in the glider rocker at the end of the living room, praying for Mother to read my mind. *Oh Mother of the word incarnate, despise not our petitions, but in thy mercy hear and answer us. Amen*

For me, these details are the difference between hope and despair:

Right before the men abandoned the sinking raft and slid into the 34-degree water to swim to Rock Island, they promised to try to stay together.

"The cold water might get us," my father said. And the last expression Dave Hymanson saw on my father's face was a smile.

I can see that smile today on my son's face. He has the same grey-green sunken Cutter eyes and the identical slow, gentle smile, sometimes, laced with acceptance and resignation all at once, and it breaks my heart every time. I want to fix whatever is broken in him.

Did my father want to survive? Were we all just too much? An unwieldy, independent pack or brood? I wanted to know if he just gave up. But in the article Mr. Hymanson said: "… Darrah managed to free a knife and cut down one side and around one leg of the waders he was wearing. He had a seat cushion sling in both arms. His life jacket was still untied."

So, he had a life jacket on! He wanted to live. He slashed his waders. I cried for two hours after reading this description of my father's last moments. And then I read it again and again before putting it away for another 32 years. And even today, I can still see him in that black water, with seat cushions strapped to his arms, trying to slash those heavy green rubber waders loose. Trying desperately to live.

They had planned to be gone only 11 days, home by August 27. Another answer to another question: he had planned to be home for my birthday.

The newspaper story ended with: "There will be other men like Darrah

Cutter, but to his many friends in this country and state, no one will ever take his place. In Anoka, like the northland he will be missed." (A complete copy of The Anoka County Union article is included at the conclusion of this story).

There will *not be* other men like Darrah Cutter, not to his wife, not to his children, his grandchildren, not even to Arbor Day. And, there were holes in the newspaper account, weak spots, where larger holes could be drilled and imagination take over, building a plausible case to strengthen Mother's suspicions—that he was still alive in 1982.

I could see myself frantically going to The Arctic, finding Stone Island, searching for the Eskimos, on the other side of the river, who kept vigil over my father's body during the storm. Or, I'd find the children of those Eskimos. I might take a picture of my father along to show Gus, the trapper and his *Indian woman*, or find the Mounties or someone who knew them at Baker Lake, or a priest at the Mission.

I'd walk right in to the general store and ask who'd heard the story or better yet, "Has any one here seen this man in the last 22 years?" I'd ask that question, holding up the photo of my father. "He'd be more tanned, of course," I'd explain. "He'd look trim from outdoor living, and happily enjoying his simple life of trapping and fishing." But, a significant discovery stopped me from making that trip.

That summer night in 1984, immediately after reading the newspaper story, I found *a* William Taft in the Minneapolis phone book. After a long cleansing breath, I called the number and introduced myself as Charlie Cutter. The man at the other end knew immediately who I was and why I would be calling him. He sounded wary but relieved, as if my call was inevitable; it was just bound to happen sooner or later.

Bill Taft was tentative and reserved but he invited me, my husband, Mike, and my youngest sister, Eightball and her husband, Mark, to his home for pizza and conversation.

Bill was a tall man, soft spoken, a little distant, and protective. The evening was tense. It felt as if the memory and the effects on the surviving men and their families had profoundly changed their lives too—*you Cutter kids weren't the only ones.* Bill gave us copies of photographs from other fishing expeditions our fathers had taken together.

"This might help you understand the territory," he said, handing over two copies of a VCR cassette he'd made titled, "The Arctic Circle." Bill explained that the movie was made from several 1958 16-mm home movies. The location of the film was the same spot where my father died.

And finally after the pizza boxes and the Pepsi bottles had been removed from the kitchen table, I asked Bill, "Do you remember that day?" At that instant, his wife and children excused themselves and left the room, as if this moment had been discussed and rehearsed earlier. My sister left the room too. She went outside for a walk, leaving Mark, Mike and me alone at the table with Bill. Eightball told me recently, that she couldn't bear to hear what Bill might say.

"Yes," Bill began, barely audible. "To answer your question, I do remember that day." We leaned closer to hear every word he was saying.

"*I* ... was the one who spotted his body from the top of the rock hill. And *I* helped lift him out of the river and into my dad's boat at 5 p.m." Bill bobbed his head with every word like a metronome forcing him to keep talking. My heart was banging. I felt oddly guilty for requesting this meeting and asking any questions at all. I could have settled for the VCR and the photographs. There was no turning back now, I rationalized.

He continued, lifting his hands up in front of us, he said, "With my own hands, *I* helped carry him back to the campsite and into his sleeping bag, and *I* helped cover his body with a boat to protect it from the rain." His statements were definitive and conclusive. He enunciated carefully and deliberately. I realized through his delivery that he was determined to finish this errand and hoped *never* to repeat the memory or these statements again in his life.

"I helped put his body in his Seabee." With tears in his eyes, Bill began to shake and his chin trembled, as he clearly articulated, what would be his final statement. "Then we had to take him out of his plane again and leave him on the island in the care of the Eskimos."

Bill had been gracious and kind, but I left his home that night with the distinct impression that he had completed an obligation, delivered a message and done what he felt was necessary. I knew, if he had his wish, we would never see him again.

Chapter 30

Carrying Her Cross

After my father died, Mother threw herself into work. In addition to raising children, she took over management as President of The Anoka County Abstract and Title Company, when Anoka was the fastest growing county in the United States. At the same time, she began dabbling—in cooking. All the years she lived with my father, she considered herself an adequate cook, but not an ecstatic cook. I was a senior in high school when, on a whim, Mother attended a benefit luncheon in Minneapolis, featuring the local French cooking teacher, Verna Meyer. Following an enchanting introduction and conversation with Verna, Mother began attending cooking classes.

Starting out slowly, Mother learned techniques of dicing, folding, mincing, pureeing, and sautéing. She mastered the tricks of: a good roux and bases for sauces, beating and folding egg whites, the perfect quiche, proper balance for herbs de Provence, and how to flip a crepe in the air. The day she came home with a recipe for homemade mayonnaise, I thought she would go into orbit.

It took a long time for Mother to regain her balance, but when she did, she virtually flew from Mexiburgers and coddled eggs to soufflés and mousses with fine herbes.

During the next year, Mother's liberal flower blossomed. There are givers and takers, in this world. Mother was a giver. When she was asked to serve as an officer on the Board of Directors for the Anoka County Office of Economic Opportunity, she said, *yes.* O.E.O. was created by the Economic Opportunity Act to address issues of poverty and basic human rights. Their mission: "Respect the right of each citizen to be healthy, secure and to achieve social and economic well being." Mother was a proactive advocate for victims of domestic violence. More than a few nights, she would offer safe haven to devastated young mothers and their children.

The International House at the University of Minnesota depended on Mother and The Last House on Park Street to serve as "home" to many Middle Eastern and Western European students. Invariably, she said, *yes.* There was always room for more at Mother's new dining room table, which she designed—with multiple leaves—to serve 22 people. Mother practiced what she had preached to me, when I was in fourth grade and had to be the judge of who was the fattest: *Take what comes by your hand.*

The Cutter children slowly adjusted to new roles in the family. Acey naturally fell into the position of second mother to the little kids. She could always find something new to teach them; she was a patient teacher. When they were hurt or sad, she knew the best way to comfort them.

Leedsie had decided that Andrew Shinski could be a great football player. Shinski was big and strong, for a tenth grader. Leedsie coached him through a summer training program, aimed at getting him a position on the varsity football team by fall practice.

Leedsie stood at the end of our driveway with a whistle and a stopwatch, directing Shinski, "First, we'll run up to the highway and back, two times." Following that, they would go to the basement and lift weights, then, 20 laps in the pool—all summer long. Leedsie didn't let Shinski neglect his music either. It was beautiful. Andrew made varsity in tenth grade, and for the first time ever, our whole family and Sesson went to a high school football game.

Through all of her parenting and professional duties, combined with her volunteer work, Mother maintained close contact with her women friends and continued to follow her bliss, her artistic passion: food preparation. Nothing imaginable could stop the momentum; she loved where she was going.

Valentine's Day 1962: A serious Minnesota snowstorm was brewing at 6 p.m., when I left with Dave for a high school basketball game. I had started dating Dave a year and a half earlier, just about two months after my father died. Dave was co-captain of the football, basketball and baseball teams. He never missed a fishing opener, fished all summer in one lake or another, hunted grouse, pheasants and ducks in the fall and deer in the early winter, then, of course, ice-fishing wrapped up the entire year. At the time, I didn't know what I was thinking—today it's crystal clear. We need be conscious of which characteristics we try to replace in our lives.

Mother said goodbye to Sesson and the little kids earlier that night, leaving in the Mercury station wagon to pick up four of her friends. They were attending an art lecture by Vincent Price at the University.

Sesson made dinner for the little kids and planned to stay until I came home from the basketball game, at 10 p.m. But, during the evening, the snow had piled high in the school parking lot. Most cars were stuck and had to be shoveled out, even towed to a main road.

By the time Dave cleaned up after the game and shoveled his '57 Oldsmobile out of the snow, it was late. Slowly navigating the drifting snow, all the way through town and down Park Street, we finally arrived in our driveway at 10:30 p.m., later than my weekday curfew by half an hour.

Mother's station wagon was not parked in its usual place by the pantry door. *Maybe she went looking for me.* Sesson's car was gone from its spot under the elm tree by the shop. *She probably had to leave early to get out to the country without getting stuck in the snow.* The porch light was on.

Dave and I sat in the car talking about the possibilities of the empty driveway, and about being the only "couple" in the whole high school, probably the whole town, maybe the whole state of Minnesota who weren't doing "it." I was tired of the conversation and thought about Father Ardolf, Father Murphy's young assistant, who taught third-hour Catholic release classes for high school students in the basement of my friend Punky's house. At moments like this, I was always grateful for his simple instruction on sex education: "Never have sex with anyone you don't want to marry." That made my decisions easy. I looked at the dim yellow light by the porch door and thought, if Mom was home, that light would be going on and off, on and off, and on and off, until the car door opened and I appeared on the porch steps.

Squinting through the rapidly fogging windows to the snow piling up in the driveway, I imagined Mother *was* there in her bathrobe, standing in a halo of soft yellow light, inside the porch door, by the light switch, right where she belonged. *Why, why, why wasn't she there?*

At the same time, 10:26 p.m., in front of Jax Truck Stop and Restaurant on Highway 47 in Coon Rapids, an 18-wheeler swerved on the ice, trying to avoid a collision with a car that was weaving back and forth across the centerline. The car, whose occupants were drunk, hit the side of the semi, spun out of control into the wrong lane and crashed, head-on, into another oncoming vehicle.

The windows of Dave's car were completely fogged over, and Dave gave up trying to get to second base, or was it third?

"Here, I gotcha something for Valentine's," he said, grabbing a ball of tightly waded newspaper out of the glove compartment. Dropping it in my lap, he said, "Go ahead, open 'er." I pulled the newspaper ball apart and one by one, out dropped four delicate gold necklaces. By the light of the glove compartment, I could see each chain different from the others. One had my birthstone in the center of the chain, another five tiny pearls, another, a rhinestone, and the fourth one: a gold locket.

All I could think of was the gift Leedsie sent to Corrine that Valentine's Day. She was a freshman at Carleton College in Northfield, and she'd taken a real interest in coffee. Leedsie found an old wood coffee grinder, in a Washington Avenue junk store in Minneapolis; it had a tiny drawer to hold the ground coffee. He took the whole thing apart; he polished all the metal parts, sanded all the wood and refinished it. Working down in the cold basement after he finished studying, the restoration job took about two weeks. That coffee grinder was a work of art, when he boxed it up and sent it "Special Delivery—Fragile" to Northfield, with a bag of coffee beans. Then he ordered a fresh bouquet of violets all the way from Europe.

"They have to be blue," he told Hazel Hoglund, the Park Street florist. "It has to be a cut bouquet of violets, they have to be tied with white ribbon." He was adamant about every detail. And, for Hazel, finding them was not an easy task in the middle of February … in Minnesota … in 1962. Boy, Corrine was lucky.

Looking at the necklaces, in the front seat of Dave's Oldsmobile, I shook my head and wondered. The locket I received from Teach, when I was 13, was still in my jewelry box. I never wore it, but I had just recently replaced the picture of Teach with a tiny oval photo of my father. Thinking about my disobedience, made me even more impatient with Dave.

"I can't keep these," I scolded, handing the necklaces back. "You know I'm not supposed to accept jewelry or clothes from boys, only stuffed animals and records."

Oh, gad, where was Mother?

"Well maybe you can just keep 'em and don't tell anyone," he said, handing the gift back to me.

Thank God for Father Ardolf. "I have to get inside, now." I returned the ball and chains to Dave, and waded through the drifts up the porch steps.

Inside the house, all was warm and quiet. I hoped Dave wouldn't get stuck in the driveway. Then what? The kitchen table was cleared, except for one place, Leedsie's. He commuted to the University with three friends. Normally he would be home by dinner time. His car pool must have had trouble in the snow. In front of his placemat, leaning against the pepper grinder was a homemade Valentine. Three colors of glitter, red, gold and silver, were glued in the approximate shape of a heart on red construction paper.

Written on the heart was a message:

Happy Valentine's Day
To the best brother
I missed you tonight.
Love, Marcus

I checked on the little kids and went to bed. At midnight, I was awakened to find two men in my room, sitting at the end of my bed. One of them, Jim, was a car pool friend of Leedsie's. Jim was on his way home from the University that night and saw an accident in front of Jax Cafe. He recognized Mother's station wagon. Jim said, "Leedsie was studying at the library tonight and decided to ride home with your mom after the lecture." The other guy on my bed was an Anoka policeman.

"I'm sorry," the policeman said, "but you'll have to come to North Memorial Hospital with us and identify the bodies. One of the deputies will stay here with the children till you come back." I was 17, the eldest child at home. Acey was a freshman at the University, studying Home Economics. She lived at Sanford Hall. Andrew Shinski, the next in line, was in tenth grade, 15 years old. As I woke him up to get ready to go with me, I wondered if Acey might have decided to ride home with Mom, too.

Andy and I dressed quickly for the trip to North Memorial Hospital. All the way there, in the back seat of the police car, the terrifying words of the policeman kept running through my mind, *identify the bodies.* I had asked him, "What do you mean identify the bodies?" He'd said, "I can't tell you until we get there, that's my orders." So, during that long ride, I was stunned silent, believing my mother and maybe my brother were dead.

The emergency room was chaotic—nurses hovering over the women, bottles hanging and tubes running in tangles everywhere. Mother and three of her friends were on gurneys unconscious, but they were alive. Oh my God! Those women all lined up. But, someone was missing. So much blood, I couldn't even tell the color of their hair. Where was Leedsie? Could Acey have been there? "What do I have to do?"

Someone asked, "Can you tell us the names of the women?"

It was hard to distinguish the women from each other, except I could easily identify my mother, by her clothing, her manicured fingernails and her wedding ring. I did know her friend's clothing, their wool suits, their jewelry—one friend had a club foot. Oh! Those poor women. They were all professional mothers, between them they had 20 children—mostly little kids. Those women, in the emergency room, swam together in our pool. They knit together, played bridge together, babysat for each other, and attended the symphony together. They went to see Vincent Price, together … tonight.

They danced with their husbands on our tennis court. Their husbands fished together. The doctors needed the names of the husbands so they could notify them. One woman's husband was the president of the bank. He had polio; she took him to work every day in his wheelchair, picked him up at noon, and took him back to work after lunch, and at 5 o'clock, she picked him up again. What would he do now? How could he even get to the hospital? Their oldest kid wasn't old enough to drive. Good thing I knew their clothes. I knew their swimming suits and their favorite sweaters, too. One of the women wrapped our birthday presents in wallpaper. Mother thought that was very clever.

The woman in the green wool suit was married to Sy, our swimming coach. It looked like her arm was broken. Leedsie wasn't anywhere in the room. Maybe Jim was wrong. Maybe Leedsie got another ride home. And someone else was missing, too.

A doctor told me two of the women had broken necks. Mother had multiple broken bones because the engine came through into the driver's seat. The nurses were cutting their wool suits, carefully prying fabric from their bodies.

"There was another woman!" I whispered. "Where is she? Where's Leedsie? Is there a boy somewhere? Is there another girl?"

The police officer answered carefully. "The passenger in the front seat was thrown from the car into the ditch … died at the scene." Oh, my God! What seat was Leedsie sitting in? Was he in the front seat? Why wasn't he in the room? Could Acey have been in the front seat? The missing woman was Peg.

Wrapping my arm around Andy, I demanded, "Where is our brother? We need to see our brother!" Leedsie was there. He was unconscious in intensive care with kidney damage and brain injury. But he was alive. And so was the guy who crashed into them. Peg was in the front seat, passenger side. She died at the scene. She had three little kids.

Acey was in her room at Sanford Hall.

During my mother's hospitalization, my father's sister, Fritzi, came to stay with us and help Sesson. I think we were a difficult brood to manage, especially without Acey at home.

We were never ready for school on time, particularly Andrew and me. I couldn't seem to get my homework done. My German II teacher, Miss Fleischmann, said, "You'll never be the student your brother is. *Denkst du nicht an ein dritten jahr Deutsch.*" (Don't even think about a third year of German.) "*Das vas gutt mit mir.*" (That was good with me.)

Acey, Andrew, Corrine, and I camped at North Memorial Hospital, playing cards and eating hospital sandwiches, with Leedsie's high school and college friends, taking turns watching my brother through the four-inch-square window in the intensive care unit door. I had to stand on a stool to see through the window, but together we kept a constant vigil. The breath of the person before was still on the window, when Corrine took her place every time someone moved away. She held her hand flat up to the glass. The window never got cold.

Each window-watcher would bring the report back to the lounge area that, by the third day, resembled our own living room on New Year's Eve. The report was always the same: No change, no change, no change. We weren't allowed into his cubicle, but we could look at his face. We could hope and pray. I went back to school, not able to concentrate on anything but Leedsie's kidneys. *Why couldn't just one kidney work?*

10:15 a.m., during third hour American History taught by the boys' basketball coach, who had not the least knack for teaching history, there was a knock on the classroom door. An office aide asked to talk to me in the hall.

During that vigilant week of card playing and tuna fish sandwiches at the hospital, we were never allowed to talk to or touch Leedsie. So, I never had a chance to tell him I dumped Beulah's milk out in the field on purpose, after she put her dirty foot in it. Sorry for all the times I teased him about his stink-pot barn boots and girls he liked that didn't like him back. Sorry about painting on the ceiling beam in the basement: Leedsie + Sarah Larson.

And, that summer day when he was 14 and I was 11. The day he swung on the grapevine out over the creek, the vine snapped and he fell and broke his leg. I tried to carry him home, but I had to leave him leaning against the dead tree limb down in the pasture so I could run faster for help. He cried from the pain, after I left him.

I would have thanked him for taking me to Punky's house for a forbidden game of spin-the-bottle that winter night, when I was 14 and Punky's parents weren't home. I never thanked him for driving through the blizzard, picking me up and lying to Mom and Dad, telling them I was attending one of Father Ardolf's special religion classes. Leedsie told me, "A little game of spin-the-bottle at 14 won't hurt you, but don't do it again." And now, on February 22, 1962, our King of the Hill, the leader of our parade was dead.

Chapter 31

Scourging at the Pillar

Mother and her friends remained somewhere between serious and critical for nine days.

KANO radio reported their conditions every day. A supposedly "wise" person suggested that we not tell Mother that Leedsie had died. "It might worsen her condition." Acey and I disagreed. And when the doctors did tell her, she whispered, "I knew, the moment he died."

Acey and I had learned a thing or two from our father's funeral. We planned a family-only, closed-casket funeral for Leedsie at St. Stephen's Church with Father Murphy officiating. Again, "someone older and wiser" recommended, "Eightball is too young for another funeral. She should not be allowed to go."

Acey and I helped the little kids dress, including Eightball. We combed their hair in front of our little bedroom vanities, allowing each one to sit on our blue and white striped upholstered chairs. Normally we wouldn't ever allow the little kids to sit on our vanity chairs in front of our mirrors. But Leedsie's funeral wasn't normal. Corrine came to our house and stayed over night in Acey's and my bedroom. We gave her the big bed and Acey and I slept together in the little one.

We held our brothers' and sisters' mittened hands as we walked through the bundled crowd of onlookers, clumped together, lining the wide stairs to St. Stephen's Church. They were there to look at us and wonder, I'm sure, why they were not allowed at another private funeral. Maybe they wondered why those Cutter men die so young. Leeds Darrah III was planning to attend law school, so he could take over the family firm. He majored in zoology and really wanted a simple life, raising sheep with Corrine.

Inside the church, we sat on The Blessed Virgin Mary's side of the aisle;

my father's sisters, Fritzi and Mary, sat on St. Joseph's side. I noticed they dressed just like they had for our father's funeral a year and a half earlier … black high heels, black hats, and black veils. Since there was so little time between the two funerals, everything would still fit.

The organist in the choir loft began the prelude to the Mass of the Dead, as Leedsie's high school wrestling buddies and his University carpool friends, serving as his pallbearers, met Father Murphy inside a fog of incense in the vestibule. Father shook his incense and blessed the casket. He led the procession as Chris and Tom, Dave, Allen, Bob, and Jim carried the rose-covered casket down the center aisle to the altar of St. Stephen's Catholic Church.

But, maybe what the people really came to witness was Mother. The North Memorial ambulance pulled up to the snow bank on the curb in front of St. Stephen's, and carefully removed my mother, placing her traveling gurney on the snowy sidewalk. She was wrapped warmly in a heavy dark blue wool blanket. A nurse held the bottle of glucose, hanging from a tower on wheels, which was attached to an I.V. in Mother's arm. We leaned into the aisles to watch as Leedsie's pallbearers carried his casket and placed it just in the center of the aisles, between the Blessed Virgin's side and St. Joseph's side.

The same boys returned to the back of the church to guide Mother's gurney down the center aisle, bringing it to rest in between two huge pillars in the aisle alongside Leedsie's casket. All I could think was: She was close enough to touch it, if only she could move her arm.

Father Murphy walked halfway around the casket anointing it with more clouds of incense. He couldn't go all the way around because Mother was blocking his way. Over our heads, in the choir loft, the fourth grade choir began singing the Requiem Mass. *"Dona eis requiem."*

Unable to move her head from side to side, Mother could only gaze at the pastel paintings of angels and clouds on the ceiling of St. Stephen's Church. From the edge of the pew, I watched her tears run down both sides of her face, landing on the stiff white hospital sheets. A High Mass is way too long, and too sad. I wanted it to end. I prayed for them to let my mother go, go back to the hospital, even though I knew this was as close to us as she would be for a long time.

Because she insisted, Mother's ambulance led Leedsie's burial procession all the way from St. Stephen's Church, slowly down Main Street, past the courthouse, past our father's office and the Post Office. We crossed over the Rum River Bridge and turned left on Park Street, past the skating rink, Hoglund's greenhouse, and Mrs. Annon's house, to Forest Hills Cemetery. The ambulance parked at the top of the hill beside the graves of my father's parents. From there, Mother would have a view of the burial of her first son. After climbing shivering out of our cars, we huddled together around the spot where the gravediggers had been the night before, building a fire to soften the ground.

Mother lay inside the ambulance, waiting till the end, while we buried Leedsie just under that same pine tree that shaded our father's grave, but we left one burial spot between the two graves.

After the funeral, Corrine told us that she didn't know how, but that she would go back to school. "I will love your brother forever and ever." The next Memorial Day, we found a bouquet of blue violets tied with white ribbons on the bare, raw dirt over Leedsie's grave.

In the spring, when Mother came home, we turned the dining room into a hospital room and she recuperated in time to attend my high school graduation. The next fall Grandpa White died of cancer.

We never saw Aunt Fritzi again. She died before we recognized the emptiness, or where it was coming from. We didn't see or hear from my father's other sister, Aunt Mary, either, for 35 years after Leedsie's funeral. My youngest sister, Eightball Sarah Doll, went to Michigan to visit Aunt Mary, specifically to ask her, why?

"Where were you all those years we needed you? We had questions. We all wanted to see your face. You look so much like our father. Why didn't you call, or write, or come to see us?"

Aunt Mary stared at Eightball for a few seconds before she finally tried to answer the question.

"I just couldn't. You were all too sad."

Chapter 32

A Joyful Mystery

Summer of 1963: Mike Ogata was employed by the Japan Travel Bureau, while he attended the University in Yamagata. He invited all of us to come to Japan for the summer. "I think so, Mom, you come here. I plan everything. We go everywhere; see all temples and parks and shrines. Let me show you Japan. We miss Dad and Leedsie all together, ney?"

Papa Ogata's parishioners built a new house, attached to the temple, for the arrival of Mike's American family—including Sesson and a widowed friend of Mother's with her young son—11 people total.

Mike met our ship in Yokohama. He shuffled us into waiting taxis and guided us up the mountain on the train, past miles of beautifully terraced rice paddies, on our way to his home, Sagae City.

Papa Ogata, and his entire congregation, greeted us with deep bows, in the temple courtyard. After a short welcoming ceremony, where Papa introduced each and every workman who contributed to the building of the new house, he shook Mother's hand and announced, "Our community wanted to thank you for all your kindness to Ryodo, while he lived with you in Minnesota. These people have donated their time and their materials to build this house for you to live in during your visit. We have everything settled. Except," he whispered, "the western toilet. We continue to work on that."

We bathed by twos, in a deep tiled tub, heated by a fire underneath. My mother had one rule regarding food in Japan: "Try it, if you don't like it, you don't have to eat any more. But you must try everything." We ate raw fish, pickled radishes, pickled cherries, rice balls, pickled horseradishes. We attended a ceremony and luncheon hosted by the Mayor and City Council of Sagae. At the end of a two-hour, 12-course lunch, the mayor rose to give a speech to Mike's American family.

He bowed deeply, to Mother, and said, "I offer you, in my humility, the key to our city." The Tadas, across the road from the temple, owned a kimono shop. They measured us and made kimonos for all 11, with fabric that personified our age and individual personalities. They bowed and thanked us for the opportunity to give us something. "*Domo arigato.*"

The family who owned the most famous Saki factory in Northern Honshu were friends of the Ogatas. They hosted an elaborate dinner at their factory, thanking us with frequent speeches. The owner's son, Yachan, would later visit us in Anoka.

The local Kokeshi doll makers turned the dolls and decorated them, while we watched, then they gave each of us our own, specially auto-graphed wooden doll. Everywhere we went, in the shops or on the streets, the Japanese people bowed, some cried. Once I asked Mike, "What are they sad about?" He said, "They are so sorry for the war. They are apologizing."

We sat on our knees, on tatami mats, in the temple house and in the res-taurants, where we cooked at our table. Each one of us learned how to eat with chop sticks, managing the delicate connection between two sticks, to pick up everything from rice and fried grasshoppers, to soba noodles with soy sauce and ginger. Mike explained that lifting a bowl to your mouth and scooping noodles in with the chop sticks, making slurping sounds, was per-fectly acceptable—even complimentary. The boys especially enjoyed hear-ing that burping at the table is also considered polite.

Silently, respectfully, we participated in tea ceremonies conducted by Mike's mother, Hama Ogata. She demonstrated how to turn our tea bowls twice clockwise so the front is away from us, sipping the tea, wiping the bowl and turning it twice counter-clockwise before placing it back on the table.

In the evenings, in the temple house, with the music of *Sakura* playing on the stereo, the Ogata sisters, Nanako and Etsuko taught us a tradition-al dance of airy movements, symbolizing the rising sun and the power of nature. As we followed their movements on the tatami mats, they explained, in sign language, that the song is played during cherry festival in Sagae.

At night, Acey and I shared a futon and slept on the same tatami mats where we ate dinner and then danced. All five girls, Sesson, Mother and Gladys, slept in one room and the boys in the other, separated by sliding rice paper doors.

We rode the bullet train to Tokyo to see Kabuki theatre and Sumo wres-tling matches. We bathed, naked, in hot springs at Mt. Zao and Mt. Fuji. We toured Zen gardens and parks in Nara and The Imperial Palace in Tokyo. We stayed at the Imperial Hotel, designed by Frank Lloyd Wright, where we ate French toast dusted with powdered sugar.

But the most important part of our visit was the morning prayer in the temple in Sagae City.

Dressed in his gold-embroidered satin robes, Papa Ogata sounded the gong outside the temple door, and lit the incense on the altar. Then we, all 11, walked the narrow hallway connecting the house to the temple and assembled, barefoot. Sitting on our heels on the tatami mats facing the massive lacquer, gold and red altar, we folded our hands, bowed our heads and listened, while Papa beat the drum and chanted the Sutra. Every day our father's and our brother's names were imbedded over and over again in the otherwise foreign sounding rhythms, "*Cutta, Cutta, Cutta.*"

Mike Ogata became a Buddhist Priest in his father's temple and, like his father, an English professor at Tohoku Fine Arts University in Yamagata, Japan. Mike's specialty: English slang.

Chapter 33

The Great Gift of Life

Pursuing the art of fine cooking sustained Mother's spirit through the years of raising her children and running my father's business and the tragedy of Leedsie's death.

After her youngest, Eightball Sarah Doll, was educated and married, Mother sold the Abstract Company and embarked on a new and exciting adventure, continuing her own transformation. She enrolled in more local cooking classes, completing a course in Hotel Restaurant Management at the Anoka-Ramsey Community College. She went to New York, where she studied East Indian cuisine with Madre Jaffre.

I was married, when I attended my first cooking classes at *La Cuvette,* the local cooking school—where Mother was now Verna Meyer's assistant. Soon, I operated a lunch restaurant at The Minnetonka Art Center. Mother frequently drove out to Minnetonka to pitch in serving soups and soufflés at lunch time. Following the lunch service, she would teach cooking classes to our customers.

You really get to know a cooking partner when there's rough-to-fine chopping and deft, light folding going on in the same small work space. When the heat and tension are high in the kitchen, cooks need to understand each other and develop a rhythm and a productive flow.

Mother and I joined forces in another restaurant adventure at The Walker Art Center in Minneapolis. Every day we managed a staff of 15, and fed hundreds of people who filed in by the busload. Between the two restaurants, our insurance was so high that at the end of our first month at The Walker, when we opened our paychecks, Mother laughed so hard, she could barely stand up. I opened my envelope and unfolded a check from our bookkeeper: $150. Still laughing, Mother said, "Well, it's better than a poke in the eye with a sharp stick," and we both laughed, until it was time to do the dishes, because the dish washer hadn't shown up, again.

Mother and I went to California to participate in The Great Chefs of France Cooking School, hosted by Robert Mondavi. The first year we prepared exotic meats with Phillip Brown. We loved the rack of lamb, rubbed with a paste of fresh chopped rosemary, garlic, salt and pepper, then roasted on a mound of shredded carrots, onions and celery tossed with grainy mustard, soy sauce, and red wine.

We also prepared a savory cow's tongue stuffed with an eggplant, tomato, garlic, rosemary, and marjoram filling, thinly sliced and served in a pool of smooth rich tomato sauce.

Our instructor the next year was Jean Troisgros, the famous three-star French chef from Roanne, France. He was accompanied by Gael Green, the inimitable, colorful food critic for The New York Times. Remarkably colorful.

Dressed in our complimentary Great Chefs aprons, we began the preparation of Troisgros' legendary lobster soup, beginning with 15 one-pound live lobsters, which were boiled whole, then separated from their shells. We ground the shells and all the roe, straining it to create an unbelievable stock with magical bursts of stars in each bowl. It was topped with a subtle and mysterious combination of delicate herbs—some secrets he would not share.

French chefs were notorious for withholding at least one ever-so-subtle ingredient that, at that instant of first taste, *would make the angels sing.*

After a day of preparation, Mother and I were seated with our classmates under the stars in the candle-lit dining area of the Mondavi Winery. The guest of honor, Robert Mondavi himself, sat between Mother and me. He charmingly, generously shared his views of champagnes, California versus French, his preferred reds and whites and the family saga of his father's early wine making and migration from northern Minnesota to California and The Napa Valley.

Still wearing his lobster speckled apron, Troisgros stood at the head of the table to begin dinner with an announcement and a toast. He passed a sample of his secret ingredients—a tiny tower of scissor-snipped fresh fine herbs, delicately placed in the center a small porcelain plate.

He had added the herb combination into the lobster soup tureen, just before serving, and just after we, the students, left the kitchen for the dining room.

Carefully monitoring the plate of herbs, as it progressed around the table, Troisgros tapped the side of his wine glass.

"If you please," he announced. "Do not touch the herbs as they are being passed. It is possible to identify most of them by their aroma, but not all, some must be tasted. And I warn you, these herbs are tender if you over-smell or over-handle them, they *will* lose their flavor. So, please be fair to the rest, do not take more than your share of aroma."

Sounded like a good philosophy for life.

As a result of our Great Chefs of France classes, Mother and I finessed an introduction to Simone (Simca) Beck's exclusive cooking school in Provence, France. *Ecole des Trois Gourmandes,* founded by Simca, Julia Child and James Beard, was the icon of French cooking schools.

Following one week of classes in Provence, we invited Simca to come to Minnesota as part of her tour to promote her new book, *Simca's Cuisine.* She accepted and made an appearance at The Minnetonka Arts Center where she demonstrated new recipes of *Poulet en persillade*, chicken baked with mustard, parsley and garlic in a cream sauce and *Le Montmorency,* chocolate cake with kirsch and cherries.

After autographing books, she was chauffeured in a Bentley, no less, to The Last House on Park Street, where she would spend two nights with

Mother. For that occasion, I remember Mother splurging on a new and expensive sitting chair for the window of the guest room, formerly the nursery—the window where she nestled herself one night to intimidate Ned.

In their short time together, Mother and Simca were almost inseparable. Mother captured Simca's eye and her heart. In 1978, when Simca returned to Park Street for another visit and more collaborative meals, she invited Mother to be her assistant in her cooking school, in the South of France. With her right hand nervously clasping the string of pearls around her neck, Mother blurted out, "Oh, I don't think I'm qualified to be your assistant."

Simca responded firmly, with her trademark authority, "I'll decide who's qualified and my dear, you are!" Mother blushed as she accepted.

Mother's duties at *La Campanette* included shopping for ingredients, assisting and translating during classes, and testing recipes for Simca's book, *New Menus from Simca's Cuisine*. She charmed Simca's students and succeeded as an effective liaison between Texas millionaires (privately jetted in) and a frequently weary Simca, who acknowledged that she wished she could teach fewer and more serious students. "Or," she demanded. "Just permit me to retire and care for my roses."

During her free time, that first year in the South of France, Mother took French lessons in Monaco two days a week, commuting back and forth on the same hairpin mountain roads where Princess Grace died. While in Provence, Mother prepared for the small workshop classes held in the kitchen of *La Campanette,* a lovely guest cottage down a terraced rose-bordered, cobblestone walkway, 200 feet from Simca's home, neighboring Julia Child's guest cottage.

Mother and Simca had made plans for travel and working together for years to come.

In 1978, Mother bought The Jackson Hotel, a run-down pit of a building, originally constructed on Jackson Street, in downtown Anoka, in 1884. Two years later, she restored the ground floor to its original beauty, adding a stellar restaurant, bar and kitchen. The Jackson was nominated to the National Register of Historic Places. For two years, Mother was the chef at The Jackson House; she worked from morning through dinner every day, and sometimes had to do the dishes—and the ironing.

By 1982, Mother's heart needed help. After several hospitalizations and procedures, she was getting weaker. Sesson was there every day to take care of her, and Eightball Sarah Doll, with her husband and daughter, moved in to be closer to Mother.

Sarah told me about Mother's last trip to the doctor before her surgery. Sarah was driving down the driveway toward the rose garden, when Mother grabbed her arm with alarming strength. She asked her to stop the car. Sarah watched from the driver's seat, as Mother walked slowly, cautiously toward the rose garden, "Like she was creeping up on something," Sarah said.

Sarah turned off the engine and heard Mother's soft, weak voice chatting and answering questions, as she stood just at the edge of the garden. Watching as Mother nodded and tilted her head, Sarah considered that Mother may have lost her mind. She was stunned at what she saw next.

Out of the rose bushes flew two cardinals, both males—one brilliant red-and-black adult, trailed by the orange and tan juvenile. Mother wrapped her arms around herself and stepped carefully back into the car. She said, with a peaceful smile, "There now, everything will be all right."

Mother underwent a routine surgery to replace a badly scarred mitral valve. At 6 a.m. the morning of her surgery, I told her doctor, "She is our Queen. Take good care of her." She died at 4 a.m. the next morning. We were told there was, ironically, an *accident* during surgery.

We buried Mother snugly nestled between the graves of my father and brother under the pine tree at Forest Hills Cemetery. During the prayers over the open grave, I could actually see the concrete corners of the adjoining vaults. I knew she was at peace between the two men whose deaths really did break her heart.

My sisters told me it was my duty to call Simca and tell her the news. I dreaded making the phone call and as I feared, Simca was inconsolable. She shouted over the phone line, "It's not true! It's impossible!" I wrote to her, trying to explain what happened, but I didn't think she understood. Finally, 15 days after Mother died, Simca wrote:

> *My dearest Charlie,*
>
> I am so depressed; my sorrow is so deep in my heart. I cannot find the words to tell you how much I have appreciated your wonderful letters. Now, I understand what happen exactly to your so dearest mother and I would like you to know how much she was in my heart and in my spirit.
>
> I still do not realize her death, she is so present in my mind and in all she gave me here, by and through her wonderful help. What about her manuscript? I was so happy to be able to help her.
>
> All my very deepest sympathy with my very sincere and sad love.
>
> I will never, never forget your dearest mother.
>
> With all my heart, Simca

To follow up on Simca's reference to *her manuscript*, I studied the scatterings of recipes and notes in Mother's box of cooking materials. My search revealed several recipes, written while Mother was in France, with Simca's handwritten notations in the margins. In addition, I found a yellow legal pad with my mother's familiar left-leaning handwriting. Possibly an introduction, titled, *A History of French Gastronomy*; maybe this was what Simca referred to. Mother begins her introduction, by giving proper definition to the often misused phrase *gourmet cook.*

> "This is a corruption of terms and has become accepted to mean one is a fine cook. But a *gourmet* is a most cherished and honored position inside the French wine industry. He is

one who tastes wine and determines its quality—so properly *gourmet* may not be used as an adjective. Nonetheless, if one examines the work of a *gourmet*, the corruption is understandable. When tasting a wine, the *gourmet* will look for color. He will swirl the wine to examine the "tearing," he will smell and check the bouquet, he will feel the glass to discover temperature of the wine and he will, at last, taste the wine. Now he has used four of the five senses. The saying is, *If all these senses are satisfied at the swallow of the wine, the gourmet will hear the angels sing."*

"So too," she continues applying the same principle to food, "If the presentation of food is pleasing, the aroma tantalizing, the serving dishes properly chilled or warmed, the first forkful a delight—then, as with the gourmet, the diner will surely hear the angels sing."

All her life, Mother did, indeed, turn mediocrity into masterpieces, and with her excellence and care, she made *the angels sing*. I placed the legal pad with Mother's words back where I found it and carried the box home for safekeeping.

The following summer, Mike Ogata returned with his mother and two sisters to Anoka and the Park Street Forest Hills Cemetery. Never questioning the incongruity of Catholics buried in the Protestant cemetery, Mike stood over the graves with his beads and incense. He cried as he bowed deeply. "I must … I must … pray for them; they are my family. We pray to release their spirits together." Mike Ogata and his family visited the homes of each Cutter family member, hanging drawings of Buddha on our walls, praying for us all including Sesson—each and every name chanted over and over, "*Cutta, Cutta, Cutta.*"

My Conclusions

As I began this memoir, I wanted the story, that Mother wrote about Bridget and Peter—the disturbing accusations, typed on blue paper, that I'd read shortly after she died. Believing that my mother's conflicts were also mine, it might be possible now to put her story into perspective. But I couldn't find the story anywhere. I unpacked long-ignored boxes of cookbooks and family photographs. I cleaned bookcases upstairs and downstairs, and in the basement. I was obsessed, flipping through old calendars and novels I'd read on mother-daughter relationships and any other related subjects, leaving a trail of unsuccessful searches behind. I re-checked the bookcase beside my bed and all the files in my desk—nothing.

Finally I spoke directly to my mother, "If you want that story on blue paper included in this document, you'll have to help me find it. I think it's important. Do you?" With that declaration, I stood up from my desk under the eaves in the loft, dropped to my knees and crawled on the floor check- ing the bottom shelf of a 20-foot long bookcase, lifting stacks of research papers, old manuscripts and notebooks … all piles I'd thoroughly checked earlier.

At the last section of the bookcase, there it was—a corner of blue, just a tag, sticking out between an issue of <u>Better Homes and Gardens</u> magazine and a copy of the book, *The Stones Remain*, written by an English friend, Kevin Crossley-Holland.

As I tugged on the blue paper and the attached menu with recipes, an old photo of my mother followed, landing face-up on the carpet. She's kneeling on the cold slate floor of the sun porch at The Last House on Park Street, tucking something deep under the Christmas tree, which is decorated in our traditional fashion with bubble lights, birds, and angels haloed in a warm glow of tinsel.

Against the wall, behind the tree, is an antique oak pump-organ, having its own story to tell. That story began somewhere in Ireland when my great grandmother, Grandpa White's mother, was orphaned and sent to live with the nuns in St. Louis, Missouri. The significance of her grandmoth- er's organ, securely installed at The Last House on Park Street, grows with every year of mother's transformation—beginning in 1956, the year Mike Ogata lived with us.

I count at least 10 envelopes, nestled into the branches of the Christmas tree, and I know they have our names written on them. The notes inside contain clues for finding our presents from Santa. Besides the presence of the organ, I can tell by the two little dolls in the child's rocking chair that this photo was taken in 1956, because that was the year my mother salvaged and restored the organ. I know the photo was taken by Santa Claus in the middle of the night, when we were all asleep. Written in gold across the front of the photo are the words: *May the Spirit of Christmas Bring Warm Memories.*

Before re-visiting the story on blue paper, I ran my fingers over the letters of each word, as I read the French menu, the dessert recipe for a raspberry and pear tart. Sitting on the floor in the middle of the mess I'd created, I smiled and cried, recalling Mother's careful, skillful movements arranging layers of fresh raspberries and perfectly poached pear slices, inside a pre-baked tart shell, glazed with apricot preserves. As we both learned from spending time in the atmosphere of Simca, the French do not waste any-thing—not even a motion.

The Menu:
Beef en Daube
Salmon Mousse with Champagne
Spanish Sparkling Wine—Freixenete Brut
Rice Salad Andolouse
French Vegetable Accompaniment
Piesporter Michelsberg Kabinet 1979
Layered Raspberry and Pear Tart

BEEF EN DAUBE

30 4 pounds bottom round roast with no fat
     ½ pound pork fat for larding
     herbes de Provence (marjoram, oregano, thyme, savory)
(24) 3 cloves garlic, minced
     pepper
(12) 2 large onions, chopped
 (12) 2 carrots, chopped
 (12) 2 stalks celery, chopped
 (12) dried orange peel
     parsley
1 or 8 ½ cup dry red wine
1 or 8 1 cup good beef stock

In a heavy fireproof casserole place the onions, carrots, celery,
orange peel, parsley and wine. Cover and sweat until the vegetables are beginning to soften. Meanwhile, cut the pork fat
into strips and make cuts in the beef at ½ inch intervals, leaving
the piece intact but somewhat resembling a book with very thick
pages. Rub the combined herbs, garlic and pepper on each cut
side of the beef and divide the pork strips among the sections.
re-forn the beef and tie securely with string in several
places. In a heavy skillet, lightly brown the meat and place it
in the casserole atop the vegetables. Add the stock to come
about 1/3 of the way up the meat. Cover with parchment, the
lid and place the casserole in a preheated 375 degree oven
for about 2 hours turning once. Let cool in cooking liquid.
Remove and wrap in aluminum foil. Degrease the cooking liquid
and reduce to about ½ the quantity. Cool.
To serve slice the beef very thnthin slices and spread with the
cooled aspic. Served garnished with minced parsley.

We will serve French bread throughout this meal.

Menu

Salmon Mousse with Champagne We will serve a Spanish sparkling
wine Freixenete Brut

Beef en daube
Rice Salad Andalouse
Fresh vegetable accompaniament
Piesporter Michelsberg Kabinet 1979

Layered raspberry and pear dessert

Coffee

SALMON MOUSSE

1 cup dreswhite wine
1 Tbsp chopped fresh tarragon
Freshly ground pepper
2 teaspoons chopped fresh dill or
¼ tsp dried
1 pound fresh or frozen boneless salmon with the bones and skin
removed
2 to 3 tablespoons olive oil
1 clove garlic, peeled and minced
½ pound smoked salmon
20 tablespoons unsalted butter
3 to 4 tablespoons vodka

In a saucepan, bring the wine tarragon, some pepper and
the dill to a simmer. After the alcohol has evaporated for a
minute or two, poach the salmon, depending on the thickness
of the pieces, it will take a minute or two. When it is done
to a state of rosy and a little creamy in the middle, remove
it to a rack to cool. Rapidly reduce the poaching liwuid to
2 or 3 tablespoons and set aside.
In a medium skillet, warm the olive oil and add the minced
garlic and cook it gently for about 1 minute. Add the smoked
salmon and saute 30 seconds on each side. Remove from the pan
and blot away the oil. Puree the two salmons in the food pro-
cessor then add the wine reduction. Add the butter by tablespoons
and the vodka. Correct the seasoning. Pack into a mold, cover
with plastic wrap and refrigerate for at least 3 or 4 hours. This
mixture can be frozen but it also keeps well merely refrigerated
for several days.

SALAD ANDALOUSE

2½ cups boiled rice
1/3 cup raisins
2/3 cup tiny green peas, cooked
6 ounces boiled ham, diced
1/4 pound sliced fresh mushrooms, marinated in olive oil,
    lemon juice, salt and pepper
1 tablespoon chives, minced
½ cup classic vinaigrette (below)
1 cup mayonnaise au pistou (below)
watercress
2 tablespoons parsley, finely chopped

Place the cold, dry rice in a salad bowl with the raisins,
peas, ham and chives and toss with the vinaigrette. Refrigerate
for 1 or 2 hours or longer.
Just before serving, prepare the mayonnaise
Remove the salad from the refrigerator, toss and pour 3/4 of the
mayonnaise over it. Toss with the marinated mushrooms, then unmold on a platter. Garnish with vegetables and watercress and
sprinkle with minced parsley. Add the remaining mayonnaise in
dollpops at strategic points.

Classic vinaigrette
salt
1 tablespoon wine vinegar
pepper, freshly ground
3 tablespoons olive oil, or 4 tablespoons peanut oil
2 tablespoons mixed parsley, chervil and tarragon minced
Mix the salt vinegar and pepper and then add the oil. Blend
thoroughly with a whisk. Add the minced herbs.

Mayonnaise au pistou
3 cloves garlic, peeled
¼ cup fresh basil, chopped
¼ cup olive oil
1 tablespoon tomato paste
½ cup cream cheese softened with 1 tablespoon cream
salt, pepper

Crush the peeled garlic with the basil and blend them thoroughly.
Stir in the oil drop by drop. Add the tomato paste and season
with salt and pepper. Blend in the cream cheese. Correct seasoning.

Layered Raspberry and Pear Dessert

1½ pounds frozen raspberries, thawed or 3 pints fresh
2 ripe pears, peeled and cored
juice of 1 lemon
1 cup sugar
4 egg whites
salt
½ cup heavy cream
¼ cup powdered sugar
¼ cup kirsch or pear brandy
24 to 30 ladyfingers
mint

In 2-6cup molds lined with parchment paper on the bottom, place
a layer of ladyfingers, sprinkled with kirsch or brandy.

Puree the berries through the fine disk of a food mill. There
should be about 2½ cups. Reserve 1 cup of the puree for the
sauce. Puree the pears in the mill and stir in the lemon juice.
Set both purees in the refrigerator to chill.
Bring the sugar and 1/3 cup water to a boil in a small saucepan,
cook for about 2 minutes until the syrup is slightly sticky.
Meanwhile beat the egg whites until soft peaks form. Beating steadily
add the syrup to the whites and continue beating until the meringue has cooled and is stiff and shiny. Set the meringue in
the refrigerator.
Whip the cream in a large bowl, sprinkling on the powdered sugar
and adding ¼ cup kirsch or pear brandy as it stiffens. Carefully
fold the pear puree into the cream, then fold in half of the
cold meringue. Fold the raspberry puree into the remaining meringue.
Spoon half of the pear mixture into each of the two molds. Make
another layer of lady fingers, and divide the raspberry mixture
between the molds. Finish with another layer of ladyfingers.
Freeze for at least 4 hours. Unmold and serve garnished with
the reserved puree which has been sweeted slightly and a few
whole berries, dusted with fine sugar. Add the mint leaves.
Serve in slices. Pass any remaining puree.

Then I turned to the pages in blue. I leaned back and breathed slowly while I read the story I'd never forgotten, even after more than 20 years. But after all the *tugging* I'd done, I had accomplished a new and more educated perspective.

The Story Mother Wrote, May 1980

His appearance in the garden was not a surprise, merely a confirmation, so Bridget didn't faint or even experience more than surprise that he looked just as she had imagined. After almost twenty years, he should look a little grayer and a little more bald. He would be very tan, of the sort that announces outdoor living, and certainly less inclined to paunch than he had as a desk-bound lawyer. He shouldn't have lost the humor in his eyes or the smile that turned the corners of his mouth down. He looked just as she knew he would. But he was surprised, and none too pleased, that his appearance did not absolutely knock her out.

"Peter," she extended her hand, didn't throw her arms about him. "I'm glad you're alive. It's been difficult making up my mind, until recently, whether or not you really were." She could tell by his eyes, that the next voice to be heard would be cutting, and the words would be meant to reduce her to compliance. Surprisingly, she knew that would not be the case. She wondered what he would say, but she knew she'd not be devastated by whatever it was.

"Instead of a welcoming wife, I walk into a scene from one of your soap operas. I assume, I'm the villain, and you're the heroine."

Twenty years ago, she would have cried, mostly because she would have known that he wanted to hurt her and make her feel that her efforts at anything were childish and silly. Today, in exactly the same setting, she felt sorry for him that he had to be in command of every situation, in order to be civil.

The children would come in, one by one, or two by two, as the case might be. She wasn't sure of the reaction of any of them to the reappearance of their father. She hadn't told them that she knew he was alive. They might have laughed it off, and she was so positive that she didn't want to say anything, until he actually came back. She had known for three months.

She awoke one morning in France, and it was as sure as anything could be. There had been many times before, that she had hoped it was true, and that the reported death by drowning in Canada was false, but only that morning, in her bedroom in Provence, was she sure that he was alive, and she knew just how the whole thing had been managed.

Three months had given Bridget plenty of time to organize her thinking and plan exactly the way this meeting would go. It had also given her a great deal of time to relive the years since she and Peter had married, and to understand what had, in his mind, justified his leaving. Even more important, it had given her time to test her own feelings for Peter and find that, instead of the old fear that he would be bored with her, she would not be nearly as compelled to accept him as the be-all of all the world. She would like to see him. She felt certain that her changed attitude would not be appealing to Peter, but it would make possible a conversation, in which her ideas didn't have to be couched, in such a way as to allow Peter to advance them.

Actually, Bridget thought, it might make for a real friendship, as opposed to the former God-devotee model, which had seemed suitable to their respective roles. She and Peter had known each other in high school, although Peter was five years her senior. School had been her favorite place. She excelled and sped through. Peter was studious and maintained an excellent scholastic standard, but advanced at the usual rate.

Upon graduation, Peter, the son of a lawyer, went on to the University to become a lawyer, but Bridget, the daughter of a school teacher, victim of bank failure, went to work at the local radio station. The job didn't pay well, but it provided Bridget with enough to be able to take advantage of a scholarship, at a fine dramatic school, in her off hours.

All in all, Bridget spent some time brooding about the loss of college, but tennis, school, work, and beaus left her with such a busy life that there was not much time to mope. Her work at the radio station was a little of all things, but the thing she most enjoyed was writing soap operas for the local performing group. The program, because this was long before television, was a local success, and when the station manager took a much better job in California, he asked Bridget to come along, as program director.

Mr. and Mrs. Collins were loath to have Bridget depart, but they knew how much she enjoyed her work, so they were helpful in getting a friend in California to invite her to visit, until a permanent housing arrangement could be made.

During the same years, Peter had been graduating with honors from law school, and because his great enthusiasm was flying, he had persuaded his family that he should enlist in the Naval Air Cadet program, in order to perfect his skill.

It was 1938, and no one thought of war involving America, and the Navy was the best training available. He distinguished himself at Pensacola by his diligence and perseverance, his respect for authority and traditional attitudes. He graduated well in his class and was assigned to the Naval Air Station at North Island near San Diego.

Letters from friends and family told him that Bridget was living in the area, and while he remembered her chiefly as a friend of his sister, who laughed a lot, played pretty good tennis and loved to dance, he got the telephone number, and called for a date. Bridget was so surprised to hear him and delighted for a voice from home, that she quickly cancelled earlier plans and accepted his offer of dinner.

From the minute she saw him, she knew he would be fun to be with. They went to dinner, came back and played cribbage, made and drank tea, went for a walk, came back and talked until three in the morning, when Peter kissed her goodnight. At four the phone rang, it was Peter to say, good almost morning. At seven it rang again, it was Peter to say, would Bridget have breakfast with him. She certainly would. From that time on, one day melted into the next, and neither Peter nor Bridget…

I think his smile *did* knock her out, but that notwithstanding, Mother helped me see a deeper significance to the short story she wrote about her life with my father, and perhaps the reason she chose the name Bridget Collins, as her protagonist.

Collins was Mother's paternal grandmother's maiden name, an excellent ancestral choice to guide her through the labyrinth of her life with my father. Raised by the nuns in a St. Louis, Missouri, Catholic orphanage, Sarah Collins was a powerful model.

Her future husband, Thomas White, was a discouraged Irish immigrant, victim of the potato famine. He lived in the hills outside Winona, Minnesota and was traveling through the southerly states when he stopped at St. Louis to watch a parade, which included a procession of Catholic school girls. Thomas was 20 years her elder when he selected the petite 16-year-old out of the parade and asked the nuns for permission to marry little Miss Sarah Collins.

Sarah Collins White raised 10 children, while her husband secluded himself reading in his room. She built a large house in a valley, now called White's Hollow, located in the hills of Pickwick, nine miles outside Winona. With her own hands, she built the first schoolhouse in Pickwick, bringing the lumber up the river on a raft from St. Louis.

Shortly after my mother died, my husband and I drove from Northfield to Winona to investigate the remains of the home where Grandpa White grew up.

We got lucky: we found an old farmer, who actually knew the story—or better, the legend—of my grandmother. The Pickwick old-timer led us to White's Hallow, where the stone foundation of their house still remained. Then we returned to his farm.

Before we left, I asked if he could direct us to the schoolhouse. Unfortunately, it was no longer standing.

"I have something, you might like," he said. "Wait here." He went into his barn and returned with a triangle of two-inch thick oak plank. The piece of wood had a one-inch hole drilled into one corner. He handed the plank to me.

"When they took the schoolhouse down a few years back," he explained, "I stored the wood in my barn. That hole right there," he said, putting his fingers through the chunk of wood. "That's where they ran the poles through for transporting the wood up the river. They actually made the barge out of the oak planks. This board right here's a good example." I thanked the man and promised him I'd take good care of it.

"You betcha," the farmer said. "Glad I kept that wood. I knew it would be important to someone, someday."

We shook hands and, as we left, he added another tidbit. "Yes Sir, that woman was a force … a powerful force they'd never seen the likes of in these hills."

Sarah Collins White could not be stopped or intimidated, even by her husband, a brooding, depressed, once wealthy potato farmer. Now Sarah returns, as Bridget, to help her granddaughter write her story.

Bridget Collins saw Peter in the garden in Provence, 20 years after he drowned. It took that many years for Bridget to come along, with enough skill and confidence, to meet him on equal terms, way beyond the former, *God-devotee* relationship she had reluctantly accepted earlier.

Mother had to invoke Bridget to get the job done; she needed Bridget to express her anger, her doubts, regrets, resentments, and her insecurities. It is no coincidence that part of Mother's story is set in Simca's garden, in the South of France, the place where Mother excelled, rose above the crowd, with respect and accomplishment for what very few of the finest cooks have ever achieved.

It is also no mistake that Bridget's story was attached so securely to a French menu and recipes: a portfolio of notable worth. Mother wanted Bridget to present her scholarship to Peter. That's why she sent it along. And, at this meeting in the garden, Mother made sure that Bridget had the upper hand, and plenty of time to organize her plan.

"Even more importantly," my mother wrote, "it had given her time to test her own feelings for Peter, and find that, instead of the old fear that he would be bored with her, she would not be nearly as compelled to accept him as the be-all of all the world."

I now realize that Mother's greatest concern was that my father would be bored with her, and perhaps desert her. I could see references to early insecurities in her letters, when she reminded him of her acumen at cribbage, and also where she seeks acknowledgement, ironically, for the skill she would later master.

"I'm a success! I made a cake today, and permit me to brag—it was good. Honest it was, at least all the family said so. Am I so bad? Even though, I admit, I'm not one of the seven best cooks. I finished the sweater I started to knit for Uncle Earl. But I must confess. It's a bit large. In fact several sizes too large. Ah me! P'raps another time I will be more successful."

From start to finish, Mother's life with my father, was ruled by having one child after the other. Outside of being a mother, she never felt totally credentialed, until she discovered the world of fine cooking, after he died.

Other examples of Mother's early insecurity:

"Be sure to come home before you change your mind about loving me."

"I'm getting awfully lucky at bridge, but afraid my luck will break soon, and you will desert me for one of those grass-skirted girls in Hawaii. You won't, will you?"

And he was after all, the self-proclaimed, seeker of adventure. My father stated in his journal:

"There is in many of us the desire to tempt the dangerous just for the self-satisfaction of getting away with it."

And, his best friend Gene Bird told me, "Darrah took chances with that flying."

How could Mother compete with the vast land that staggers the imagination, the wonderful Arctic country, full of exploration that can, and did, excite men?

But at this meeting with my father in the garden, Bridget would not allow Mother to be seen as insignificant, *childish or silly*, as Mother once feared. She was strong, accomplished, and proud. And, as Bridget began the process of examining her feelings for Peter, we returned to my parent's first date in San Diego in 1939.

"From the minute that she saw him she knew he would be fun to be with." Bridget reminds Mother of their innocence, their first kiss, and the phone call, just hours later at 4 a.m. wishing her, "a good almost morning."

"At seven (the phone) rang again, it was Peter to say, "Would Bridget have breakfast with him. She certainly would. From that time on, one day melted into the next and neither Peter nor Bridget…""

Mother's story of Bridget and Peter ends abruptly, because at that precise moment of typing the phrase, *she certainly would*, while sitting at her desk upstairs, in what had been the boys' bedroom, at The Last House on Park Street, Mother didn't need Bridget anymore. She was ready to meet my father, on her terms. And, after she died at 4 a.m. on September 10, I discovered, that just before surgery, she changed her burial instructions. She no longer wished to be cremated; she wanted to leave the same way he did, and be buried next to him, in the Protestant cemetery.

Today, as I reflect on the three graves, shaded by one pine tree at Forest Hills, I think of the words of the new mother, just days before the outbreak of World War II, days before her first wedding anniversary.

Filled with love and hope, as she looked into the face of her baby boy, she could almost touch the idyllic, uncomplicated, and predictable journey she imagined was her future.

"I am not at all interested in living in Waikiki. In fact for me there is one person living in Honolulu and if I never see anyone except you and 3.2 Darling, I can think of it only as—close to being in heaven. I love you so very, very much."

Healing from the wounds of war began in 1956 with the arrival of Ryodo "Mike" Ogata. The process of healing continues today, as we strive for peace through understanding and acceptance.

A few years ago, my Japanese daughter-in-law drove me to the airport in Bellingham, for a trip back to Minnesota.

My two-year-old Japanese-Irish-American granddaughter, CharlaAnne, and nine-month-old grandson, Theodore Edwin, were in car seats behind me. I asked CharlaAnne what she'd like for lunch. She said, with perfect acceptance, "Oh whatever you have."

"Wow," I said. "You're a diplomat. You know you could be President, if you want."

She turned sideways in her car seat and looked out the window at the airplanes resting on the tarmac. "No, I no want President. I want fry airpranes."

I wondered what my parents would think of this precise moment. My father, an aviator wounded by the Japanese during the war, or my mother, who intentionally brought a young Japanese Buddhist boy to live with us as part of our family, to heal the wounds of war. What would they think of this moment—in that car with these people?

Albert Einstein said, *"The distinction between past, present, and future is only a stubbornly persistent illusion. Time is not at all what it seems. It does not flow in only one direction, and the future exists simultaneously with the past."*

We are connected not only with everything in our lives today but also with everything that's ever been, as well as with future events. What we're experiencing *now* is the outcome of events that have occurred, in part, in a realm of the universe that we can't even see.

The bridges we build, and the messages we send today, affect not only the present, but the future. Over 600 years ago, St. Francis said, *"There are beautiful and wild forces within us."* We *do* have the power to change the world, to heal and create peace, if we are conscious of the messengers, and accepting when a message is delivered. That is what we *get* to do in our lives.

Sarah Collins' organ *lives*, as a totem in our family. After Mother's death, the organ was naturally bestowed upon her grandmother's namesake, Sarah Collins (Eightball Sarah Doll). In 2003, when my daughter, Sarah Anne Conroy, was married and moved to the country—to live in the house where her husband and his father grew up—the Cutter sisters collaborated to restore our great grandmother's organ, as a wedding gift to another namesake.

Final Messages From My Parents

Shortly before she died, Mother wrote this poem to be discovered later.

I want to say something to all of you
Who have become a part
Of the fabric of my life

The color and texture,
Which you have brought into my being,
Have become a song,
And I want to sing it forever.

There is an energy in us,
Which makes things happen,
When the paths of other persons,
Touch ours,
We have to be there,
And let it happen.

When the time
Of our particular sunset comes,
Our thing, our accomplishment,
Won't matter a great deal,
But the clarity and care,
With which we have loved others,
Will speak with vitality,
Of the great gift of life,
We have been for each other.

Four years before I was born, two months after his 25th birthday, and one year before Pearl Harbor was bombed by Japan, my father left a message, for me, in his journal. It must have been intended for me, because I participated in the answers to my questions. I participated in the outcome of my story and my parents' story, heeding the advice of Eugene Bird, years ago when he advised, *Read all the letters and study all the entries. Make sense of things.*

On January 20, 2006, 61 years after the U.S. dropped the atom bomb on Japan, I found this message from my father, buried behind pages of pencil drawings of airplane carburetors, pressure valves, flight and dive-bombing formations.

> **1939:** It is the lot of those, who are literate in the arts of government, to define the place of each specialist, and all have fallen woefully behind them. They have gone so far ahead, that the negative friction their knowledge and advanced state has created, threaten to destroy us. We have toyed with petty things—adjourned our minds to deal with lower tasks.
>
> Our task is far greater, far more significant, and attended with more difficulty than the mere ministering to the social ills of our fellowmen. It is our task to discover and prescribe the social use, to which all that is known can be put.
>
> Our means of living together must be amended so that no man's efforts are wasted. It can only be the hope of those who teach, that some among the thousands who are taught, will use their minds to solve the riddles that face us.

The Anoka County Union, Anoka, Minnesota, Friday, Sept. 23, 1960:

Darrah Cutter's Life, Death in the North He Loved
Attorney Leeds Darrah Cutter left Anoka August 16 for the North Country he loved so well.

He and a fellow pilot and friend, Dave Hymanson, a hardware and lumber dealer, flew Darrah's Seabee, and Robert Taft and son Robert William, 13, went with them in the Taft Seabee, to enjoy the vast expanses of the Canadian Territories and to sink a hook into the huge 50 pound trout that lie waiting in the cold waters north of the Arctic Circle.

Darrah was returned to Anoka and was buried in private ceremony Sept. 12 after he lost his life in a tragic drowning near the Arctic Ocean, Aug. 29 that almost claimed the life of his companion Dave Hymanson.

The events leading to and surrounding Cutter's death is a tale of northern life … and death … and raw courage, rescue and survival.

It didn't start out quite that eventfully.

The four left about 7 a.m. in two planes, went through customs at International Falls, then flew to Winnipeg, landed and lunched. They spent the night at Lynn Lake.

They next flew to the Great Slave Lake and were to stay ... although they didn't know it at the time ... for the next nine days with a trapper in his cabin. Gus DaOust, had spent some 33 years working his trap line with his Indian woman. Gus's trapping days may be numbered, however. The sight in his one good eye is gradually going bad.

Gus and Darrah hit it off real well and Darrah had planned to visit him on a return flight to the North Country this winter. They spotted a nearby herd of Musk ox. Musk ox is a large ruminant mammal with an ox-like body and long, woolly brown coat, short legs and curved horns. They travel mostly in herd and live on mosses and grass.

Darrah wanted air pictures of the herd. The first indication of trouble to come then arose.

While taxiing off the lake they noticed oil pouring from the tail of the Taft Seabee. They stopped and spent the rest of the day trying to fix the oil cooler.

Darrah took his plane and he and Bob flew to Yellowknife 140 miles away to have the proper repairs made. They returned the next day and this time, not to take chances, took off with both planes to try to photograph the Musk ox herd.

They saw caribou but no Musk ox. Bob's oil cooler began giving them trouble again so they went for parts. Bob sent his wife a wire to fly an oil cooler to Winnipeg and that he would be in Yellowknife Monday. Dave and Darrah stayed two nights there until the parts came.

They attempted to fly back to Fort Reliance late Tuesday afternoon but the wind was too strong. They managed to leave Thursday morning and got to Fort Reliance at 8 a.m. They then left the trapper's cabin Friday after being there the better part of nine days.

On Saturday they assembled their boats and fished Dubawnt, catching a few, but nothing large. It was there that Taft remarked that the boat Darrah was using was good, but not stable for real rough water.

Sunday they flew to Baker Lake, got their license for Northwest Territory fishing, gassed their planes, got extra gas and took off. They flew north of the Arctic Circle to the Back River that flows into Chantrey Inlet. This is 2000 miles from Anoka.

The Arctic Ocean is a mile and a quarter away. One can see the blue, black darker water of the Back River meeting the robin egg blue of the Arctic. One can stand on a hill and see waves of the two waters meeting.

They set up camp on a fairly large island in the Back River. The river is about a mile and a quarter wide at this point.

On a hill on the island is a rock image of a man and on that fateful Monday morning the four walked to it and took turns taking pictures of each other. They started to fish about 11 a.m. They got their boats off together on the west side of the island. Dave and Darrah's boat was collapsible, rubber canvas held together with wire ribs.

The four were going to cross the Back River to an Eskimo settlement. Eskimos from King William island to the north come south to Chantrey Inlet and the Back River to catch the huge trout nearby. Caribou hunting is also considered excellent in the Back River region.

Dave noticed two top rods in the boat's structure were not in solidly and one had come out. They stopped their boat in the water to fix it.

Taft and his son came from behind and asked what the trouble was and if they could help. Darrah told them to go ahead. They would meet them later.

Darrah and Dave stopped back on the island and ate two candy bars Dave had in his pocket. Dave smoked a cigarette and they took off again. It had been about 20 minutes since they had seen the Taft boat.

Taft had come out on the east side of the island, saw what looked like wind approaching and took the back side of the river to reach the Eskimo settlement.

Dave and Darrah were about half way across the Back River when a sudden … and devastating wind squall hit them. The waves went to five feet high.

One wave hit Dave in the shoulder. It swamped a third of the boat.

Dave tried desperately to start their swamped three-horse outboard engine while Darrah lost an oar trying to get the oars into the oar locks. Darrah saw two big waves coming. Dave couldn't get the motor started.

The full force of the squall was behind those waves when it hit the boat and filled it. As it started to sink both men grabbed their life jackets and pulled loose seat cushions. Darrah didn't tie the front of his jacket.

Before they sank completely they spotted a rock island south of them in the river. Both men agreed they should stick together if possible and try to make the island. Darrah smiled, shook his head in acknowledgement and the two went into the rough 34-degree cold, dark water of the Back River, now alive with wind and wave. Darrah told Dave the cold water "might get us." The two men struggled in the swirling, frigid water, fighting to stay alive as they bounced along like corks, being struck often by the force of the waves.

Dave looked back, Darrah was swimming behind him, doing a breast-stroke. Another wave hit and Dave ducked. When a big one came, Dave would duck, then ride the crest. For two or three minutes he didn't see Darrah. "Is he ahead of me or behind me," flashed through Dave's mind. The last he saw of Darrah he was swimming. Dave, altogether was in the water an estimated 40 minutes, which is about 20 minutes longer than most people have lived in water that cold. He was dressed in rubber pack boots, quilted undergarments, shirt, cap and other clothing … plus a pair of pliers in his pocket. He kept swimming for the island nearly a quarter of a mile away.

Meanwhile, on the opposite shore, Eskimos had seen the two go into the water and quickly summoned Taft.

Bob left his son on shore, locked an oar in his motor, placed himself low on the bow of his rubber boat and took off into the teeth of the squall to try and rescue his companions.

"It took a hellava lot of guts," Dave said, "for a man to come out into that stuff. A wave could have flipped his boat and he would have been in the same fix we were in."

In about 20 minutes after their boat sank the wind receded a bit and "it wasn't quite as wild." Dave was about 100 feet from the rock island when Bob found him. Dave isn't at all positive he could have made that last 100 feet by himself.

Bob luckily spotted him between alleys of waves and grabbed him by the wrist. Bob asked where Darrah was. Dave told him he hadn't seen him in some time. Bob dropped Dave off at the island then went searching for Darrah for the next 25 minutes. Dave, on the island, began to shake. "I never shook like that before," Dave said.

Bob picked up his son, came back, then spent the next two and a half hours searching for Darrah in a criss-cross pattern of the area. All he found was their gas can.

They picked up Dave and took him to a point on the island about a quarter of a mile from where they had camp. Dave walked to the tent to get the stiffness out of his numbing legs.

Bill Taft, standing on a hill, spotted Darrah's brightly colored life jacket floating in the water. They recovered his body about 5 p.m., near the spot where the boat swamped four and a half hours earlier.

Darrah had managed to free a knife and cut down one side and around one leg of the waders he was wearing. He had a seat cushion slung in both arms. His life jacket was still untied.

Bob got Darrah back to the island and the three of them put him in his sleeping bag and covered him with an air mattress. The disheartened trio went back to their tent. No one ate much and no one got much sleep that night.

Their troubles weren't yet over. They got up about 4 a.m. Tuesday and it started to rain. Bob went back to Darrah and covered him with a boat. It rained until about 2:30 p.m.

To make matters worse the wind had beached their planes. They got help from the Eskimos, however, who came over and worked for two hours to get the planes into deeper water. "We would have been in rough shape without their help," Dave said. They were 190 miles north of Baker Lake.

Now they had another problem. How to get Darrah back. Neither felt up to flying with the body of their friend sitting alongside them. They made a decision and told the Eskimos in pictures and sign language what they were going to do … take off for help and return soon for the body.

They took off in both planes, but soon ran into heavy fog and had to return. When they landed this time, they left their planes in deeper water and anchored them securely. Again, no one slept too well that night.

On Wednesday they arose at daybreak. It was still foggy. About three hours later a small wind came up, clearing the sky somewhat, so they loaded and again took off from the Back River. They got 80 miles and fog set in. They were forced to set down on a small, unnamed lake for about three and a half hours. They ate and went up again.

They now had another problem—gas. They almost had to go on. They got another 60 miles and set down on another small lake for another three and a half hours until 4 p.m. By this time they were about 60 miles from Baker Lake. The fog was still heavy but they decided to try it. They flew only about 50 feet off the ground.

Twenty minutes from Baker Lake they ran completely out of the fog into a nice blue sky and flew the remaining distance to Baker Lake in comparative ease. They looked back and could see the dark stuff that had caused them so much air trouble. They landed about 5 p.m.

At Baker Lake there is a town consisting of a Hudson Bay store, Catholic and Protestant missions and a DOT (Department of Transportation). Here they informed the Northwest Mounted Police of Cutter's death, then sent a telegram to Anoka.

They never did get a confirmation to the telegram during the entire eight days they spent there, although they inquired each day.

They spent the eight days—from Wednesday to Wednesday—in three extra upstairs rooms at the Catholic mission with Father Choque, 39, a Belgian who has been in the north country for about 15 years.

"He tried to assist us in every way," Dave said.

Father Choque soon found that Dave plays cribbage and they spent many hours over the board. Dave won most of the games.

"There we were," Dave recalled, "a Catholic priest, a Jew and a

Methodist. We got along real good." On Thursday night the Mounties arrived and with Bob took off in an eight-place large single engine rescue plane called the Otter, to try and bring back Darrah's body. The Otter can take off in a comparatively small area.

They got only 80 miles from Chantry, then ran into wind and had to come back. The wind damaged the plane and at Baker Lake blew the two Seabees eight feet on shore. They repaired the plane Friday, went up and again had to return. They made it to the Back River Saturday and returned with Darrah's body at 2 p.m.

"To be with Darrah on a camping or hunting trip was to know him," Dave said. "He loved the north woods, understood the people, their food and ways. When he lived there he lived like the trapper. Darrah was a wonderful guy."

Bob and Dave signed releases for the planes. The Mounties flew Darrah to Churchill. The Mounties treated them quite well, Dave said. Darrah's body was later shipped to Anoka.

The wind started howling again that night and continued to do so for three days, again beaching the aircraft. They finally pulled the planes further on the beach to prevent more damage.

They got airborne Wednesday morning for Churchill. On Thursday they were fogged in and stayed at Ilford. They left there Friday morning, gassed at Red Lake and got to International Falls at dark Friday night. They stayed Friday night Fort Francis.

Saturday, they put their wheels back on, gassed the planes, drained off the water, then bad luck gave them a last parting shot. Bob's plane began having oil trouble again so they landed at Grand Rapids, repaired it and landed at Anoka at 4 p.m.—back home after 27 days. They had originally planned to be gone only 11 days and be back Aug. 27.

They were glad to be back. Will they ever return to this land of moss and rock? To the place where their friend met his tragic death?

"Definitely," Dave says. He plans to return when he can for a fishing trip.

"This land is a vast area that staggers the imagination," Dave said, "a wonderful country full of exploration that can excite men."

Darrah Cutter loved the northland with its vast wilderness and places of exploration in a world entirely different from his everyday life.

There will be other men like Darrah Cutter, but to his many friends in the country and state, no one will ever take his place. In Anoka, like the northland, he will be missed.

Afterword

Our stories like our dreams are as individual as our palm prints and DNA. We now know that it is never too late to rewire our brains, to open new connections with fresh insights. If we do, we will shine a light on all that existed in the past and remains within us to be shared, in one way or another, with the next generation and the next.

Naturally, the story of Mary Helen and Darrah is fascinating to me. The path my parents chose and the decisions they made shaped my life and my dreams. *Time does not flow in only one direction, and the future exists simultaneously with the past.* My parents continue to affect the choices I make every day.

Writing down whatever they said was my job description, as the eight-year-old owner and only reporter for The Shanty Town News. I hid under the sofa, behind doors or nestled in the shrubbery, writing down everything my parents said.

No wonder I write today. No surprise either that I'm married to an artist or that I've spent the major portion of my professional life creating with food. It makes sense that, as one of my careers, I chose to help a bunch of teenagers build their own youth-run center. The Northfield Union of Youth, Inc., was designed as a safe, creative space to give voice to youth and empower them to be active in their dreams and their community.

Also, not a mystery that it is impossible for me to make creamy oatmeal.

Our parents demonstrated how to *come to the edge*—to live not as bystanders, but as active participants in our own outcomes. It did not happen by accident that two of my siblings emerged as extremely talented teachers, one of them founding the first charter school in the nation. One brother majored in music and considered studying to be a conductor, but instead owns a spectacular California home and winery—all built from found materials. Another sibling was a philosophy major and then spent many years building homes using the mortise and tenon joint, simple and strong, constructed to last a lifetime. One of my sisters plays the flute, is a lawyer and a champion swimmer. Eightball plays violin, teaches piano and manages a bookstore.

Altogether, we have 16 children.

Mike Ogata and his family are forever connected to this family portrait, because once something is joined, it is always connected whether it remains physically linked or not.

The messages from my parents, grandparents and great-grandparents live and flow freely, over all barriers down through the generations. Their words and their love will continue to *speak with vitality of the great gift of life we have been for each other.*

Other Books by Anne Cutter Mikkelsen

"Take Charge of Parkinson's Disease"
Dynamic lifestyle changes to put you in the driver's seat.
ISBN: 978-0-9823219-3-5

Praise for Take Charge of Parkinson's Disease:

"Through Anne's powerful storytelling and practical information about stress management, exercise, and caregiving, we are inspired to consider the things we can control: our outlook, what we eat, and the power of sharing our story with others. Simply reading this book is a healing experience for anyone touched by PD."

~Susan E. Ouellette, CRNP, CSP, APRN-PMH, Psychiatric Nurse Practitioner, Patient Advocate

"The meaning of life is not where-you-get-to-in-the-end, but rather, the journey you take along the way. Anne Mikkelsen's book describes the bitter, sweet, complicated, funny, and very human path that she and her husband have followed over almost 30 years with Parkinson's disease.

~ Martha A. Nance, M.D., Medical Director, Struthers Parkinson's Center, Minneapolis, MN, and Adjunct Professor, Department of Neurology, University of Minnesota

"Thank you, Anne, for sharing your journey. Your candid saga of the delicious lifestyle that you and Mike created in spite of PD will inspire others who find themselves traversing a similar life path with chronic disease. Your brain healthy recipes are a welcome addition to the PD armamentarium."

~ Becky Dunlop, RN, BSN, Nurse Coordinator, The Johns Hopkins Parkinson's Disease and Movement Disorders Center, Baltimore, MD

Please visit the Author's Website
www.annecuttermikkelsen.com

CPSIA information can be obtained at www.ICGtesting.com

226881LV00002B/205/P